한 권으로 끝내는

해외여행 영어회화

(소설형식 + 50섹션 2400핵심문장)

해외여행 필수 지참서!

한국인의 마음을 알려주는 여행영어!

한 권으로 끝내는 해외여행 영어회화
(소설형식 + 50섹션 2400핵심문장)

제 1부
Travel Story (여행 이야기)
: 소설형식으로 배우는 해외여행 영어!
Novel (소설)
: Travel brings happiness back into your life.
(여행은 당신의 삶에 행복을 되돌려 준다.)

제 2 부
Most Practical English Expressions for Travel
(여행에서 가장 실용적인 영어 표현들)

제 3 부
Basic Practical English for Daily Life
(기본적인 일상생활 영어)

부록
Visiting Korea
(한국 방문)

목차

제 1 부 Novel(소설) - Travel Story   10   -   127
    Travel brings happiness back into your life.
    (여행은 당신의 삶에 행복을 되돌려 준다.)
제 2 부 Most Practical English Expressions for Travel
    (여행에서 가장 실용적인 영어 표현들)

	실용적인 표현들 (Practical Expressions)	스토리 본문 (Text of Story)
1. 비행기 예약 (Booking Flight)	131	14
2. 비행기 스케줄 변경 (Change of Flight Schedule)	134	
3. 비행기 연착 (Flight Delay)	136	
4. 공항 발권 (Airport Ticketing)	138	19
5. 공항 검색 및 탑승 수속 (Security Check & Boarding)	141	20
6. 수하물 찾기 (Baggage Claim)	143	
7. 수하물 분실 신고 (Baggage Lost & Found)	144	
8. 비행기 기내에서 (On the Plane)	146	95
9. 입국 수속 (Immigration Procedure)	150	21

10. 세관 수속 (Customs Procedure)	152	22
11. 호텔 예약 (Hotel Reservation)	154	16
12. 호텔 체크인 (Hotel Check In)	157	27
13. 호텔 체크아웃 (Hotel Check Out)	159	93
14. 호텔 생활 영어 (Practical English at Hotel)	160	29
15. 호텔 불편 사항들 (Complaint Details at Hotel)	164	77
16. 버스 이용 (Taking a Bus)	168	31
17. 지하철 이용 (Taking a Subway)	171	34
18. 택시 이용 (Taking a Taxi)	173	106
19. 기차 이용 (Taking a Train)	175	
20. 렌터카 이용 (Rent a Car)	177	59
21. 자가 운전 (Car Driving)	180	61
22. 교통사고 (Traffic Accident)	182	65
23. 교통신호 위반 (Traffic Violation)	183	62
24. 길 묻기 (Asking for Directions)	184	46
25. 관광지 정보 (Tourist & Sightseeing Information)	186	57

26. 관광지 생활 영어 (Practical English at Tourist Attractions)	187	79
27. 선택 관광 및 야외 활동 (Optional Tours & Outdoor Activities)	190	
28. 사진 촬영 (Taking Pictures)	193	35
29. 쇼핑 (Shopping)	194	68
30. 편의점, 식료품점에서 (At Convenience, Grocery Store)	200	
31. 식당에서 (At Restaurant)	201	36
32. 패스트푸드점에서 (At Fast Food Restaurant)	206	81
33. 화장실 (Restroom, Toilet)	208	88
34. 미용실, 이발소에서 (At Beauty Shop, Barbershop)	209	
35. 환전 및 은행 (Currency Exchange & Bank)	210	90
36. 우체국 (Post Office)	213	
37. 도둑 및 범죄 (Getting Stolen & Crime)	214	
38. 분실 (Missing and Loss)	216	
39. 여행 중 공감 대화 (Empathy Conversation while Traveling)	217	98
40. 질병 및 응급상황 (Disease & Emergency Situation)	219	

제 3부 Basic Practical English for Daily Life
(기본적인 일상생활 영어)

(41) 인사   225
      (Greeting & Farewell)

(42) 대화 및 자기소개   226
      (Conversation & Self Introduction)

(43) 날씨   229
      (Weather)

(44) 전화   231
      (Phone)

(45) 취미   232
      (Hobby)

(46) 렌트 하우스 찾기   234
      (Finding Rental House)

(47) 친구 사귀기   235
      (Making Friends)

(48) 약속과 만남   238
      (Appointment & Meeting)

(49) 데이트   240
      (Dating)

(50) 일과   244
      (Daily Work)

부록 (Appendix)

Visiting Korea

(한국방문)

250 – 283

한국인의 철학과 우정이 담긴

해외여행 영어회화 책

PART I (제 1부)
Travel Story (여행 이야기)

Travel brings happiness back into your life.

여행은 당신의 삶에 행복을 되돌려 준다.

(K : Mr. Kim J : Mr. James C : Miss Charlotte F : Other Foreigners)

Life is a challenge and response.
인생은 도전과 반응이다.

My motto is
'Think globally, act locally and always inspire creative ability'.
나의 좌우명은 '국제적인 생각으로,
실천은 지역에서부터 시작하고 항상 창조적 능력을 고취시켜라' 이다.

When I was a child,
my dream was a writer who travels around the whole world.
어렸을 적 나의 꿈은 세상을 여행하는 작가가 되는 것이었다.

But the reality is quite different from dream.
하지만 현실은 꿈과 상당히 다른 법이다.

Life seems to be a path and it's not the way we imagine it.
인생이란 길과 같은 것인데 우리가 생각한 것과는 다르게 간다.

Life is not designed to make us comfortable.
It's designed to make us strive for achievements.
인생이란 우리를 편하게 하기보다는 성취를 위해 분투하게 만든다.

We should be self-determined and self-motivated
to make one's own life a better stage.
우리는 자신들의 삶을 더 좋은 무대로 만들기 위해
스스로 결정하고, 스스로 동기부여를 해야 한다.

I am a businessman who works for a company.
나는 회사를 위해 일하는 회사원이다.
I want to enjoy my work and be a hard working person.
일을 즐기며 열심히 일하는 사람이 되고 싶다.
But I've been quite busy these past few months and exhaust myself basically.
최근 몇 달 동안 너무 바빠 나 자신이 완전히 탈진했다.
Actually I am totally pissed off and tired from work.
사실 정말 짜증이 났고 일에 지쳐버렸다.
Patience is a necessary ingredient of success,
but the first thing I have in mind is to take some time off.
인내는 성공에 필요한 근원이라지만,
지금 나에게 떠오르는 건 휴가를 좀 내야겠다는 것이다.
I need something refreshing for mental relaxation.
정신적인 휴식을 위해 뭔가 새로운 것이 필요했다.
So I apply for a regular vacation to the company.
그래서 회사에 정기 휴가를 신청했다.
New York is the one of the most popular tourist destinations.
뉴욕은 여행자들이 가장 선호하는 곳 중 하나이다.
I send an email to James who lives in New York.
나는 미국에 살고 있는 제임스에게 이메일을 보냈다.

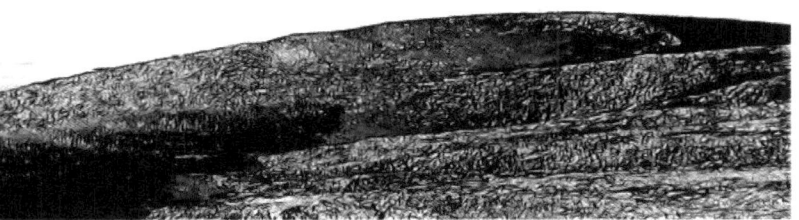

Dear Mr. James.
제임스에게.

How have you been?
어떻게 지내세요?

Thank you for your recent e-mail regarding an invitation to New York.
뉴욕에 초대해준 최근 이메일 정말 고맙습니다.
I am pleased that I could afford to accept your kindness.
당신의 친절을 받아들일 수 있는 여유가 되어 기쁘군요.
I am sending information concerning my visit to New York.
뉴욕 방문에 관한 사항을 보냅니다.
The last item is my travel itinerary from Seoul to New York.
끝부분에 서울에서 뉴욕으로 가는 여행일정이 있습니다.
My hotel reservations are at the Manhattan Hotel.
호텔예약은 맨해튼 호텔로 되어있습니다.
I look forward to seeing you in New York.
뉴욕에서 당신을 만나는 것이 기대가 되는군요.
I will be staying about 10days looking around New York.
약 10일정도 머무르며 뉴욕을 둘러보고 싶군요.
I appreciate your offer to meet me at the airport.
공항에서 저를 만나기로 한 제안에 고맙게 생각하고 있습니다.
But I think it would be best if I were able to call you from the hotel after I arrive in New York to make an arrangement of our meeting if that is convenient for you.
하지만 당신이 괜찮다면, 뉴욕에 도착한 다음에 제가 호텔에서 전화를 걸어 약속을 잡는 것이 어떨까 생각됩니다.

Sincerely yours
당신의 진정한 친구로부터

Dear Mr. Kim.
미스터 김에게.

I'm so excited to hear that you are finally going to visit me.
마침내 저에게 온다는 소식을 듣고 무척 기쁩니다.
In the past couple of years, you have been in a hell of a lot of stress from your business.
몇 년 동안 당신은 일 때문에 많은 스트레스 속에서 살아왔습니다.
This can't be how you feel about the rest of your life.
이런 느낌으로 평생을 살 수는 없지요.
Money can't buy happiness.
돈으로 행복을 살 수는 없는 것입니다.
You deserve to find time for the things that make you feel happy.
당신을 행복하게 해주는 것들을 찾는 시간을 가질 필요가 있습니다.
And you seem to finally realize, it's time to travel.
마침내 당신은 그걸 깨닫고 여행을 하려 하는군요.
I always keep in mind your kindness in Korea.
한국에서의 당신의 호의를 항상 기억하고 있습니다.

I would like to return your kindness.
저도 당신의 호의를 되갚고 싶군요.
So I have been waiting for you to come for so long.
그래서 당신이 오기를 오랫동안 기다렸습니다.
I can't make an arrangement to take a few days off from work.
직장에서 며칠 휴가를 받기는 어렵습니다.
But I will be able to come to meet you at airport.
하지만 공항에서 당신을 만날 수는 있을 것 같습니다.
I hope to do many things with you during the weekend.
주말에 당신과 많은 것들을 할 수 있길 바랍니다.

             Sincerely
           진정한 친구로부터

F : Delta Airline. How can I help you?
델타 에어라인입니다. 무엇을 도와 드릴까요?

K : I would like to book a flight from Seoul to New York.
서울에서 뉴욕으로 가는 비행기를 예약하고 싶은데요?

F : What date will you be traveling?
언제 가실 거죠?

K : Next Friday. March 11. How many flights do you have?
다음 주 금요일, 3월 11일입니다. 몇 편이 있나요?

F : Hold on please. Let me check. We have 2 non-stop flights. All seats of morning flight are booked. We've got only 7:30 P.M. flight. Is that OK?
잠깐 기다리세요. 확인해 보겠습니다. 직항 비행기편이 2대 있는데, 아침 비행기 좌석은 모두 다 예약이 되었습니다.
저녁 7시30분 비행기만 있습니다. 괜찮습니까?

K : All right. Book me for the flight. What's the round trip fare?
알겠습니다. 오후 비행기로 예약해주세요. 왕복 요금이 얼마지요?

F : Do you want to go Economy, Business or First Class?
이코노미, 비즈니스, 일등석 중 어느 좌석을 원하시죠?

K : Economy. And I'll be returning 10 days later. March 21.
이코노미석입니다. 그리고 10일 뒤, 3월21일에 돌아오려고 합니다.

F : $1900 plus tax. Would you like booking up?
1900불에 세금이 더해집니다. 예약을 하시겠습니까?

K : Yes, please.
예.

F : For how many people?
몇 명이죠?

K : Just me.
저 혼자입니다.

F : On your return flight, would you prefer morning or afternoon?
돌아오실 때 아침 또는 오후 어느 비행기를 원하시나요?

K : I'd like to leave in the afternoon.
오후에 출발하고 싶군요.

F : I will put you on afternoon flight, March 21.
Returning flight will depart from JFK at 2:00 P.M.
3월 21일 오후 비행기에 예약을 하겠습니다.
오는 편은 JFK 공항에서 오후 2시에 출발합니다.

K : OK.
알겠습니다.

F : May I have your name please? How do you spell?
성함이 어떻게 되시죠? 스펠링이 어떤가요?

K : My first name is Joonhyung, that is -. Last name is Kim, -.
이름은 준형이고 철자가 -이고, 성은 김, -입니다.

F : Please, tell me your cell phone number.
휴대폰번호를 말씀해 주실래요?

K : My number is ****-****.
제 번호는 ****-****입니다.

F : You need to reconfirm your reservation at least 3 days before departure date.
떠나기 3일 전까지 재확인 하여야 합니다.

K : I see. How long before a flight should I check in?
알겠습니다. 탑승 시간 얼마 전에 체크인 해야 되죠?

F : You have to check in 2 or 3hours before your flight.
2-3시간 전까지 체크인 해야 됩니다.

I make a call to Manhattan Hotel in New York.
나는 뉴욕의 맨해튼 호텔에 전화를 걸었다.

F : Thank you for calling Manhattan Hotel. How may I help you?
맨해튼 호텔입니다. 무엇을 도와드릴까요?

K : I'd like to reserve a room.
   방 하나를 예약하고 싶은데요.

F : What days are you going to stay in this hotel?
   언제 머무르실 거죠?

K : I am planning to stay from next Friday for 10 nights.
   다음 주 금요일부터 10일 밤을 머무를 예정입니다.

F : Wait a minute. I'll check the reservation.
   What kind of room do you want?
   잠깐 기다리세요. 예약을 확인해 보겠습니다. 어떤 방을 원하세요?

K : I'd like to get a single room.
   싱글 룸을 예약하고 싶습니다.

F : I am afraid there is no single room available.
   죄송하지만 싱글 룸이 없군요.

K : How about a double standard room?
   더블 스탠다드 룸은 어떤가요?

F : All right. How many people will be staying in the room?
   Are you coming alone?
   좋습니다. 몇 명이 머무를 거죠? 혼자오세요?

K : Yes. It's just me. By the way what's your rate?
   예. 저 한 명입니다. 헌데 가격이 얼마이죠?

F : The doubles are $200 during off season.
   비수기 때는 더블 룸이 200불입니다.

K : OK. The price is acceptable.
   알겠습니다. 가격이 괜찮군요.

F : Do you prefer a smoking or non smoking room?
   흡연 또는 금연 방 중 어디를 원하시나요?

K : I would like a non smoking room.
   금연 방을 원합니다.

F : May I have your full name and phone number?
   당신의 이름과 전화번호를 알려 주실래요?

K : My name is Joonhyung Kim, my number is -.
　　저는 김준형이고 전화번호는 - 입니다.
F : When do you expect to arrive at the hotel, sir?
　　호텔에는 언제쯤 도착하실 예정이신가요?
K : I think I can arrive there by 8:00 in the evening.
　　저녁 8시까지는 도착할 수 있을 것입니다.
F : Thank you very much. We have booked a room for you.
　　감사합니다. 예약이 완료되었습니다.
K : Thank you.
　　감사합니다.
F : Please be sure to arrive before 8 P.M. on your check-in date.
　　If you have any change in your reservation, please let us know.
　　Thank you for your reservation.
　　체크인 하는 날 저녁 8시까지 와 주시기 바랍니다.
　　만약에 예약에 변화가 있으시면 연락 주세요. 감사합니다.

　　James calls me directly on my cell phone after sending an email.
　　제임스는 이메일을 보낸 후 나에게 직접 휴대전화로 전화를 걸었다.

J : Hi. Mr. Kim. It's been a long time to hear your voice.
　　미스터 김. 안녕하세요. 오랜만에 목소리를 듣는군요.
K : Hi. James. I am glad to hear you.
　　안녕하세요. 제임스. 당신의 목소리를 들으니 반갑군요.
J : Is your family doing well?
　　가족들은 잘 지내시죠?
K : Things are going well for everyone.
　　How about you?
　　모두가 좋습니다. 당신은 어떤가요?
J : I am fine.
　　좋습니다.

K : What's up?
　　무슨 일이세요?

J : I am calling you, because I'd like to pick you up at the airport.
　　공항에서 당신을 픽업하고 싶어 전화를 했습니다.

K : I really don't want to bother you.
　　정말로 당신에게 폐를 끼치고 싶지는 않습니다.

J : Don't worry. I want to see you at JFK airport.
　　걱정 마세요. 케네디 공항에서 당신을 뵙고 싶군요.

K : If you are so minded, you may do it.
　　마음이 불편하시다면 그렇게 하도록 하세요.

J : What time are you arriving?
　　언제 도착하시죠?

K : I will be arriving at 6:30 P.M.
　　오후 6시30분에 도착합니다.

J : Arrival procedure at airport will take about 30 minutes.
　　How about if I meet you there at 7 P.M.?
　　공항 입국수속이 약 30분 정도 걸릴 것입니다.
　　저녁 7시에 그곳에서 만나면 어떨까요?

K : All right. But there may be delays due to overcrowding and
　　long queues. If I am late, I will call you.
　　좋은 것 같군요. 하지만 붐비고 기다리는 줄이 밀려서 시간이
　　걸릴 수 있습니다. 늦으면 제가 전화하겠습니다.

J : I'll wait for you. If something happens, just let me know.
　　당신을 기다리겠습니다. 무슨 일 있으면 알려주세요.

K : OK. Thank you.
　　알겠습니다. 감사합니다.

　　　The journey begins and there is a huge smile on my face.
　　　여행이 시작되었고 내 얼굴에는 미소가 가득했다.

K : I'd like to check in.
　　체크인 하고 싶은데요.

F : Where are you flying today?
　　오늘 어디로 가시죠?

K : I am flying to New York.
　　뉴욕으로 갑니다.

F : May I see your ticket and passport?
　　티켓과 여권 좀 주실래요?

K : Here you are. Can I have a window seat, please?
　　여기 있습니다. 창가 좌석이 있습니까?

F : I am sorry, there are only aisle seats available.
　　죄송합니다. 안쪽 좌석밖에 남은 것이 없습니다.

K : That's okay
　　알겠습니다.

F : How many pieces of luggage?
　　짐이 몇 개이지요?

K : Two.
　　2개입니다.

F : Did you pack the bags yourself?
　　가방들을 직접 싸셨나요?

K : Yes.
　　예.

F : Are there any electrical items like lap top in your baggage?
　　가방에 노트북 같은 전자제품들이 있습니까?

K : No.
　　없습니다.

F : Please put your baggage up here, one by one.
　　Oh, one of your bags is overweight.
　　I'm going to have to charge you for the excess weight.
　　가방을 이 위에 하나씩 올려 주실래요?

아, 가방 하나가 중량 초과이군요.
초과 중량에 대해 비용을 지불하셔야 합니다.

K : I see. How much extra do I have to pay?
알겠습니다. 초과부분에 대해 얼마를 지불해야 하나요?

F : $50 dollars.
50달러입니다.

K : Can I pay by credit card?
신용카드로 되나요?

F : Yes. We do accept credit cards.
네. 신용카드로 됩니다.

K : Sure. Can I bring this carry-on suitcase on the plane?
알았습니다. 이 휴대용 가방은 비행기로 가져가도 되나요?

F : Yes. Here is your boarding pass and baggage claim tickets.
예. 여기 탑승권과 수하물표가 있습니다.

New York is the most diverse and multicultural city in the world.
뉴욕은 세계에서 가장 다양하고 다문화적인 도시이다.
The airport is crowded with tourists all the year round.
공항은 일 년 내내 관광객들로 붐비는 곳이다.
I line up and go through Immigration and Customs after arriving
John F Kennedy International Airport.
JFK 국제공항에 도착한 후,
나는 줄을 선 다음 입국수속과 세관통과를 했다.

F : Welcome to the United States. Where do you live?
　　미국에 오신 걸 환영합니다. 어디에 사시죠?

K : South Korea.
　　남한입니다.

F : May I see your passport?
　　여권 좀 주실래요?

K : Here it is.
　　여기 있습니다.

F : What's the purpose of your visit?
　　미국은 무슨 일로 오셨죠?

K : I am here on sightseeing.
　　관광차 왔습니다.

F : Have you ever been issued a VISA?
　　비자를 발급받으신 적이 있습니까?

K : Yes. But my VISA has expired 2 years ago.
　　So I have previously received approval for travel via the ESTA.
　　예. 하지만 저의 비자는 2년 전 기간이 만료되었습니다.
　　그래서 사전에 ESTA로 여행허가를 받았습니다.

F : OK. Where are you going to stay here?
　　알겠습니다. 어디에서 머무르실 겁니까?

K : Manhattan Hotel in New York.
　　뉴욕의 맨해튼 호텔입니다.

F : How long will you be in the United States?
　　미국에는 얼마나 있으실 계획입니까?

K : For about 10 days.
　　약 10일 있을 것입니다.

F : What do you do for a living?
　　직업이 무엇이죠?

K : I am a businessman.
　　회사원입니다.

F : Your customs declaration?
세관신고서는요?

K : Here it is.
여기 있습니다.

F : How was your flight?
비행기 여행은 어땠어요?

K : Very comfortable.
좋았습니다.

F : Do you have anything to declare other than what you have got here?
이곳에 적은 것 말고 또 신고하실 것이 있으십니까?

K : No, I don't.
없습니다.

F : Will you open your bag?
가방을 좀 열어 주실래요?

K : OK.
알겠습니다.

F : Are you bringing in fruits?
과일을 가지고 있나요?

K : No. Just my personal belongings.
아닙니다. 개인적 물건들만 있습니다.

F : What do you have in this pack?
이 포장 안에는 무엇이 있죠?

K : This is Korean food, Kimchi. I put a check mark in food item.
이것은 한국의 김치입니다. 음식반입 항목에 체크하였습니다.

F : Ok. Everything is cleared.
됐습니다. 끝났습니다.

K : May I close my bag?
가방을 닫아도 될까요?

F : Yes, you may. Enjoy your trip.
   예, 좋습니다. 즐겁게 보내세요.

   I meet James at the airport. He works at a big company.
   나는 제임스를 공항에서 만났다. 그는 큰 회사에서 일을 하고 있다.
   He gets up at 5:00 A.M. and jogs every morning,
   so he is a healthy and good looking guy.
   그는 아침 5시에 일어나 날마다 조깅을 하여 건강하고 멋진 남자이다.

J : Hi. Mr. Kim. How are you? Long time no see.
   안녕하세요. 미스터 김. 오랜만이네요.
K : Pretty good. It's been so long. How about yourself?
   안녕하세요. 정말 오랜만이군요. 어떻게 지내세요?.
J : Great. I am glad to see you here.
   아주 좋습니다. 이곳에서 보니 기쁘군요
K : Thank you for coming to the airport.
   공항까지 나와 주셔서 감사합니다
J : My pleasure. You have taken a long haul flight.
   천만에요. 장거리 비행을 하셨군요.
K : I am suffering from jet leg. Long distance air travel is not easy.
   지금 시차적응이 안 되는군요. 장거리 항공여행은 쉽지가 않군요.
J : I felt the same way when I came to Korea.
   Let's go to the parking area.
   한국에 갔을 때 저도 똑같았습니다. 주차장으로 가시죠.
K : Yes. How long does it take to get to Manhattan?
   네. 맨해튼까지는 얼마나 걸리지요?
J : About 50 minutes if we don't get stuck in bumper to bumper traffic.
   차가 막혀 밀리지 않는다면 50분 정도 걸립니다.
K : Are there serious traffic jams frequently?
   심한 교통체증이 자주 있나요?

J : Yes. New York's rush hour traffic congestion is the worst in the nation. City's residents are always complaining about that, but there is no way.
네. 뉴욕의 러시아워 교통 체증은 미국에서 가장 최악입니다.
시민들은 항상 그것에 대해 불평을 하고 있지만 방법이 없어요.

Fortunately, traffic jam isn't as bad as he thought.
다행히 교통체증은 그가 생각한 만큼 심하지 않았다.
I have a conversation with him in his car.
나는 차 안에서 그와 대화를 나누었다.

K : How is your job going?
당신의 일은 잘되나요?

J : My business is doing very well. How is your work getting along?
일은 잘되고 있습니다. 당신의 일은 어떤가요?

K : Things are great. How is your life in New York?
좋습니다. 뉴욕생활은 어떠세요?

J : I am always tied up with work. New York is the most expensive city in the world to live. Rental payment is extremely high.
항상 일 때문에 묶여 있습니다. 뉴욕은 살기에 가장 비싼 도시이죠. 임대비용이 매우 높아요.

K : But everybody seems to envy New Yorker.
하지만 모두가 뉴요커들을 부러워하는 것 같아요.

J : Things have gotten a lot worse here, too many guns and terror threats.
총도 많고 테러위협으로 이곳 상황이 많이 나빠졌습니다.

K : It's not possible for a city to be crime-free.
범죄 없는 도시란 불가능한 법이죠.

J : New York is popular, but I advise you to avoid it at night.
뉴욕은 꽤 인기 있는 곳이지만 밤에는 피하라고 권하고 싶군요.

K : That is the Janus face of US.
    미국의 양면성이로군요.
J : Welcome to America. But don't worry. Police officers have
    spread throughout the downtown. You feel protected here.
    이게 미국이죠. 하지만 걱정 마세요. 경찰들이 시내에 깔려있어
    안전하다고 느낄 것입니다.
K : Would you tell me any good places to visit in New York?
    뉴욕에서 관광할 만한 장소들을 가르쳐 주실래요?
J : Where would you like to go?
    There are many attractions in New York.
    어디를 가고 싶은데요? 뉴욕에는 매력적인 곳이 많아요.
K : Where are the most popular sights and attractions?
    어디가 가장 인기가 있고 좋은 곳들이죠?
J : I recommend you Must-See places. Natural History Museum,
    Museum of Modern Art(MOMA), Guggenheim Museum,
    Metropolitan Museum of Art, Central Park, Times Square,
    Empire State Building and the Statue of Liberty.
    꼭 봐야 할 곳들을 추천하자면, 자연사 박물관, 현대 미술 박물관,
    구겐하임 박물관, 메트로폴리탄 미술박물관, 센트럴 파크, 타임스퀘어,
    엠파이어 스테이트 빌딩, 자유의 여신상 등입니다.
K : How can I get some tour information about those places?
    그곳들에 관한 관광안내 정보들을 어디서 얻을 수 있나요?
J : Buy the New York CityPASS ticket.
    New York CityPASS ticket is a booklet of admission tickets to
    6 Must-See best attractions in New York.
    You'll save 41% compared to combined regular box office prices.
    뉴욕 시티패스 표를 사세요. 시티패스 표는 뉴욕에서 가장 좋은 볼만한
    6곳의 입장표 책자인데 정식 입장 가격보다 41% 저렴합니다.
K : How can I buy it?
    어디서 살 수 있죠?

J : It's sold at all CityPASS attractions for the same low price.
　　같은 할인 가격으로 시티패스의 관광지 어디에서든 살 수 있습니다.
K : OK. I will check New York tour web site through internet.
　　알겠습니다. 인터넷으로 뉴욕 관광 사이트를 살펴보아야겠네요.
J : You can get more details.
　　자세한 것들을 더 알 수 있을 것입니다.

　　　　　　James drops me off at Manhattan hotel.
　　　　　　제임스는 나를 맨해튼 호텔에서 내려주었다.
Manhattan hotel is in a fantastic location, so my first impression is positive.
　　　　맨해튼 호텔은 좋은 위치에 있어서 첫인상은 좋았다.
Hotel is centrally located enough to walk to most of the major midtown sights.
　　　호텔은 주요 미드 타운 장소를 걸어서 갈 정도로 중심부에 위치했다.
James would like to treat me to tomorrow dinner to show his appreciation.
　　　제임스는 감사의 표시로 내일 저녁을 대접하고 싶어했다.
　　　　　　James makes a call to the restaurant.
　　　　　　그는 식당에 전화를 했다.

J : I need a reservation for tomorrow night.
　　내일 밤 예약을 하고 싶습니다.
F : How many in your party?
　　몇 명이나 되지요?
J : Two.
　　2명입니다.
F : What time would you like?
　　몇 시에 예약해 드릴까요?
J : We would prefer 6:30.
　　저녁 6시 30분에 해주세요.
F : OK.
　　알겠습니다.
J : My name is James.
　　제 이름은 제임스입니다.

F : Yes. Do you have a preference?
  알겠습니다. 좋아하시는 곳이 있나요?
J : I'd like a table near the window if possible.
  창가 근처 테이블이면 좋겠는데요?
F : I'll try.
  노력해 보겠습니다.

J : White restaurant is famous for great food in Times Square.
  화이트 식당은 타임스퀘어에서 좋은 음식으로 유명합니다.
K : What is the dress code for the restaurant?
  식당 드레스 코드가 어떤가요?
J : The attire is business casual. It would be OK if you wear a collared shirt and trousers.
  복장은 비즈니스 캐주얼입니다. 옷깃 있는 셔츠와 바지면 괜찮습니다.

> He promises to call me back tomorrow and leaves.
> 그는 내일 전화하기로 약속하고 떠났다.

K : I'd like to check in, please.
  I have a reservation under the name of Joonhyung Kim.
  체크인 하려는 데요? 김준형이란 이름으로 예약하였습니다.
F : OK. Are you staying for 10 nights, Nonsmoking, Double room?
  알겠습니다. 금연실, 더블 룸, 10일간 머무르실 거죠?
K : Yes.
  네.
F : Could you fill out this registration card?
  Name, address and phone number.
  이 등록카드를 작성해 주실래요? 이름과 주소와 전화번호를 써 주세요.
K : OK. Do I need to guarantee lodging charge with a credit card?
  알겠습니다. 숙박료를 카드로 미리 보증해야 하나요?

F : Yes. Guests must present the credit card at check in.
네. 손님들은 체크인할 때 신용카드를 보여주셔야 합니다.

K : Here is my VISA card. Does this hotel have a fitness facility?
여기 비자카드가 있습니다. 이 호텔에 피트니스 룸이 있나요?

F : Yes. We have an exercise facility.
예. 운동시설이 있습니다.

K : Do I have to pay extra?
비용을 따로 지불하나요?

F : The gym is free to guests.
숙박 손님에게는 무료입니다.

K : What time does it close?
언제까지 하죠?

F : The gym is open from 5:00 A.M. till 11:00 P.M.
아침 5시부터 밤11까지 개방하고 있습니다.

K : Can I use the internet in this room?
이 방에서 인터넷을 사용할 수 있습니까?

F : Yes. Guest room has free high-speed internet access.
Just plug the Ethernet cable into your computer.
예. 객실에 무료 인터넷이 있고 케이블을 컴퓨터에 꽂으시면 됩니다.

K : How can I use WiFi? Could you let me know ID and Password?
와이파이는 어떻게 사용하죠? ID와 비밀번호를 알려 주실래요?

F : It's written on room key card. But wireless internet access can be available in all public areas like lobby.
방 카드에 적혀있는데 무선 인터넷은 로비같은 공공장소를 이용하세요.

K : Where is the restaurant?
식당은 어디에 있지요?

F : The restaurants are on the second floor.
식당들은 2층에 있습니다.

K : Does the room rate include breakfast?
숙박료에 아침이 포함되어 있나요?

F : No, Sir. Meals are charged separately.
   아닙니다. 식사 계산은 각각 입니다.
K : OK.
   알겠습니다.
F : Here is your room key. If you need anything, just dial 0 on your room phone. Do you need help with your baggage, sir?
   여기 룸키가 있습니다. 만약 필요한 것이 있으시면 방 전화 0번을 누르십시오. 가방을 들어줄 분이 필요한가요?
K : No. Thank you.
   아뇨. 감사합니다.

I have a beer can on my right hand and a book on my left hand.
오른손에 캔맥주를 들고 왼손에 책을 들고 있다.
It gives me happiness. I feel like I unplug myself from the competitive world.
행복감이 느껴진다. 경쟁만이 존재하는 세계에서
나 자신을 빼 논 느낌이랄까?
Travel seems to allow myself to be myself.
여행은 나 자신에게 진정한 나 자신을 주는 것 같다.
Traveling is a very important part of life and it makes people open-minded.
여행은 인생의 중요한 일부이며 사람들의 마음을 열게 만든다.
Travel is more than the seeing of sights, it's a chance that goes on the deep of living and makes travelers know the value of people.
여행은 관광 이상의 의미로써 삶의 깊은 곳으로 가게 만들며,
인간들의 가치를 알게 만드는 기회이다.
I am convinced that knowledge and wisdoms gained in travel will reside in my spirit.
여행으로 얻어진 지식과 지혜들은 나의 정신에 흡수될 것이라고 확신한다.

F : May I help you?
   무엇을 도와 드릴까요?
K : Could you give me a wake-up call tomorrow morning?
   내일 아침 모닝콜 좀 부탁합니다.
F : What time would you like?
   언제 원하세요?

K : I'd like to get up at 6:00.
　　6시에 일어나길 원합니다.
F : Wake-up call, 6:00. Tomorrow morning. We will call you at 6.
　　모닝콜, 내일 아침 여섯 시입니다. 6시에 모닝콜 하겠습니다.

　　　　The following day, I plan to get around New York on my own
　　　　　　　with the intention of taking photos.
다음날 나는 사진을 찍기 위해 스스로 뉴욕을 돌아다니기로 계획을 세웠다.
Many tourists from all over the world flock to the restaurants, cafes and shops
　　　　　　　　like clouds in downtown New York.
세계 곳곳에서 온 많은 관광객들이 뉴욕 시내의 식당, 카페, 쇼핑가로
　　　　　　　　구름처럼 몰려들었다.
The color of New York gives me a significant impact on the perception of
　　　　　multicultural environment of the international city.
뉴욕의 국제도시적 다문화 환경적 색깔은 나에게 강한 인상을 주었다.
　　　I ask a passerby for directions and transportations.
　　나는 지나가는 사람에게 방향과 교통편들을 물어보았다.

K : Excuse me. This area is not familiar to me.
　　Could you please tell me how much it will cost if I take a taxi from here to the Museum of Modern Art(MOMA)?
　　실례합니다. 이곳을 잘 모르는데 택시를 타고 현대미술관까지 가면 얼마나 들죠?
F : Taxi would probably cost $20.
　　Bus is the cheapest ride to get there.
　　택시는 20불 정도 됩니다. 버스가 그곳으로 가기에 싼 교통편입니다.
K : Where do I take the bus?
　　버스를 어디서 타지요?
F : Right in front of that building.
　　저 건물 앞에 있습니다.

K : Is there a bus that goes the Museum of Modern Art(MOMA).
　　현대 미술관에 가는 버스가 있나요?
F : Try bus M 1,2,3.
　　M 1,2,3번을 타세요.
K : How much is the fare?
　　요금이 얼마죠?
F : $2.75 per way.
　　편도에 2.75달러입니다.

K : Is there a pass card?
　　교통카드가 있나요?
F : Yes. There is a 7-day unlimited ride Metrocard that offers unlimited subway and bus rides for $31.
　　You can buy Metrocard at subway stations with cash or credit.
　　네, 7일 동안 지하철과 버스를 제한 없이 탈 수 있는 31불 메트로 카드가 있습니다. 지하철 역에서 현금이나 신용카드로 살 수 있습니다.
K : How often is it running?
　　얼마나 자주 오죠?

F : Every 10 minutes.
　　10분마다 옵니다.
K : How long does it take from here?
　　여기에서 얼마나 걸립니까?
F : It takes about 15 minutes by bus.
　　버스로 약 15분 걸립니다.

K : Excuse me. Do you go to the MOMA.
　　현대 미술관까지 가나요?
F : Yes I do. But this bus stops near the museum.
　　맞습니다. 하지만 미술관 근처에서 섭니다.
K : Do I have to transfer?
　　갈아타야 하나요?
F : No. Get off at 53th street.
　　And go straight 2 blocks.
　　You can easily find it. Get on.
　　53번가 앞에서 내리세요.
　　그리고 2블럭을 계속 걸어가면
　　쉽게 찾을 수 있습니다. 타세요.
K : How can I use this traffic card?
　　이 교통카드를 어떻게 사용하죠?

F : Hold the Metrocard name facing you. And put the card into the
　　slot of the farebox machine, and then the card will pop back out.
　　카드의 글자 쪽을 보며 요금박스 기계에 넣으면 저절로 나오게 됩니다.
K : Thank you. Could you let me know where to get off?
　　감사합니다. 내릴 곳에서 말씀해 주실래요?
F : OK.
　　알겠습니다.

The Museum of Modern Art (MOMA)
opens at 10:30 A.M,
but there are many people,
which makes me wait in line.
현대미술관은
오전10시 30분에 열었는데,
사람이 많아 줄을 서서 기다렸다.
It is exhibiting many wonderful
collections of modern art.
미술관은 많은 훌륭한 현대미술
작품들을 전시하고 있었다.
I have a talk with a few people
while looking around the museum.
나는 박물관을 돌아보면서
몇몇 사람들과 대화를 나누었다.

After having a light meal for lunch, I go to the Museum of Natural History by taxi.
가벼운 점심을 먹은 후, 택시를 타고 자연사 박물관으로 갔다.
The Museum collections contain over 32 million specimens of various
life forms on earth, fossils, meteorites and human cultural artifacts.
박물관에는 3200만 종류의 지구상에 있는 다양한 생명체들과
화석, 운석, 문화재들이 있었다.
I enjoy looking around till closing time and head for Times Square.
나는 문 닫을 시간까지 구경하고 타임스퀘어로 향했다.

K : What's the easiest way to get to Times Square from here?
   타임스퀘어까지 가는데 어떤 방법이 가장 쉽죠?

F : Subway will make getting around easy and inexpensive.
   지하철이 돌아다니기 쉽고 저렴하여 좋습니다.

K : Is there a subway to go to Times Square?
   타임스퀘어로 가는 지하철이 있나요?

F : You actually need to take two subways to get to Times Square.
   타임스퀘어로 갈려면 지하철을 2번 타야 됩니다.

K : Which subway will I have to take?
   어느 지하철을 타야 하죠?

F : First, you need to take subway line A or C.
   먼저 A나 C라인 지하철을 타세요.

K : Then what do I do next?
   그 다음에는 어떻게 하죠?

F : Get off on Columbus Circle station.
   콜럼버스 서클 역에서 내리세요.

K : What's next?
   그 다음은요?

F : Take the subway line 1. It'll take you to Times Square station.
   지하철 1호선을 타세요. 타임스퀘어로 갈 것입니다.

K : How often does the subway run?
   지하철이 얼마나 자주 있지요?

F : It runs every few minutes.
   몇 분마다 있습니다.

K : Where do I get on a subway?
   지하철을 어디서 타죠?

F : Right over there.
   바로 저기 있어요.

K : How can I use Metrocard on the subway?
   지하철에서 교통카드를 어떻게 이용하죠?

F : With the Metrocard name facing toward you, quickly swipe your card through the turnstile in one smooth move.
Walk through when the turnstile screen says GO.
메트로카드 글자가 있는 쪽을 보며 가볍게 회전문 개찰구에 긁으세요.
회전문에 가라는 표시가 나면 지나가시면 됩니다.

K : Thank you.
감사합니다.

F : Your welcome. Don't forget to check out the subway map.
천만에요. 지하철 노선도를 꼭 확인하세요.

Times Square is the world's most visited tourist attraction, gleaming neon signs and billboards are dazzling with brilliance.
타임스퀘어는 세계에서 가장 방문하고 싶은 관광지로 밝은 네온사인들과 간판들이 휘황찬란했다.

K : Will you take my picture in front of this place, please?
이곳에서 사진을 좀 찍어 주실래요?

F : Okay.
좋습니다.

K : Could you make sure that building is in the background?
저 빌딩이 뒤에 나오게 해주실래요?

F : Sure.
알겠습니다.

James and I meet at Times Square and go to white restaurant in the early evening.
제임스와 나는 타임스퀘어에서 만나 초저녁에 화이트 식당으로 갔다.

F : Do you have a reservation?
예약을 하셨습니까?
J : We have a reservation under the name of James for 2 people.
제임스란 이름으로 2명 예약했습니다.
F : I'll show you to your table. This way, please.
제가 안내해 드리지요. 이쪽입니다.
J : Thanks.
감사합니다.
F : Is this all right?
자리 괜찮으세요?
J : This will be fine.
괜찮을 것 같군요.
F : I'll be your waiter for this evening.
Let me tell you about tonight's specials.
오늘 저녁 담당 웨이터인데 오늘의 스페셜 메뉴를 말씀 드리겠습니다.
J : Thank you for explaining, but I think we'll order from the menu.
설명 감사합니다만 메뉴를 보고 주문할게요.
F : All right. I'll bring you the menu.
알겠습니다. 메뉴판을 가져다 드리겠습니다.

J : How was today?
오늘 어땠어요?
K : I had fun.
재미있었어요.
J : Are you free tomorrow evening?
내일 저녁 시간이 되세요?

K : Yes. I have no plans.
    네. 별다른 계획이 없습니다.
J : I would like to fix you up with my younger sister tomorrow night.
    내일 저녁 제 여동생을 소개해 주고 싶군요.
K : What are you talking about all of sudden?
    갑자기 무슨 말이죠?
J : She has been working as a freelancer journalist, magazine writer in Cleveland and is coming here tomorrow morning.
    She has a big interest in Korean culture such as KPOP.
    그녀는 클리블랜드에서 프리랜서 기자로 잡지 기고를 하는데 내일 아침 이곳에 옵니다. KPOP 같은 한국 문화에 큰 관심을 가지고 있지요.
K : Oh, now I am catching on.
    아, 이제야 알겠군요.
J : She wants to cover the story. But she really wants Asian culture to be a part of her life. She likes KPOP music very much.
    취재를 하고 싶은 것이지요. 하지만 그녀는 아시아 문화가 그녀 생활의 일부이기를 바래요. KPOP 음악을 무척 좋아하죠.
K : I'll do whatever you say.
    당신이 말하는 데로 할게요.

J : Do you have a particular place in mind?
    어디에서 만나는 것이 좋을까요?
K : Has she ever tried Korean food before?
    그녀가 한국 음식을 먹어본 적이 있나요?
J : Maybe not yet.
    아직까지는 아닐 것입니다.
K : I'd like to treat her to dinner at Korean restaurant?
    그녀에게 한국음식점에서 저녁을 대접하고 싶군요.
J : That would be very good. What time is good for you?
    아주 좋을 것 같군요. 어느 시간이 좋죠?

K : Any time will be fine in the evening, but it would be good to see her at 6:00 P.M. in front of Hanahreum Asian Mart in Korea Town.
저녁에는 아무 때나 좋은데, 코리아타운의 한아름 아시아마트 앞에서 저녁 6시에 보는 것이 어떨까 싶습니다.

J : Do you know how to get there?
그곳에 어떻게 가는 지는 아시죠?

K : Yes. I can find my way.
네. 혼자 갈 수 있습니다.

J : OK. She'll be there on time.
알겠습니다. 그녀가 시간에 맞추어 나갈 것입니다.

K : I am looking forward to meeting with your sister.
당신 여동생을 만나는 것이 기대되는군요.

F : Here are your menus.
Can I get you a drink while you are looking over your menu?
여기 메뉴가 있습니다. 메뉴를 보시는 동안 마실 것을 드릴까요?

J : Sure. We'd like to have cold beers.
What kind of beer do you have?
차가운 맥주를 마시고 싶군요. 어떤 종류의 맥주가 있지요?

F : Heineken, Budweiser, Corona beer, sir.
하이네켄, 버드와이저, 코로나 맥주가 있습니다.

J : We'll have two Budweiser.
버드와이저 2병 주세요.

F : Would you like anything else?
또 다른 것은요?

J : That'll be fine for now, thank you.
I'll call you when we're ready to order.
충분합니다. 감사합니다. 준비가 되면 다시 부를게요.

F : OK. Let me know when you're ready.
알겠습니다. 준비되면 알려주십시오.

F : Before your main course, would you like to order an appetizer?
　　메인 코스를 주문하기 전에 에피타이저를 주문하실래요?
J : Do you have a special appetizer menu?
　　특별한 에피타이저 메뉴가 있나요?
F : Grilled shrimp salad with a peanut dressing is very good.
　　땅콩 드레싱에 볶은 새우야채가 좋습니다.
J : I'd like to have just mixed green salad as a starter.
　　전채 요리로 혼합 샐러드를 먹겠습니다.
F : That would be a great choice. What kind of dressing would you like? French, Italian, Honey mustard, Thousand island.
　　좋은 선택인 것 같군요. 드레싱은 어떤 것으로 하시겠습니까? 프렌치, 이탈리안, 하니 머스터드, 싸우젠 아일랜드가 있습니다.
J : Honey mustard.
　　하니 머스터드로 해 주세요.
F : What for you?
　　손님께서는 무엇을 드시겠습니까?
K : Smoked Chicken Nachos.
　　훈제치킨 나쵸를 주세요.

F : What soup would you like to have?
　　수프는 어떤 것으로 하시겠습니까?
J : What soup do you have today?
　　오늘 수프는 어떤 것이지요?
F : We've corn, broccoli, mushroom and clam chowder.
　　옥수수 수프, 브로콜리, 버섯, 조개 수프가 있습니다.
J : I'll have broccoli.
　　브로콜리 수프로 주세요.
K : Clam chowder.
　　조개 수프로 할게요.

F : May I take your main order, sir?
메인 요리를 주문하시겠습니까?

J : I'd like to order filet mignon.
필레미뇽을 주문하고 싶군요.

F : I'm sorry. We're currently out of filet mignon.
죄송합니다. 지금 필레미뇽이 다 떨어졌습니다.

J : Is there any good steak menu for today?
오늘 다른 좋은 스테이크 메뉴가 있습니까?

F : May I suggest T-bone or porterhouse steak instead?
대신 티본 스테이크나 포터하우스 스테이크를 권하겠습니다.

J : I'll take the T-bone steak.
티본 스테이크를 먹겠습니다.

F : How do you want your steak? Rare? Medium? Well done?
고기는 어떻게 익힐까요? 설익게, 중간, 아니면 잘 익힐까요?

J : Medium please.
중간으로 익혀주세요.

F : What would you like for your side dishes?
곁들이는 음식은 어떤 걸로 하시겠습니까?

J : Baked potatoes.
구운 감자로 주세요.

F : Our vegetable today is carrot or peas.
오늘 야채는 당근과 콩입니다.

J : I'll have carrot.
당근을 주세요.

F : OK, the other guest?
알겠습니다. 다른 손님께서는?

K : I'll have the same. Make it two. And Medium-Well done, please.
같은 것으로 하겠습니다. 2개 준비해 주세요. 그리고 약간 익혀 주세요.

F : OK. Would you like anything else?
네. 다른 필요한 것은 없습니까?

K : That'll be fine for now, thank you.
지금은 이것이면 됩니다.

F : Would you like to something to drink wine?
The wine list is posted on the menu in the middle of the table.
Vintage wines are very good.
와인을 드시겠습니까? 와인 종류는 테이블 중간의 메뉴판에 있습니다.
빈티지 와인들은 아주 좋습니다.

J : This King Estate wine. Please.
이 킹 에스테이트 와인을 주세요.

F : Thank you, sir. It shouldn't take too long.
감사합니다. 오래 걸리지 않을 것입니다.

F : What would you like to have for dessert?
Ice cream, sherbet or lemon cake with blue berry sauce?
디저트는 어떤 것으로 하겠습니까? 아이스크림이나 셔벗,
블루베리 소스의 레몬케이크, 어느 것으로 하시겠습니까?

J : What flavors of ice cream do you have?
아이스크림 향은 어떤 종류가 있지요?

F : We have Vanilla and Chocolate.
바닐라와 초콜릿입니다.

J : I'd like a Vanilla
바닐라를 주세요.

F : OK, the other guest?
알겠습니다. 다른 손님께서는요?

K : No, thanks. May I have some water, please?
저는 먹지 않을게요. 물 한잔 먹고 싶군요.

F : OK. Don't you want anything else, sir?
알겠습니다. 그 외에 다른 필요한 것은 없습니까?

J : Could you bring us some more bread and butter?
빵과 버터를 좀 더 주실래요?

F : Coming right up.
   곧 가져오겠습니다.

J : May I have the check, please?
   계산서를 주실래요?

F : Have you finished?
   식사를 다 마치셨어요?

J : Yes. That was a good dinner. I'm satisfied.
   예. 좋은 식사였습니다. 만족합니다.

F : Thank you, sir. I'll be right back with that.
   Do you want to pay separately?
   감사합니다. 계산서를 곧 가져 오겠습니다. 각자 계산하실 건가요?

J : No, you can put it all on one bill.
   아뇨. 청구서 하나로 해주세요.

F : There you go.
   여기 있습니다.

J : This was great service.
   I am thinking that 20% service charge would be just right.
   서비스가 아주 좋았습니다. 20% 팁이 괜찮다고 생각됩니다.

F : Thank you sir.
   감사합니다, 손님.

The dinner was excellent. I have expressed my sincere gratitude to James.
저녁식사는 아주 훌륭했다. 나는 제임스에게 고맙다고 말했다.
After returning to the hotel, I am having a long soak in the hot bath.
호텔로 돌아온 후 뜨거운 욕조에 오랫동안 몸을 담갔다.
Steam rises from the bath and various thoughts rise up from deep inside of my mind.
욕조에서 피어나는 수증기처럼 여러 생각들이 마음 깊은 곳에서 떠올랐다.
Thoughts are the ripples of the mind. Nobody can reverse the wave.
생각들이란 마음의 잔물결이다. 아무도 그걸 막지 못한다.
To awaken alone in a strange city is one of the exciting sensations.
생소한 도시에서 홀로 깨어있는 것은 흥미로운 느낌들 중 하나이다.

The greatest reward of travel is
to be able to experience new things which are not familiar.
여행의 가장 큰 보상은 친숙하지 않은 새로운 것들을 경험한다는 것이다.

F : Laundry service. May I help you, sir?
　　세탁 서비스입니다. 무엇을 도와드릴까요.
K : I have something to be laundered and pressed.
　　세탁과 다리미질 할 것이 있습니다.
F : We'll send up a person to you right away.
　　지금 곧 사람을 보내겠습니다.
K : When will I get it back if I send it out now?
　　지금 세탁을 맡기면 언제 돌려받을 수 있지요?
F : Are you in a hurry?
　　급하신가요?
K : I have an appointment with my friend tomorrow.
　　내일 친구와 약속이 있습니다.
F : I think they can be done by 7 A.M.
　　We will bring them up within that time.
　　아침 7시까지는 가능합니다. 그 시간 안에 가져다 드리겠습니다.
K : Okay.
　　알겠습니다.

The world is a travel book for someone who wants to read whole pages.
I want to be an avid reader.
세상이란 모든 페이지를 읽고 싶은 사람에게는 여행책자 같은 것으로
나는 열혈 독자가 되고 싶다.
I always believe that new experiences in travel will be my wealth for all life.
여행에서 얻은 새로운 경험들은 내 인생의 재산이 될 것이다.
From early morning, I am getting around the whole downtown.
아침 일찍부터 시내 모든 곳을 돌아 다녔다.

K : How do I get to Metropolitan Museum of Art from here.
이곳에서 메트로폴리탄 박물관까지는 어떻게 가죠?

F : Get in the S shuttle at Times Square subway station. Then get off at Grand Central station and transfer to the 4,5,6 subway going uptown to 86th Street.
타임스퀘어 역에서 셔틀 S라인을 타고 가세요. 그리고 그랜드 센트럴역에서 내려 업 타운 86번가로 가는 4,5,6번으로 갈아타세요.

K : Is there any other way?
다른 방법은 없나요?

F : You can take the bus heading toward uptown at 5th Avenue.
5번가에서 업 타운으로 가는 버스를 타셔도 됩니다.

K : Do you know where I get off at?
어디서 내리는지 아세요?

F : If you tell the bus driver where you're going, he'll announce to you when to get off. And you have to walk a little bit.
버스 기사에게 어디를 가는 지 말하면 내릴 때 말해 줄 것입니다. 그리고 약간 걸으셔야 합니다.

K : Excuse me. Does this bus go to Metropolitan Museum of Art?
죄송한데 이 버스가 메트로폴리탄 박물관까지 갑니까?

F : Yes. Get in.
예. 타세요.

K : Where do I get off at?
어디서 내려야 하죠?

F : I'll let you know.
제가 알려드리겠습니다.

K : Did I miss my stop?
제가 내릴 곳을 지나쳤나요?

F : You still have more to go.
좀 더 가야 합니다.

K : I'm not sure, is this my stop?
　　이곳이 제가 내릴 곳인지 모르겠군요.
F : We've arrived at the Museum. Get off the bus.
　　박물관에 도착했습니다. 버스에서 내리세요.

Metropolitan Museum has more than 2 million works,
span more than 5,000 years of world culture, from every part of the globe.
메트로폴리탄 박물관은 약 200만개 이상의,
지구 모든 곳에 온 5000년 세계 역사를 아우르는 작품들을 가지고 있었다.
It offers a good mix of kinds of art.
박물관은 여러 종류의 훌륭한 작품들로 조화를 이루었다.
I take my time at the exhibits and enjoy it to the fullest.
나는 전시관에서 시간을 보내며 최대한 즐겼다.
After seeing the exhibition, I walk to a nearby Guggenheim Museum.
전시된 것들을 보고 난 후,
나는 근처에 있는 구겐하임 박물관으로 걸어서 갔다.

F : Can I help you find something?
어디를 찾고 있으세요?

K : I'm looking for the Guggenheim Museum, but I think I'm lost. How do I get there?
구겐하임 박물관을 찾는데 길을 잃은 것 같아요. 그곳까지 어떻게 가죠?

F : The Museum is located at 89th Street, 5th avenue.
5번가, 89번가에 있습니다.

K : Is it close by?
이 근처에 있나요?

F : It's not far from here. It's just a couple of minutes walk from here.
이곳에서 멀지 않습니다.
걸어서 몇 분 거리입니다.

K : Which way do I go?
어디로 가야 하죠?

F : Go straight down this street and make a right at the intersection.
이 길을 따라 쭉 가다가 첫 번째 교차로에서 우측으로 가세요.

K : Pardon me?
예?

F : You need to walk west and turn right at 5th Avenue. And go toward the north to 89th Street.
서쪽으로 가다가
5번가에서 우회전하여
89번가까지 북쪽으로 가세요.

The form of Guggenheim gallery is a spiral ramp and lined with modern art exhibits.
구겐하임 갤러리 모양은 나선형으로 현대미술 작품들이 전시되어 있었다.
I have a great chance to see Picasso's and Van Gogh's paintings.
피카소와 반고호의 그림들을 볼 수 있는 좋은 기회였다.
After looking around the museum,
I go to Korea Town to meet James's sister, Charlotte.
미술관을 둘러 본 후,
제임스 여동생 샬럿을 만나러 코리아타운으로 갔다.

Korea Town is located on 32th Street between 5th Avenue and Broadway.
코리아타운은 5번가와 브로드웨이 사이의 32번가에 있다.
Korea Town is well known fantastic place to grab lunch or dinner.
It's one of the few places in New York which one can have a dinner till midnight.
코리아타운은 점심이나 저녁 먹기에 좋은 곳으로 알려져 있다.
뉴욕에서 자정까지 저녁을 먹을 수 있는 여러 곳들 중 하나이다.
I meet Charlotte in front of Hanahreum Asian Mart.
나는 샬럿을 한아름 아시아 마트 앞에서 만났다.
She is a beautiful lady with short blond hair.
샬럿은 짧은 금발의 아름다운 아가씨였다.

C : Hi, how are you doing?
    안녕하세요.
K : I'm fine. How about you?
    네. 안녕하세요.

C : I'm pretty good. Is this your first trip to New York?
좋아요. 뉴욕에는 처음이신가요?

K : No, This is my second visit.
아뇨. 2번째 방문입니다.

C : I've heard a lot about you. How do you like New York?
당신에 대해 많이 들었어요. 뉴욕이 어떠세요?

K : I like it very much.
아주 좋아요.

C : How long do you plan to stay in New York?
뉴욕에 얼마나 머물 계획이시죠?

K : About 10 days. Have you ever tried Korean food before?
10일간입니다. 한국 음식을 먹어본 적이 있나요?

C : Not yet.
아직 안 먹어봤어요.

K : How about having dinner with me at Korean restaurant?
저와 함께 한국음식점에서 저녁을 먹으면 어떻겠습니까?

C : Sounds great.
좋아요.

We have a dinner at Wonjo restaurant and talk about many things.
우리는 원조식당에서 저녁을 먹으며 많은 이야기를 나누었다.
She always says with a smile in her eyes.
그녀는 눈에 항상 웃음을 머금고 말을 했다.
Conversation makes a new connection when people are face to face.
얼굴을 맞대고 대화를 나눌 때 새로운 연결고리가 만들어진다.
She pays attention to what I am saying
and always looks me in the eye while I am listening to her.
그녀는 내말에 집중을 했고 그녀의 말을 듣는 동안에도 내 눈을 응시했다.
Spending time with her elevates my mood and boosts my sense of curiosity.
그녀와 함께 보내는 시간은 기분이 좋았고 호기심을 자극했다.
She smiles at me across the table
and asks me many questions as if she would like to get to know Korea better.
그녀는 식탁 너머로 미소를 지으며 한국을 알고 싶어 많은 질문들을 했다.

K : I'd like to feel New York as much as possible until the last day of my schedule. Have you ever used chopsticks?
떠나기 전까지 뉴욕에 대해 가능한 많이 느껴보고 싶습니다.
젓가락을 사용해 본 적 있으세요?

C : No. But I have seen wooden chopsticks in the Asian restaurant.
아뇨. 하지만 동양계 식당에서 나무젓가락은 본적이 있어요.

K : Let me teach you how to use it. It's not difficult.
어떻게 사용하는 지 가르쳐 드리죠. 어렵지 않습니다.

C : OK. How can I use this?
알았어요. 어떻게 사용하죠?

K : Pick up the first chopstick with 1st web space and fourth finger. And grip the second chopstick with index and third finger. Finally place your thumb over the second chopstick. Now try to move the upper chopstick and pinch the food.
첫 번째 젓가락을 첫 번째 손가락 사이와 4번째 손가락으로 잡으세요.
그리고 두 번째 젓가락을 2,3번째 손가락으로 잡으세요.
마지막으로 엄지손가락을 두 번째 젓가락에 올려놓으세요.
이제 윗부분 젓가락을 움직여 음식을 집으려고 해보세요.

C : It's hard to use.
사용하기 힘들군요.

K : Try doing it like me. You will soon get used to it. This is a spoon. Koreans usually eat rice with a spoon.
저처럼 해보세요. 곧 익숙해질 것입니다. 이것은 숟가락입니다.
한국인들은 밥을 숟가락으로 먹습니다.

C : OK. I'll try.
알겠어요. 사용해보죠.

K : Enjoy Korean food.
한국 음식을 맛있게 드세요.

C : Thank you. Every dish is delicious.
감사해요. 음식들이 다 맛있군요.

K : Are you interested in things of Korea?
한국에 대해 관심이 많나요?
C : Yes.
네.

K : What sort of things?
어떤 것들이 그렇죠?
C : What's the reason of current Korean success in business?
최근 한국의 비즈니스에서의 성공은 무엇 때문이죠?
K : Koreans are diligent and dynamic in doing business.
한국인들은 부지런하고 일을 할 때 역동적입니다.
C : Korean-made home appliances are popular in US.
한국 가전제품들은 미국에서 인기가 많아요.
K : Yes. Korean electronics companies have come to own a significant share of the world market today. There are lots of big conglomerates that own many world-class products. Especially Samsung is a world leader in display and smart phone technology.
예. 한국 전자회사들이 요즘 세계시장에서 상당한 점유율을 가지고 있습니다. 세계적인 제품을 소유한 재벌 기업들이 많습니다. 특히나 삼성은 디스플레이와 스마트 폰 기술에서 세계를 선도하고 있습니다.
C : I like Korean high-tech appliances like cell phone and TV. Times Square in New York has been the Mecca of advertising. I've seen many ads of Korean companies, Samsung, Hyundae, LG in Times Square.
저는 한국의 휴대폰, TV와 같은 첨단제품을 좋아해요. 뉴욕의 타임스퀘어는 광고의 중심이에요. 타임스퀘어에서 삼성, 현대, LG 같은 많은 한국 기업들의 광고를 보았어요.
K : We are proud of that.
그것이 자랑스럽습니다.

C : I could see patriotism at sport events. Korean fans wearing red T-shirts were cheering national teams in unison, banging on drums and waving a massive flag.
스포츠 행사들에서 애국심을 볼 수 있었어요. 붉은색 티셔츠를 입은 한국 팬들이 북을 치고 커다란 국기를 흔들며 대표 팀을 응원하더군요.

K : Koreans are extremely proud people.
But all other countries have similar minds to patriotism.
한국인들은 자부심이 아주 강한 민족입니다.
하지만 다른 모든 나라들도 애국심은 비슷할 것입니다.

C : By the way, I really like Korean drama and KPOP.
Korean dramas have attractive characters. It deals with emotions, pain and love so delicately and tenderly without losing the feel and spirit of it. And KPOP idols are pretty, gorgeous and very talented. Their dances make me mimic.
아무튼 저는 한국드라마와 KPOP을 정말 좋아해요. 한국드라마들은 매혹적인 캐릭터들을 가지고 있어요. 그리고 드라마들이 감정이나 고통, 사랑 등을, 느낌이나 내용을 잃지 않고 세밀하고 부드럽게 표현을 해요. 그리고 KPOP 아이돌들은 예쁘고, 멋있고, 아주 재능이 많아요. 그들의 춤은 나를 따라 하게 만들어요.

K : You are a big KPOP fan.
당신은 KPOP 열광 팬이군요.

C : Absolutely. I listen to KPOP every day.
물론이죠. KPOP을 날마다 듣는 걸요.

K : Korean Pop Music is very popular in Asia and it has been gaining much fame worldwide.
한국 대중음악은 아시아에서 아주 인기가 많고 세계적으로 명성을 얻고 있습니다.

C : KPOP is refreshing and singers are cute.
KPOP은 신선하고 가수들이 귀여워요.

K : Korean wave is taking around the globe. KPOP concerts take place in many international cities. Do you know that?
한류 물결이 세계적으로 유행이죠. KPOP 공연들이 많은 국제도시에서 열립니다. 알고 계세요?

C : Oh yes. I saw many Korean live music concerts on youtube. Many Idol dances were fantastic and amazing.
아 예. 유튜브에서 많은 한국 라이브 음악 공연들을 보았어요. 많은 아이돌 춤들이 환상적이면서 놀랍더군요.

K : KPOP singers can perform their unique dances and various styles of music, because they have a long period of training before the debut. People get to experience the variety of vocals and dance styles from different singers within the same group.
KPOP 가수들은 데뷔 전 오랫동안 훈련을 하여 독특한 춤들을 추고 여러 가지 스타일의 음악을 할 수 있습니다. 사람들은 같은 그룹이지만 서로 다른 가수들로부터, 다른 음색과 춤을 느끼며 다양함을 경험할 수 있는 것이죠.

C : That is the reason why Korean Idol groups have huge fan bases around the world.
그것이 바로 한국 아이돌 그룹들이 세계적으로 많은 지지 팬들을 가지고 있는 이유인가 보군요.

K : Yes. I am proud that Korean dramas and KPOP have gained mass popularity worldwide. And Korean films, computer games and fashion styles have become more popular in Asia. Korean spirit is alive and dynamic.
예. 한국드라마나 KPOP이 세계적으로 대중적 인기를 얻고 있는 것이 자랑스럽습니다. 한국의 영화, 컴퓨터 게임, 패션스타일도 아시아에서 점점 인기를 끌고 있습니다. 한국의 정신들은 살아있고 활동적이죠.

C : Fantastic! I'd like to feel the colorful variety of Korean culture.
놀라워요! 다양한 한국적 문화들을 느껴보고 싶어요.

K : Why don't you visit Korea? Come and see me, no matter when. I'll play cicerone to you.
한국에 오세요. 언제라도 저에게 오면 관광 안내를 해 드릴게요.

C : Thank you, I will if I get the chance.
고마워요. 기회가 되면 그럴게요.

K : I'll be expecting you.
기대하고 있겠습니다.

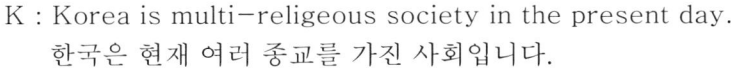

C : How about religion in Korea?
한국의 종교는 어떤가요?

K : Korea is multi-religeous society in the present day.
한국은 현재 여러 종교를 가진 사회입니다.

C : Korea seems to respect the diversity of free expression.
한국은 자유로운 표현의 다양성을 존중하는군요.

K : Yes. I think that Buddhist's mercy and Christ's love may be the common principle of the universal love.
부처의 자비나 예수의 사랑은 똑같이 넓은 사랑을 의미할 것입니다.

C : I think Buddhism is more about an ethic and philosophy than an actual religion. Christ's love is God's love, but Buddhist's mercy is developed human nature.
저는 불교는 종교라기보다는 윤리나 철학이라고 생각해요. 예수의 사랑은 신의 사랑이고, 부처의 자비는 발달된 인간의 본성이라고 생각해요.

K : There is no difference between them in essence. Both can embrace all living beings. Human being is a small part of god with connecting system of the whole spirit.
둘 다 본질의 차이는 없습니다. 양쪽 다 모든 생명체를 끌어안을 수 있습니다. 인간이란 존재는 전체적 정신과 연결된 신의 작은 일부분이죠.

C : Whole spirit? What does that mean?
전체적 정신이라뇨? 무슨 뜻이죠?

K : It means nature's will to evolve. Every will and love in the

nature is same in essence. Conflicts of religions could be avoided if we could understand that all religions are dynamic evolutionary processes of the nature.
진화하려는 자연의 의지를 말합니다. 자연의 모든 의지와 사랑은 본질적으로 똑같은 것입니다. 우리가 만약 모든 종교들이 자연의 능동적인 진화과정이라는 것을 이해한다면 종교적 갈등들은 없어질 것입니다.

C : You are a great thinker.
It's a pleasant surprise to hear that.
생각이 아주 깊으시네요. 그런 말을 듣다니 정말 놀라워요.

K : I am very flattered. Nowadays enjoying life by having fun has mushroomed into every corner of the country. Traditional customs have undergone transition period due to the rapid change of society.
과찬의 말씀입니다. 요즘은 즐거움으로 삶을 즐기려는 풍토가 나라 구석구석 파고들고 있습니다. 전통적인 관습들이 급격한 사회의 변화로 과도기에 있습니다.

C : It seems to be worldwide trend. Modern people are in a hurry.
세계적인 흐름인 것 같아요. 현대인들은 항상 마음이 급해 있어요.

K : I agree with you. Many people have a quick and hot temper.
동의합니다. 많은 사람들이 성격이 급하고 다혈질인 것 같습니다.

C : Sure. The world is moving fast. Information is overflowing. Modern people miss the sense of where they are going and why.
맞아요. 세상은 너무 빨리 변하고, 정보는 넘치고 있어요.
현대인들은 어디로, 왜 가는지도 모르고 있어요.

K : We need to take time to slow down and enjoy the simple life.
시간을 가지고 느리게 살면서, 평범한 일상을 즐길 필요가 있습니다.

C : We think alike.
우리는 생각이 비슷하군요.

K : Do you have any close friends in Korea?
한국에 가까운 친구가 있습니까?

C : No. I haven't.
　아뇨. 없어요.
K : Let's keep in touch.
　연락을 주고받을까요?
C : Sure.
　그러죠.
K : This is my business card. Do you have your business card?
　제 명함입니다. 명함이 있으신가요?
C : No, I don't have it now.
　지금은 없어요.
K : Give me your email address and mobile number.
　당신의 이메일 주소와 핸드폰 번호를 주세요.
C : OK. Let me get a pen. Here you are. E mail me. I'll be in touch.
　알았어요. 펜 좀 준비 할게요. 여기 있어요. 메일 주세요. 연락할게요.
K : OK. Feel free to give me a call or email anytime.
　알았습니다. 언제든지 저에게 전화나 메일 주십시오.

　　　　　I wave goodbye to her and go to the hotel on foot.
　나는 그녀에게 손을 흔들어 작별인사를 하고 걸어서 호텔로 갔다.
　　　When I travel alone, I learn how to trust someone bit by bit.
　　여행을 혼자 하면 사람들을 믿는 방법을 조금씩 배우게 된다.
　　　　And travel gives me a taste of different sides of the world.
　　　그리고 여행은 다른 세계의 또 다른 느낌을 나에게 던져준다.

The following morning, I oversleep and take a nice long shower,
have a brunch around 11 A.M. at Times Square.
다음날 아침 나는 늦잠을 자고 기분좋게 오랫동안 샤워를 한 후,
타임스퀘어에서 오전11시경 브런치를 먹었다.
The Staten Island ferry run every 30 minutes between 7 A.M. and 11 P.M.
스태튼 섬 페리는 아침 7시부터 밤 11시까지 30분 간격으로 운행하였다.
Travel time is approximately 25 minutes and free.
운행 시간은 25분 정도이며 무료였다.

K : Does the ferry leave from here?
    페리가 이곳에서 출발하나요?
F : Yes, I think so. I am also waiting for the ferry to arrive.
    네 그런 것 같아요. 저도 페리가 도착하기를 기다리고 있어요.
K : Isn't the ferry supposed to arrive now?
    페리가 지금쯤 도착되어야 하지 않나요?
F : I guess the ferry is running a little late.
    페리가 조금 늦게 오나 보네요.

The ferry gives me a great view of the New York Harbor
and a chance to see the Statue of Liberty from a distance.
페리는 뉴욕항의 멋진 풍광과
멀리서 자유의 여신상을 볼 수 있게 해주었다.

Double-decker sightseeing bus tour is a great way to see New York.
2층 투어버스가 뉴욕을 구경하기에 좋은 방법이다.
Hop-on, hop-off bus tour is fun.
타고 내리며 구경하는 버스 투어는 재미있었다.
One visitor sitting next to me asks kindly.
옆에 앉은 한 관광객이 친절하게 물었다.

F : Where are you come from?
어디에서 오셨어요?

K : I am from Korea.
한국에서 왔습니다.

F : Did you see Broadway Musical? It's very wonderful.
브로드웨이 뮤지컬 쇼를 보셨나요? 정말로 대단합니다.

K : How can I see a Broadway Show?
브로드웨이 쇼를 어떻게 보죠?

F : Times Square is the heart of the Theater District.
But tickets for Broadway shows can be very expensive.
타임스퀘어가 극장가의 중심부입니다.
하지만 브로드웨이 쇼 티켓은 매우 비쌉니다.

K : What is the best way to get a good deal on theater ticket?
표를 적당한 가격에 살 수 있는 좋은 방법이 있나요?

F : The best way to get discount theater tickets is to visit a TKTS booth. You get in line and buy 50% off tickets for that night.
표를 할인 받으려면 TKTS 부스로 가는 것이 좋습니다.
줄을 서서 50% 할인된 저녁시간 표를 사세요.

K : How can I get there?
그곳에 어떻게 가죠?

F : TKTS booking office is under the red stairs in Times Square.
TKTS 매표소는 타임스퀘어의 붉은 계단 아래에 있습니다.

K : Are there going to be long lines?
기다리는 줄이 길까요?

F : Lines can get long, but it is worth saving money on something you really want to see.
줄이 길지만 보고 싶은 것을 싸게 볼 수가 있어 그럴 가치가 있습니다.

Many tourists are buying discounted theater tickets at the TKTS Booth, but there is no ticket for Lion King which I want to see.
많은 관광객들이 TKTS부스에서 할인표를 사고 있었는데, 내가 보고 싶은 라이언 킹은 팔지 않았다.
The Lion King is playing eight times a week at the Minskoff Theater, I have bought directly a ticket in theater.
라이온 킹은 민스코프 극장에서 일주일에 8번 공연을 하는데, 극장에서 직접 표를 샀다.
The play is fantastic. I get back hotel at night and put my feet up.
연극은 환상적이었다. 밤에 호텔로 돌아와 편히 쉬었다.

Next day, I wake up early to go to the Woodbury Common Premium Outlet.
다음 날, 우드버리 커먼 프리미엄 아울렛으로 가기 위해 일찍 일어났다.
It's so far away. I decide to rent a car.
그곳은 너무 멀었기에 차를 렌트하기로 했다.

K : Excuse me. I'd like to rent a car.
　　차를 렌트하고 싶습니다.
F : What kind of car would you like?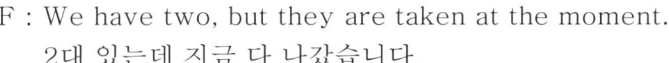
　　무슨 차를 원하세요?
K : Do you have Hyundae Sonata?
　　현대 소나타는 있나요?
F : We have two, but they are taken at the moment.
　　2대 있는데 지금 다 나갔습니다.
K : How about compact car?
　　소형차는요?
F : We're out of that. How about other medium sized sedan?
　　그것도 다 나갔습니다. 다른 중형차는 어떻습니까?
K : OK.
　　좋습니다.
F : Automatic or manual?
　　오토입니까 수동입니까?
K : Automatic, please.
　　오토입니다.
F : How long will you have it for?
　　얼마나 사용하실 거죠?
K : One day. What's the rate?
　　하루입니다. 사용료가 얼마죠?
F : Rental fee is $50 per day.
　　렌트료는 하루에 50 달러입니다.

K : What does the rental price include?
렌트료에 무엇이 포함되죠?

F : The price includes limited mileage and tax.
가격에는 제한된 거리와 세금이 포함되어 있습니다.

K : Doesn't that include auto insurance?
자동차 보험은 포함되지 않았나요?

F : No. Insurance will cost you extra.
Car insurance is mandatory.
예. 보험은 요금이 추가됩니다. 차 보험은 의무입니다.

K : I'd like to be insured.
Just Collision Damage Waiver(CDW) Insurance.
보험에 들겠습니다. 차량 손해보험만 들겠습니다.

F : Did you ever get into an accident and need your insurance?
사고가 난 적이 있거나 보험이 필요했던 적이 있나요?

K : I had a traffic accident last month, but it wasn't my fault.
It was the other person's fault and their insurance covered it.
지난 달 교통사고 난 적이 있는데, 제 잘못은 없고 상대방 잘못이라,
그쪽 보험회사에서 비용처리 했습니다.

F : You need bodily injury and property damage liability (No fault insurance). And it doesn't cover roadside service.
대인, 대물 책임보험은 꼭 필요합니다. 또 긴급출동 지원은 안됩니다.

K : OK. I want to buy full coverage including roadside assistance.
And I need a GPS for navigation.
종합보험, 긴급출동 다 들겠습니다. 그리고 네비게이션도 필요합니다.

F : Sure. You need to fill out this form.
그러죠. 이곳에 기입해 주세요.

K : Is there a spare wheel in the car?
예비 타이어가 있나요?

F : Yes. All cars have a spare wheel.
예. 모든 차량에 예비 타이어가 있습니다.

K : Should I fill it up before returning the car?
　　차를 돌려주기 전에 기름을 가득 채워야 하나요?
F : If the car is not returned with a full tank of fuel, then we will charge you for the fuel service fee.
　　연료를 가득 채워 반환하지 않으시면 연료서비스 비용이 추가됩니다.
K : I'd like to take a look at it if it has any problems.
　　무슨 문제가 있는지 보고 싶습니다.
F : Car is parked there, in the parking lot.
　　Let's go out and check the condition of car.
　　차는 저기 주차장에 있습니다. 나가서 차 상태를 체크해 보죠.

　　There is no road signs to indicate how to get to outlet.
　　어떻게 아울렛으로 가야 하는 지 교통 표지판이 없었다.
　　I depend on navigation, but it's not accurate.
　　네비게이션에 의존했으나 정확하지가 않았다.

K : Pump number 3, regular, $30, please. How far is Woodburry Outlet from here? Am I going the right way?
　　주유펌프 3번, 보통 휘발유 30불어치요. 우드버리 아울렛까지 이곳에서 얼마나 되죠? 제가 올바른 길로 가고 있나요?
F : Yes, you are in the right direction. It's about 40 miles from here.
　　예. 올바른 방향으로 가고 있어요. 이곳에서 40마일 거리입니다.
K : What's the best way to get there?
　　그곳까지 가는 가장 좋은 길이 어디죠?
F : Take the palisades interstate parkway.
　　That will take you all the way to there.
　　팰리세이드 인터스테이트 파크웨이를 타세요. 그 길로 쭉 가면 됩니다.
K : Do I keep going straight?
　　똑바로 가라고요?
F : Yes, but turn left at the Queensboro brook intersection.
　　네 하지만 퀸스보로 브룩 교차로에서 좌회전 하세요.

K : Can you show me where it is on the map?
　　이 지도에 표시를 해주실래요?
F : Sure, it's right here.
　　Take a right at the next signal to enter the parkway.
　　그러죠. 바로 여기입니다. 다음 신호에서 우회전하여 파크웨이로 들어가세요.

K : Is there a problem, officer?
　　무슨 문제가 있나요 경관님?
F : You didn't stop for the stop sign.
　　And you ran a red light.
　　정지신호에서 멈추지 않았네요.
　　그리고 빨간 불에서 지나치셨어요.

K : I'm sorry for running it.
　　지나쳐서 죄송합니다.
F : Didn't you notice it?
　　보지를 못하셨나요?
K : I honestly see it yellow light.
　　솔직히 노란색으로 보았습니다.
F : You know better than that, yellow means slow down.
　　아시겠지만 노란색은 속도를 줄이라는 뜻입니다.
K : I swear that I didn't mean to run it.
　　정말로 지나치려는 생각은 없었습니다.
F : I can understand.
　　이해합니다.
K : Can't you give me a warning? I am a foreign tourist.
　　I am not familiar with this road. I got confused.
　　경고만 해 주실 수는 없나요? 저는 외국 관광객입니다.
　　이 길에 익숙하지 않고 혼란스러웠습니다.

F : OK. I will let you go with a warning.
  알겠습니다. 경고만 하고 보내드리겠습니다.
K : Thanks for being so understanding.
  이해를 해 주셔서 감사합니다.
F : Make sure to pay closer attention. Buckle your seatbelt and don't exceed the speed limit.
  주의를 기울여주세요. 안전벨트를 매시고 속도제한을 넘지 마세요.

F : Pull up over there.
  저곳에 세우세요.
K : Why do you pull me over?
  왜 저를 세우셨나요?
F : I am an undercover police officer.
  일반 차량을 탄 경찰관입니다.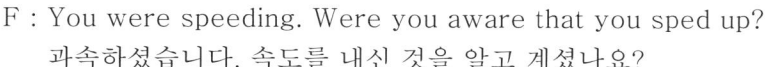
K : What's wrong? officer?
  무슨 일이죠? 경관님?
F : You were speeding. Were you aware that you sped up?
  과속하셨습니다. 속도를 내신 것을 알고 계셨나요?
K : I'm not sure.
  잘 모르겠습니다.
F : Do you have any idea how fast you were going?
  얼마나 빨리 달렸는지 아세요?
K : I think I was going about 40mph.
  40마일로 달린 것 같은데요.
F : You were going 50mph. The speed limit is 40mph.
  50마일로 달리고 있었습니다. 40마일이 속도제한입니다.
K : Sorry. I was not aware of that.
  죄송합니다. 모르고 있었습니다.
F : I'm going to give you a ticket for this.
  교통위반 딱지를 발부하겠습니다.

K : Please, I entreat you. Let me go with warning.
I am a foreign visitor and not familiar with this area.
부탁인데, 저에게 경고만 해주시고 보내주시길 바랍니다.
외국인 방문객이고 이곳을 잘 모릅니다.

F : I'm just doing my job.
제 일을 할 뿐입니다.

K : I understand. I'm sorry.
이해합니다. 죄송합니다.

F : Do you have a valid international driver's license from your country and rental agreement?
당신 나라에서 받은 유효한 국제면허증과 렌터카 계약서가 있습니까?

K : Yes, here you are.
네. 여기 있습니다.

F : If you don't pay the ticket fine, you could be denied next entry into the U.S.
교통위반 벌금을 내지 않으면 다음 미국 입국이 금지될 수 있습니다.

I drive car again. I am at a red light, but a car has hit me from behind.
나는 다시 차를 몰았다. 빨간 신호등에 서 있는데 차가 뒤에서 차를 받았다.
I move my car off to the side of the road
and out of the path of oncoming traffic to keep me at a safe distance.
나는 지나는 차량과의 안전거리를 위해 차를 도로 옆에 세웠다.

K : Hello. You hit my car.
제 차를 받으셨네요.

F : I didn't mean to. It was an accident. Does anyone get hurt?
의도적으로 그런 것이 아닙니다. 사고입니다. 누가 다쳤나요?

K : My car is damaged.
제 차가 다쳤네요.

F : Your car looks okay to me.
당신 차는 괜찮은 것 같은데요.

K : My rear bumper is scratched and smashed in.
뒤 범퍼가 긁히고 들어갔잖아요.

F : I don't see anything wrong with it.
아무 이상 없는 것 같은데요.

K : My car got dent. I'll make the call to request police assistance.
제 차가 찌그러졌잖아요. 경찰을 불러 판가름해야겠습니다.

F : Hey, man. If no one is hurt, the cars involved are not
blocking traffic and damage is under $1000,
reporting the accident to the police is not required.
이봐요. 아무도 다치지 않았거나, 교통을 방해하지 않거나, 손해가
1000달러 이하이면 경찰을 부르지 않아도 되잖아요.

K : But I think getting a report of the accident would be helpful in
establishing fault.
하지만 잘못을 가리기 위해 경찰의 도움이 필요할 거라 생각합니다.

F : I'll take care of it.
제가 고쳐드리겠습니다.

K : Can you handle this?
책임질 수 있나요?

F : Yes I can. Please, give me your rent car phone number.
예. 렌터카 회사 전화번호를 알려주세요.

K : Here you go. And I need your information too. I need your name, address and phone number. Do you have your registration and driver's license?
여기 있습니다. 당신의 정보도 주세요. 당신의 이름, 주소, 전화번호가 필요합니다. 차량 등록증이나 운전면허증이 있으세요?

F : OK. I hate fender benders. I have had twice a month.
알겠습니다. 접촉사고가 정말 지겹군요. 이달에 2번이나 발생했어요.

I take car accident scene photos
and write down his car model, year and license plate number of vehicle.
나는 교통사고 현장을 촬영하고 차 모델, 연식과 차량번호를 기록했다.
After exchanging information, I immediately report the car accident to my rent car company and provide the company with information on the other driver.
정보를 교환한 후 렌터카 회사에 차 사고에 대한 보고를 하고
상대 운전자의 정보를 회사에 제공했다.

K : Pardon me, do you know where Woodburry Outlet is? Someone told me it's around here somewhere.
죄송한데 우드버리 아울렛이 어디인지 아세요?
누가 이 근처에 있다고 하던데요?

F : You have to turn around and drive that way and when you get to Averill Avenue, turn right.
돌아서 저 길로 간 다음 애버릴 가에서 우측으로 도세요.

K : So, I have to make a U turn and go back the other way?
그러니까 U 턴을 한 다음, 다른 길로 가라는 거군요?

F : Yes.
네.

When I get there, the parking lot is full.
The Woodbury Outlet looks massive.
그곳에 갔을 때는 주차장이 만원이었다.
우드버리 아울렛은 거대하게 보였다.

K : All of parking spots are gone. Can I park on the street?
　　주차 장소가 다 차서 없네요. 길가에 차를 주차해도 되나요?
F : You have to pay attention to the parking tickets.
　　주차위반 딱지에 주의하세요.

There are not available parking spots anywhere.
주차장 어디에도 주차할 곳이 없었다.
I circle multiple times around the parking lots and barely find the parking area.
주차할 곳을 찾아 여러 차례 돌아서 가까스로 주차할 장소를 찾았다.
I wouldn't be able to hit every store, but try to be in full shopping mode.
나는 모든 가게를 둘러볼 수는 없었지만, 쇼핑만 한다는 생각으로 다녔다.
The prices are much cheaper compared to other shopping malls,
but they also have the most expensive items.
가격들은 다른 쇼핑몰보다 상당히 저렴했지만, 아주 비싼 품목들도 많았다.

F : Can I help you?
　　어서 오세요.
K : I am looking for T-shirt.
　　티셔츠를 찾고 있습니다.

F : What size do you wear?
어느 사이즈를 입으세요?

K : X Large, I think.
X 라지 사이즈를 원합니다.

F : How do you like this one?
이것은 어떠세요?

K : Can I try it on?
입어 봐도 될까요?

F : You can try it on in the fitting room over there.
저곳 탈의실에서 입어보세요.

K : Does it look too big?
너무 크지 않나요?

F : It looks like it's a perfect fit.
아주 잘 맞는 것 같습니다.

K : Yes, I like it. I'll get it.
네. 좋습니다. 살게요.

F : Is there anything else you'd like to get?
맘에 드시는 것이 또 있으신가요?

K : No. This will be fine.
아뇨. 이것이면 됩니다.

F : How would you like to pay for it?
어떻게 지불하시겠습니까?

K : Here's my credit card.
여기 신용카드가 있습니다.

F : Your signature here. Here's your receipt. Have a nice day.
여기 사인해 주세요. 여기 영수증이 있습니다. 좋은 하루 되세요.

K : Is this dress on sale?
이 옷 세일하나요?

F : No, it isn't. 아닙니다

K : How much are they?
저것들은 얼마죠?

F : They are each 70 dollars.
각각 70달러입니다.

K : Are they on sale?
저것들은 세일하나요?

F : Some of them are, and some of them aren't.
어떤 것은 하고 어떤 것은 안 합니다.

K : I'd like to try this clothes on.
이 옷을 입어보고 싶군요.

F : Try on.
입어보세요.

K : How do I look?
이 옷이 어떤가요?

F : It's wonderful on you.
훌륭하군요.

K : I'll take this.
이것을 살게요.

F : Cash or charge?
현금이나요 카드이나요?

K : Here is my card.
여기 카드가 있습니다.

F : Have you found anything that you like?
마음에 드는 것을 찾으셨어요?

K : I am interested in buying this. How much is this?
이것을 사고 싶군요. 이것은 얼마죠?

F : This is $220 dollars.
220달러입니다.

K : You can't be serious. That's too expensive for me.
  진짜요? 제겐 너무 비싸군요.
F : This is of very high quality.
  질이 아주 좋습니다.
K : Could you lower the price a little? I can't afford that.
  가격을 좀 낮추어줄 수 없나요? 그럴 여유가 없군요.
F : I can't go down on that price.
  저 가격에서 더 내릴 수는 없습니다.
K : I want something inexpensive. Do you have anything cheaper?
  저는 싼 것을 원합니다. 좀 더 싼 것은 없습니까?
F : How about this one?
  이것은 어떻습니까?
K : How much?
  얼마죠?
F : 130 dollars.
  130달러입니다.

K : Can you come down a little?
  I would buy it if the price is reasonable.
  조금 깎아 줄 수 있나요? 가격이 맞으면 살게요.
F : How much are you talking?
  얼마를 말하시나요?
K : I'll buy it for $100.
  100달러에 사겠습니다.
F : I'm sorry, but $110 is the final price.
  That's the lowest price I can get you for today.
  죄송합니다. 110달러가 최종가격입니다.
  그것이 오늘 당신에게 줄 수 있는 가장 낮은 가격입니다.
K : Okay. Do you accept VISA card?
  알겠습니다. 비자카드로 되나요?
F : Yes. 예

F : May I help you find something?
    도와드릴까요?
K : Yes. I am looking for an attractive T-shirt.
    네. 좋은 T셔츠를 찾고 있습니다.
F : I think you'll like this one.
    이것이 마음에 드실 것입니다.
K : I want a more attractive one.
    좀 더 좋은 것을 원합니다.
F : Come this way.
    이곳으로 오세요.
K : Is there anything on sale today?
    오늘 세일하는 것이 있나요?

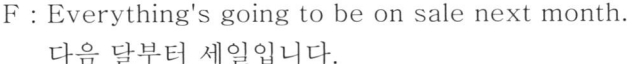

F : Everything's going to be on sale next month.
    다음 달부터 세일입니다.
K : OK. I like that style over there.
    알겠습니다. 저 스타일이 좋군요.
F : How about this one?
    이것은 어떻습니까?
K : It's too dark. Do you have any other color?
    너무 어둡군요. 다른 색깔은 없습니까?
F : How about this?
    이것은 어떻습니까?
K : Do you have this style in yellow?
    이런 스타일의 노란색은 없나요.
F : I'll have to check.
    찾아볼게요.
K : Can you guess my size?
    제 사이즈를 아시겠습니까?

F : Try this on.
이것을 입어보세요.

K : What size is this?
이 사이즈가 몇이죠?

F : Large X.
라지 X 사이즈입니다.

K : Where is the fitting room?
옷 입는 곳이 어디죠?

F : Follow me. Right here.
따라오세요. 여기입니다.

K : I can't make up mind.
결정할 수가 없군요.

F : It looks good.
좋은데요.

K : It's too big. Do you have a smaller one?
너무 큽니다. 더 작은 것은 없나요.

F : We have all sizes available.
모든 사이즈가 있습니다.

K : Can I try this?
이것을 입어보아도 되겠습니까?

F : Yes, you can. Try on it.
예. 좋습니다. 입어보세요.

K : This size seems to fit me. How does it look?
이 크기가 저에게 맞는 것 같군요. 어떤가요?

F : It suits you.
잘 어울립니다.

K : How much is this?
얼마죠?

F : 140 dollars.
140달러입니다.

K : It costs me too much. Can't you give me a better price?
너무 비싸군요. 좀 더 좋은 가격에 줄 수 없나요?

F : It's not on sale at the moment. But I will give you 10 percent off.
지금은 세일이 아닙니다. 하지만 10% 할인해 드리겠습니다.

K : Thanks. I'll take.
고맙습니다. 이것을 사겠습니다.

F : How would you like to pay for this?
어떻게 결제하시겠습니까?

K : Cash.
현금입니다.

K : It really appeals to me. I was wondering what the price is.
제 취향이군요. 가격이 얼마인지 궁금하군요.

F : Come on in. How much do you want to pay?
I'll give it to you for 200 dollars.
들어오세요. 얼마를 원하세요? 당신에게 200달러에 드릴게요.

K : The price is a little high for this. I think that 100 dollars would be fair for this. Could you lower the price a bit?
가격이 이것에는 조금 비싸군요. 이것은 백 달러면 합당할 것 같군요. 가격을 조금 깎아 주실래요?

F : Isn't that a great?
좋지 않나요?

K : I need to compare this to others.
이것을 다른 것과 비교하고 싶습니다.

F : So do you think that you would like to buy this?
그래서 이것을 사시겠습니까?

K : I am not interested in buying this right now.
But I appreciate your time.
지금 이것을 바로 사고 싶지는 않습니다.
아무튼 시간을 내 주셔서 감사합니다.

F : Why don't you take a second look at others?
다른 것들도 좀 더 보시지 그러세요?

K : I was thinking a little lower than that.
I will continue to look around and will come back to you.
그것보다는 가격을 낮게 생각했습니다.
더 둘러보고 당신에게 오겠습니다.

F : What can I do for you?
무엇을 도와드릴까요?

K : Is this on sale?
이것 세일하는 중이나요?

F : I'm sorry. It's not for sale.
죄송하지만 그것은 세일하지 않습니다.

K : I really like this, but I want to pay the sale price.
How much are you selling it for?
정말 이것이 좋은데 세일가격에 사고 싶군요. 얼마에 파나요?

F : This is $300.
300달러입니다.

K : You can't be serious.
너무하군요.

F : Design is smart and outstanding.
디자인이 아주 멋있고 훌륭합니다.

K : I think that price is too high for this.
가격이 이것에겐 너무 비싸게 생각되는군요.

F : I might be able to come down a little on the price.
가격을 낮추어 드릴 수 있습니다.

K: I'll buy it for $200.
200달러에 사고 싶군요.

F : I'm sorry, $250 is a low as I'll go.
죄송합니다. 250달러가 제가 할 수 있는 최저가입니다.

K : That's too expensive for me. I appreciate your time.
저에겐 너무 비쌉니다. 시간을 내주셔서 고맙습니다.

F : What price were you thinking would be a good deal for you?
어느 가격이 적당하다고 생각하셨나요?

K : I will continue to look around for others.
다른 것들을 더 둘러볼게요.

F : How much do you want to pay?
얼마를 원하시죠?

K : I will come back to you if I change my mind.
마음이 변하면 다시 오겠습니다.

K : Does this T-shirt come in blue?
이 티셔츠로 파란색이 있나요?

F : No, we don't have it in blue, only in yellow and red.
파란색은 없고 노란색과 빨간색만 있습니다.

K : Is it on sale?
세일하나요?

F : Yes, it's on sale. All T-shirts are 30% off this month only.
네, 세일 중입니다. 이번 달만 모든 티셔츠가 30% 할인입니다.

K :What about Y-shirts?
와이셔츠는 어떤가요?

F : 20% off sale.
20% 할인입니다.

K : This Y-shirt don't have a price tag. How much is it?
이 와이셔츠는 가격표가 없는데 얼마이죠?

F : That is $29.
29달러입니다.

K : I'll take this. Could you wrap it up for me?
이것을 살게요. 포장을 해주시겠습니까?

The road traffic is heavy. I spend a lot of time to come back to the hotel.
길이 밀렸다. 호텔까지 돌아오는데 많은 시간이 걸렸다.

I want to go out and around somewhere, not stay in hotel.
나는 호텔에만 있지 않고 어디에든 나가 돌아다니고 싶었다.
I take a look around 5th avenue
which is one of the world's most expensive streets at night.
나는 밤에 세계에서 가장 비싼 거리 중 하나인 5번가를 둘러보았다.
Street lights help to keep everything visible.
거리의 불빛들은 모든 것을 볼 수 있게 했다.
Splendid neon signs, busy sidewalks,
a variety of products displayed in the show windows,
all of them stimulate tourist's curiosity.
화려한 네온사인들과 붐비는 인도,
쇼 윈도우에 전시된 다양한 상품들이
관광객들의 호기심을 자극하고 있었다.

The next morning, I plan to see
the UN building and the Stature of Liberty.
다음 날 UN 빌딩과 자유의 여신상을 보려고 계획했다.
I order breakfast through room service.
룸 서비스로 아침을 시켰다.

F : Room service. May I help you?
룸 서비스입니다. 무엇을 도와 드릴까요?

K : I'd like to order some breakfast.
아침을 주문하고 싶습니다.

F : Yes, sir. What would you like to order?
예. 손님 무엇을 원하십니까?

K : Continental breakfast with fried eggs.
콘티넨털 식사와 계란 프라이 부탁 드립니다.

F : What would you like, Toast, Bagel or Muffin?
토스트, 베이글, 머핀 중에서 어느 것을 드실래요?

K : Toast.
토스트를 주세요.

F : Would you like some coffee or orange juice?
커피나 오렌지 주스 어느 것을 드실래요?

K : Coffee please.
커피로 주세요.

F : Anything else?
다른 것은 없나요?

K : Bring me a couple of bananas. Will that be possible?
바나나 2개 가져다 주세요. 가능할까요?

F : OK. Room service will be charged to your room account. It will be up shortly.
알겠습니다. 룸 서비스는 호텔 비용에 추가 될 것입니다.
곧 준비될 것입니다.

K : Hello, room service?
룸 서비스인가요?

F : Yes. May I help you?
예. 무엇을 도와 드릴까요?

K : I ordered some breakfast. I have been waiting for almost 30 minutes. What happened to it?
아침을 시켰는데요. 거의 30분이나 기다렸습니다. 어떻게 된 일이죠?

F : We are very sorry for being late. Would you please wait another 5 minutes?
늦어서 죄송합니다. 오 분만 더 기다려 주실래요?

K : I am in a hurry.
지금 급합니다.

F : Yes, sir. It will be delivered as soon as it's all ready. We are very busy this season. Please accept our apologies. Staff will be up shortly with your order, sir.
네. 알겠습니다. 준비 되는대로 가져갈 것입니다. 지금 매우 바쁜 시기라 정말 죄송합니다. 곧 주문하신 것을 직원이 가지고 갈 것입니다.

At the front desk, I ask concierge for sightseeing advice.
프런트 데스크에서 컨시어즈에게 관광안내를 받았다.

K : I was wondering if you could recommend me special tourist attractions?
관광객들이 가볼 만한 특별한 곳 좀 추천해 주실래요?

F : What did you see?
무엇을 구경하셨나요?

K : Most of Museums, Times Square, Down Town. Today, I'll see the UN building and the Statue of Liberty. Can you recommend somewhere good to go?
대부분의 박물관과 타임스퀘어, 시내중심가를 보았습니다.
오늘 유엔 건물과 자유의 여신상을 볼 계획입니다.
어디 갈만한 좋은 곳을 추천해 주실래요?

F : By any chance, did you see the bridges in the city?
혹시 도시의 다리들을 보셨나요?

K : No. Come to think of it, I'd really like to see the bridge.
아뇨. 생각을 해 보니, 정말 다리를 보고 싶군요.

F : I would suggest the Brooklyn Bridge.
You can enjoy wonderful seaside skyline. Then you can visit the famed Grimaldi's Pizzeria after crossing the bridge.
브루클린 다리를 추천합니다. 멋진 해안가 도시경관을 즐길 수 있을 것입니다. 그리고 다리를 건너 유명한 그리말디 피자가게를 가세요.

K : That sounds like a good plan.
Could you tell me the best way to get there without taking a cab?
좋은 계획인 것 같군요.
택시를 타지 않고 그곳으로 가는 가장 좋은 방법이 무엇입니까?

F : Take the subway to Brooklyn Bridge-City Hall and you can walk across the bridge from Manhattan.
If you do get lost, just ask someone to point the way.
지하철을 타고 브루클린 다리-시청역까지 가면 맨해튼에서 다리를 건널 수 있습니다. 만약 길을 잃으면 다른 사람에게 길을 물어보세요.

K : I'd like to go to UN building. Can I get there by bus?
UN 빌딩을 가고 싶은데, 버스로 갈 수 있나요?

F : You can take M6. Get on the bus heading south.
It will take you there.
M6번 버스를 타는데, 남쪽으로 가는 버스를 타세요.
당신을 그곳으로 데려다 줄 것입니다.

K : Does it stop right in front of UN building?
바로 UN빌딩 앞에서 멈추나요?

F : No. Bus doesn't make stops at UN building.
It's very near from there. Go east on foot.
아뇨. 버스는 UN 빌딩에서는 서지 않아요.
그곳에서 아주 가까워요. 걸어서 동쪽으로 가세요.

K : When is the bus going to get here?
　버스가 이곳에 언제 오죠?
F : It was supposed to be here 5 minutes ago.
　I think it's running late. It will come soon.
　5분전에 왔어야 되는데요. 제 생각에 늦는 것 같은데 곧 올 것입니다.
K : Thanks for letting me know.
　가르쳐 주셔서 감사합니다.

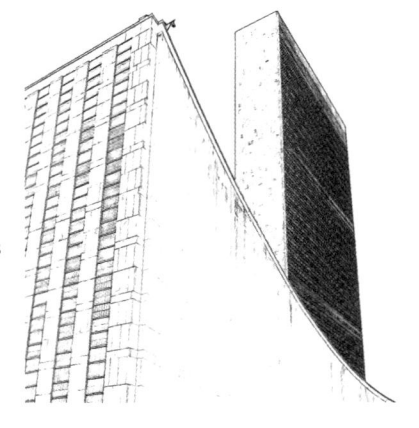

The United Nations Headquarters stands on the eastern shore of Manhattan along East River.
UN본부는 이스트 강을 따라 있는 맨해튼 동쪽 기슭에 자리 잡고 있다.
This is the building where the world leaders gather to make decisions that can alter the history of the world.
이곳은 세계의 지도자들이 모여 세계의 역사를 바꾸는 결정을 하는 곳이다.
　　UN is a symbol of peace and a beacon of hope.
　　UN은 평화의 상징이고 희망의 등불이다.
　The knotted Gun Sculpture in front of building means non violence.
　　빌딩 앞 총열이 묶인 총 조각상은 비폭력을 의미한다.
　　　It has become the essential photo-op for UN visitors.
　UN 방문객들에게 기본적으로 찍어야 할 사진촬영 장소가 되었다.
After doing the guided tour, I go to Times Square and have lunch at cafeteria.
가이드 관광 후, 타임스퀘어로 가서 카페테리아 식당에서 점심을 먹었다.

F : What would you like to order?
무엇을 주문하실래요?

K : What's the most delicious food in here?
이곳에서 가장 맛있는 음식이 어떤 것이죠?

F : Would you like some chicken curry?
닭고기 카레를 드실래요?

K : I don't like chicken. A small pizza and a cup of coffee.
치킨을 좋아하지 않습니다. 작은 피자와 커피 한 잔 주세요.

F : What kind of toppings would you like?
토핑을 어떤 것으로 하실래요?

K : I'd like pineapple and pepperoni.
파인애플과 페퍼로니로 주세요.

F : Do you put cream in your coffee?
커피에 크림을 넣습니까?

K : Yes, just a touch. Weak.
예, 조금만 넣으세요. 약하게요.

F : Is there anything else?
더 필요한 것은 없으세요?

K : No, that's it for now.
아닙니다. 그것으로 충분합니다.

F : Your total comes to $21. Here are your receipt and change.
모두 21달러입니다. 여기 영수증과 잔돈이 있습니다.

K : I want to see the Statue of Liberty. How can I get there?
자유의 여신상을 구경하고 싶군요. 어떻게 가죠?

F : You have to go to the Battery Park for riding the Statue Cruises Ferries.
크루즈 페리 호를 타기 위해 배터리 공원까지 가야 합니다.

K : How do I get there on public transportation?
대중교통으로는 어떻게 가죠?

F : Ride the subway.
지하철을 타세요.

K : Which line should I take?
몇 호선을 타야 되나요?

F : Take the subway line 1 and get off at Chambers street.
From there, you will have to walk several blocks southwest.
1번 지하철을 타고 챔버 가에서 내리십시오.
그곳에서 남서쪽으로 몇 블록 걸어가세요.

K : Can I take a bus there?
그곳에서 버스를 탈 수 있나요?

F : Yes. You can also take a bus from subway station to there.
네. 지하철역에서 버스를 타고 갈 수도 있습니다.

K : Could you tell me in more detail?
좀 더 자세하게 설명해 주실래요?

F : After getting out of the subway, turn around the corner and you can find the bus stop. And take the bus heading toward west and get off at the second stop. You won't miss it.
지하철 출구로 나와 모퉁이를 돌면 버스 정류장을 발견 할 수 있을 것입니다. 그리고 서쪽 가는 버스를 타고 두 번째 정거장에서 내리세요. 쉽게 찾을 수 있을 것입니다.

K : Where is the subway station around here?
이 근처에 지하철이 어디에 있습니까?

F : It's across the street.
길 건너에 있습니다.

Battery park is located on the southern shoreline of Manhattan Island.
배터리 공원은 맨해튼 남쪽 해안가에 있다.
 It was a military post which artillery battery had served to protect New York.
그곳은 뉴욕을 방어하기 위한 포병대가 있었던 군 주둔지였다.

Battery Park is the only departure point in Manhattan
where board a ferry to Liberty Island.
배터리 공원은 맨해튼에서 리버티 섬으로 가는
페리 호를 탈 수 있는 유일한 곳이다.
The ticket office is located
inside Castle Clinton at Battery Park.
매표소는 배터리 공원의 클린턴 성 안에 있었다.
The ferry to Liberty Island
also stops at Ellis Island.
리버티 섬으로 가는 페리는 엘리스 섬에도 들렸다.

The Statue of Liberty is the icon of freedom
and one of New York's most popular attractions.
자유의 여신상은 자유의 상징이며, 뉴욕의 가장 인기 있는 관광지이다.
The Statue was built in Paris, and originally the statue was meant to be placed in
Egypt, but the France gave it to America in response to their help in their war in 1886.
조각상은 파리에서 만들어져 원래 이집트에 세워질 예정이었는데,
프랑스는 1886년 그들의 전쟁에서의 도움에 대한 보답으로 미국에 주었다.
The height of statue is 46m tall
and it is about 93m tall from the ground to the tip of the flame with the pedestal.
조각상의 높이는 46미터이고
받침대를 포함하여 땅에서 횃불 끝까지는 약 93미터이다.

After returning to Battery Park,
I go to the Brooklyn Bridge
and walk across the bridge
to get to Grimaldi's Pizzeria.
배터리 공원으로 돌아온 후
그리말디 피자집으로 가기 위해
브루클린 다리를 걸어서 건넜다.

The waiting line is long but it's worth waiting.
기다리는 줄이 길었지만 그럴 가치가 있었다.
Grimaldi's thin crust pizza is really good,
freshly made in a charcoal oven and no greasy.
It's very delicious.
그리말디의 얇은 크러스트 피자는
석탄 오븐에 신선하게 구워져 느끼하지 않고
정말 맛있었다.

Charlotte emails me and invites me to her dinner party in Cleveland.
샬럿이 이메일을 보내
나를 그녀의 클리블랜드에서의 저녁파티에 초대했다.
I am hesitant at first, but decide to go to Cleveland.
처음엔 주저했지만 클리블랜드로 가기로 했다.
I'd like to enjoy looking around new cultures and discovering the unique idea.
나는 새로운 문화를 구경하고 독특한 생각을 발견하는 것을 즐기고 싶다.
I change my flight schedule.
나는 비행기 스케줄을 변경했다.
I plan to go back home via San Francisco from Cleveland.
클리블랜드에서 샌프란시스코를 거쳐 집으로 돌아갈 것이다.

K : Hello. I am Mr. Kim. How are you?
여보세요. 미스터 김입니다. 안녕하세요.

C : Hi. Mr. Kim. What's going on with you?
안녕하세요. 미스터 김. 어떠세요?

K : Fine. Did you get a chance to read my email?
좋습니다. 혹시 제 이메일을 읽었나요?

C : I'm sorry, I was busy doing something. I forgot to check email.
죄송해요. 무언가를 하느라 바빠서 이메일 체크를 잊었어요.

K : Why were you so busy?
왜 그렇게 바쁘세요?

C : I had a lot of work to do. So I've been very busy until now.
할 일이 많았어요. 그래서 지금까지 매우 바빴어요.

K : Did you finish all of your work?
일은 다 끝내셨나요?

C : Yes. Almost done. Can you come to my Saturday party?
예. 거의 다 했어요. 제 토요일 파티에 올 수 있나요?

K : Yes. I'm going to Cleveland on this Friday.
네. 이번 금요일에 클리블랜드로 갑니다.

C : Oh! Sounds good.
아! 좋아요.

K : Where will it take place?
어디에서 하죠?

C : It will be at my house. Do you need my home address?
제 집에서 열어요. 집주소가 필요한가요?

K : Yes. email me your address.
이메일로 주소를 보내주면 고맙겠습니다.

C : That would be no trouble at all.
그렇게 할게요.

K : Is it formal or casual?
정장인가요? 일상복 차림인가요?

C : Just casual dinner party.
　　일상적인 저녁파티에요.
K : Can I bring something to drink?
　　마실 것 좀 가져갈까요?
C : Everything is taken care of, but if you want to bring along,
　　wine would be appreciated.
　　모든 것이 준비되었지만 가져오길 원하신다면 와인이면 고마워요.
K : What time will it start?
　　몇 시에 시작하죠?
C : It will start at 6:30 P.M.
　　저녁 6시30분에 시작해요.
K : I'll be there on time. Thank you for inviting me.
　　제시간에 그곳으로 가겠습니다. 초대해 주셔서 감사합니다.

　　　　I always try to embrace the history of the world I'm in.
　　　　나는 내가 속한 세계의 역사를 끌어안으려 항상 노력한다.
　　People never know their boundaries until they have reached it on their own.
　　사람들은 스스로 자신의 한계까지 가 보기 전에는 자신의 한계점을 모른다.
　　　　Where can I find my latent ability to overcome my limitation?
　　어디에서 나 자신의 한계를 극복할 수 있는 잠재적 능력을 찾을 수 있을까?

　　　　　　　　I am so tired that I go to bed early.
　　　　　　　　너무 피곤하여 일찍 잠을 잤다.
　　　　During next several days, I try to see everything of New York.
　　　　　다음 며칠 동안 뉴욕의 모든 것을 보려고 노력했다.
I go around many places, such as Empire state building, Yankee stadium in Bronx,
New York University, Wall street, Chelsea, Soho, Harlem, China town, High line in
　　　　Manhattan, Flushing in Queens, Coney island in Brooklyn.
　　　　나는 엠파이어 스테이트 빌딩, 브롱크스의 양키 스타디움,
　　　뉴욕 대학, 월 스트리트, 첼시, 소호, 할렘, 차이나타운, 하이라인,
　　　퀸스의 플러싱, 브루클린의 코니아일랜드 등 여러 곳을 돌아다녔다.
　　　　　All places are usually crowded with natives and tourists.
　　　　　대부분의 장소들이 미국인들과 관광객들로 붐비었다.

K : I need to get a taxi.
택시가 필요합니다.
F : Where will you be going?
어디로 가시나요?
K : Empire state building.
엠파이어 스테이트 빌딩으로 갑니다.
F : What time would you like to be picked up?
언제쯤 타실 거죠?
K : The sooner the better.
빠를수록 좋습니다.
F : A taxi will be here shortly, sir.
택시가 곧 올 것입니다.

K : Is there a bus to go to New York University?
뉴욕대학으로 가는 버스가 있습니까?
F : Yes. Buses run every 15 minutes.
15분마다 버스가 있습니다.
K : Is it too far to walk there?
그곳까지 걸어가기는 너무 먼가요?
F : Yes, you'll have to take a bus.
네, 버스를 타야 될 것입니다.
K : Where do I take the bus?
버스를 어디서 타지요?
F : You can see the bus stop right in front of that building.
저 건물 바로 앞에 정류장이 있습니다.

I sometimes want to get a feel
for the atmosphere of a tour place.
나는 간혹 여행 장소의
분위기를 느끼고 싶었다.

After having a lunch
at fast food restaurant,
I spend 30 minutes
walking through the maze shops
in the Union Square Holiday Market.
패스트푸드점에서 점심을 먹은 후,
유니언 공원의 휴일 시장의
미로 같은 상점들을
돌아다니며 30분을 보냈다.

K : Excuse me, where is the public restroom near here?
  실례합니다. 가까운 공중화장실이 어디 있습니까?
F : It's just a few blocks away.
  Go straight this road and turn right at the intersection.
  몇 블록 거리에 있습니다.
  이 길을 따라 가다가 교차로에서 오른쪽으로 도세요.

K : Thank you.
감사합니다.
F : You might try to use the restroom at the nearby fast food restaurant or shopping mall.
가까운 패스트푸드점이나 쇼핑몰의 화장실을 이용하세요.

F : May I help you?
어서 오세요.
K : I'd like a hamburger and a medium coke.
햄버거와 콜라 중간 컵 주세요.
F : Would you like everything on it?
토핑을 다 할까요?
K : Yes, everything on it.
네, 전부 해주세요.
F : Here or to go?
여기서 드실래요? 가지고 가실래요?
K : Here.
여기서 먹겠습니다.

F : Would you like fries with that?
감자튀김도 드실래요?
K : No, thanks.
아닙니다.
F : It won't be long. Would you like anything else?
오래 걸리지 않을 것입니다. 다른 것은 없나요?
K : No, thank you. That's it.
네, 감사합니다. 그것이 전부입니다.

I take the subway to Flushing.
지하철을 타고 플러싱에 갔다.
Flushing is the second largest china town in the New York
and there are many Koreans who live there.
플러싱은 뉴욕에서 2번째로 큰 차이나타운으로
많은 한국인들이 살고 있다.
Asians have been creating a new Asian American mixed culture.
아시아인들은 새로운 아시아 아메리카 복합적 문화를 만들어가고 있었다.

I go to the bank to exchange money.
돈을 바꾸기 위해 은행에 들렸다.

K : Where can I change money?
   어디서 돈을 바꾸지요?
F : The bank is not too far from here.
   은행은 여기서 멀지 않아요.
K : How do I get there?
   어떻게 가죠?
F : It's just one block away, keep going straight.
   똑바로 한 블록만 가세요.
K : Thanks for your help.
   도와주셔서 감사합니다.
K : I'm looking for the bank. Is it on this floor?
   은행을 찾고 있습니다. 이 층에 있나요?

F : No, It's on the 2nd floor. Go back to the elevators and ride up one floor. And it's down the corridor on the right.
Hallway signs will direct you. You'll find it easily.
아뇨. 2층에 있습니다. 엘리베이터를 타고 한 층 더 올라가세요.
오른쪽 복도 끝에 있습니다. 복도의 표지판이 알려줄 것입니다.
쉽게 찾을 것입니다.

F : May I help you?
무엇을 도와드릴까요?
K : I'd like to exchange some money.
돈을 좀 바꾸고 싶습니다.
F : What currency do you want to exchange?
어떤 돈을 바꾸시길 원하시죠?
K : I want to change Korean money into U.S. dollars.
한국 돈을 미 달러로 바꾸고 싶습니다.
F : Yes. How much do you want?
예. 얼마를 원하죠?
K : About 1000 dollars.
약 천 달러정도입니다.
F : How would you like it?
어떻게 가져가시겠습니까?

K : Nine hundreds, nine tens and the rest in ones.
100달러 9장, 10달러 9장, 나머지는 모두 1달러로 주세요.
F : Here you are.
여기 있습니다.

Most of the people I've met are friendly and helpful.
내가 만난 대부분의 사람들은 친절하고 도움이 되었다.
I would like to remember tour places forever with plenty of photos.
나는 많은 사진으로 여행 장소를 영원히 기억하고 싶었다.

Coney Island is well known as a famous amusement area and hot dog eating contest.
코니 아일랜드는 놀이공원과 핫도그 먹기 대회로 유명하다.
I sit at the beach by myself just watching peoples
and paying close attention to the details around me over a cup of coffee.
나는 혼자 해변에 앉아 커피를 유유히 마시며
사람들을 구경하고 주변을 관심있게 둘러보았다.

I wander around several places in Brooklyn and go back to the hotel.
브루클린 여러 곳을 돌아다닌 후 호텔로 돌아갔다.

K : How do I get to Manhattan hotel from here?
　　Can I take a bus or do I have to take a taxi?
　　이곳에서 맨해튼 호텔까지 어떻게 가죠?
　　버스를 탈수 있나요? 아니면 택시를 타야 하나요?
F : There are no buses that go to downtown from here.
　　 You'll have to take a cab.
　　시내중심가로 가는 버스는 없습니다. 택시를 타야 합니다.
K : How much will it cost?
　　비용이 얼마나 될까요?
F : The fare to downtown is usually about $30.
　　시내중심가까지는 항상 대략 30불입니다.

I am leaving New York today.
오늘이 뉴욕을 떠나는 날이다.
I go to the Visitor's Center, take a map
of the Central Park and stroll the beautiful grounds.
나는 센트럴 공원의 방문객 센터로 가서
지도를 가지고 아름다운 지역을 걸어 다녔다.
Trees and fountains are beautiful and
various statues stimulate my curiosity.
나무와 분수대는 아름다웠고, 다양한 조각상들이 나의 호기심을 자극했다.

After sitting on a park bench for a little while, I go back to the hotel.
잠시 동안 공원 벤치에 앉아있다가 호텔로 갔다.

K : I'd like to check out.
　　체크아웃 하겠습니다.
F : I'll print out your receipt. Here you are.
　　영수증을 프린트해 드리겠습니다. 여기 있습니다.
K : What are all these charges?
　　이 요금들은 무엇이죠?
F : They are minibar charges and movie fees.
　　미니바와 영화채널 이용료입니다.

K : There is a charge on my bill that I never made.
   I discover that I owe $15 for a movie that I never ordered.
   청구서에 내가 하지 않은 것이 청구되어 있네요.
   보지 않은 영화에 15불이 계산되어 있군요.

F : Let me check, sir. You were charged for watching movie last night.
   잠깐 볼게요. 어제 밤에 영화를 보았다고 되어 있는데요.

K : That is absolutely incorrect. I didn't see the movie
   잘못 되었습니다. 영화를 보지 않았는데요.

F : Are you sure that you didn't make?
   결제 안 하신 것이 확실합니까?

K : Yes. It looks like there is a mix up.
   네. 아마도 혼동이 있는 것 같습니다.

F : Okay, let me see what I can do. Let me correct this error.
   제가 할 수 있는지 살펴보겠습니다. 잘못된 실수를 고치겠습니다.

K : Thank you.
   감사합니다.

F : Here is your receipt.
   여기 영수증 있습니다.

K : I need to get to airport. How do I take the airport shuttle bus?
   공항으로 갈려는 데요. 어떻게 공항으로 가는 셔틀버스를 타지요?

F : Take the NYAS express bus at Penn Station.
   펜 역에서 NYAS 익스프레스 버스를 타세요.

K : What time does airport shuttle bus leave for the airport?
   공항까지 가는 셔틀버스가 언제 있습니까?

F : The buses operate once every thirty minutes between 7 A.M. & 8 P.M. The fare is $16. You can pay in cash to the bus driver.
   아침 7시부터 저녁 8시까지 30분 간격으로 운행합니다.
   요금은 16불이고 버스 기사에게 현금을 내면 됩니다.

K : Is it a long ride?
오래 걸리나요?

F : It doesn't take long at all. 50 minutes to an hour.
오래 걸리지 않습니다. 시간은 50분에서 1시간 걸립니다.

I arrive at airport on time and take an airplane.
나는 제시간에 공항에 도착하여 비행기를 탔다.

F : May I get through?
지나가도 될까요?

K : Yes you may.
예.

F : I am sorry. Would it be possible to change seat with you?
죄송한데 자리를 바꿀 수 있겠습니까?

K : Yes. But may I ask why?
예, 그런데 무슨 이유가 있습니까?

F : My wife and I would like to sit together.
집사람과 제가 함께 앉고 싶습니다.

K : Okay. I will move over there.
알았습니다. 제가 저쪽으로 옮기지요.

F : Thank you.
감사합니다.

K : Could I get another blanket please? I feel a little cold.
조금 추운데 담요 한 장 더 줄 수 있나요?

F : Certainly, sir. Would you like a pillow as well?
물론입니다. 배게도 필요하시나요?

K : No thank you. And could you also lend me a pen?
아닙니다. 그리고 펜 좀 빌려주실래요?

F : I don't have it right now, but I'll get one for you.
지금 저에게 없는데 곧 가져다 드리겠습니다.

K : Do you know when we will be landing?
언제 도착하지요?

F : In about 2 hours.
2시간 안에 도착합니다.

F : I see your seat light is on. May I help you?
좌석 등이 켜 있더군요. 무엇을 도와 드릴까요?

K : Could I have some water?
물 좀 주실래요?

F : Sure. Would you like ice in that?
물론입니다. 얼음을 넣어 드릴까요?

K : Yes. Thank you.
네. 감사합니다.

K : I am getting thirsty, may I order a drink?
목마른데 마실 것 좀 주문할 수 있을까요?

F : We have coffee, tea, or soda as well as alcoholic beverages.
커피, 차, 음료수 및 주류가 있습니다.

K : Do you charge for beer?
맥주는 돈을 받나요?

F : Beers are five dollars each.
맥주는 각각 5달러입니다.

K : Do you offer nonalcoholic beverages for free?
알코올이 아닌 음료는 무료인가요?

F : Yes.
네.

K : One beer please, and could you give me a small snack?
맥주 하나 주세요. 그리고 작은 스낵도 같이 주실래요?

F : We are taking orders for dinner.
Would you prefer chicken or beef steak?
저녁 식사로 치킨과 비프스테이크 중 어느 것을 원하세요?

K : Beef steak, please.
비프스테이크를 주세요.

F : Please put your tray down in front of you.
선반을 앞으로 내려 주실래요?

K : OK.
알겠습니다.

F : Would you like to have something to drink?
음료수는 무엇을 드릴까요?

K : Orange juice, please.
오렌지 주스 주세요.

A middle aged man is sitting next to me on the plane
중년 남성이 비행기 옆 좌석에 앉아있었다.
He speaks to me in a kind way.
그는 친절하게 나에게 말을 걸어왔다.

F : Are you traveling on business?
일 때문에 가시나요?

K : No. I'm going to visit my friend.
아뇨. 친구를 만나러 갑니다.

F : If you don't mind me asking,
may I ask your age?
실례하지만 나이가 어떻게 되세요?

K : I am thirty one.
31세입니다.

97

F : You look younger than your age.
나이보다 훨씬 젊게 보이시는군요.

K : Thank you.
감사합니다.

F : How old do you think I am?
저는 몇 살처럼 보이시나요?

K : About 33?
33세 정도인가요?

F : I am 38 years old.
저는 38살입니다.

K : You look much younger than you are. Are you married?
당신도 나이보다 젊어 보이는군요. 결혼 하셨나요?

F : Yes. I have two children.
My wife is expecting our third child.
네. 아이들이 2명이 있습니다. 아내는 세 번째 아이를 임신하고 있죠.

K : Congratulations.
축하드립니다.

F : Thank you.
감사합니다.

K : How old are they?
애들이 몇 살이죠?

F : My son is 6. My daughter is 3.
아들은 6살이고 딸은 3살입니다.

K : Does your son go to school?
아들은 학교에 다니나요?

F : Yes, he does. He is in the first grade.
Do you want to see a photo of my family?
네. 1학년입니다. 가족사진을 보여 드릴까요?

K : Sure. Oh. Your children are good looking. Who is this?
네. 아이들이 잘생겼군요. 이 사람은 누구죠?

F : The lady on the left is my younger sister.
　　왼쪽의 여자가 여동생입니다.
K : Is the man on the right your brother?
　　우측 남자가 형제 이신가요?
F : Yes. He is my elder brother.
　　네. 제 형님입니다.
K : All people look very happy. You have a very nice family.
　　모두가 행복해 보이는군요. 화목한 가족이군요.
F : Thank you. Do you have any brothers or sisters?
　　감사합니다. 형제나 누이가 있으십니까?
K : I have an elder brother and one elder sister. They are married.
　　I'm the youngest of my siblings.
　　저는 형님과 누나가 있습니다. 그들은 모두 결혼했습니다.
　　저는 형제 중에 가장 젊습니다.
F : Are your parents still living?
　　당신의 부모님은 모두 살아계시나요?
K : Yes. We have 3 generations of family living in father's house.
　　예. 삼대가 아버지 집에서 살고 있습니다.
F : My parents passed away.
　　저의 부모님들은 돌아가셨습니다.
K : I am sorry to hear that. Does your wife have any business?
　　아 그러셨군요. 당신의 아내는 무슨 일을 하고 계십니까?
F : My wife is a nurse. She really has been busy.
　　저의 아내는 간호사입니다. 그녀는 아주 바쁩니다.
K : Many Korean wives stay at home and look after children,
　　focusing on their education.
　　많은 한국의 아내들은 집에서 아이들 교육에 집중하고 있습니다.
F : My wife sometimes wants to be a full time mother.
　　저의 집사람은 가끔씩 하루 종일 엄마 노릇만 하길 원하죠.
K : Korea is definitely the land of private tutoring. Other countries

also have cram schools that help get a high score in tests, but Korea has a wide variety of private institutes. My nephew learns not only English and Math but also Taekwondo and drawing through private tutoring.
한국은 과외의 나라입니다. 다른 나라들도 시험 점수를 높이기 위해 학원들이 있기는 하지만, 한국은 아주 다양한 사설 학원들이 있습니다. 제 조카는 영어, 수학뿐만 아니라 태권도와 미술 과외도 하고 있습니다.

F : It's a hard life. Children need to play.
어려운 삶이군요. 아이들은 놀 필요가 있어요.

K : Yes, I know. But playing children couldn't catch up with the others. We have no choice. And it's very hard for parent to pay the tutoring expenses. Because the private tutoring isn't over until children go to college.
예. 압니다. 하지만 노는 아이들은 다른 아이들을 따라 갈 수가 없어요. 어쩔 수 없지요. 그리고 과외공부 비용을 대는 것이 부모들에겐 아주 힘이 듭니다. 왜냐하면 과외공부는 아이들이 대학을 들어갈 때까지 계속되기 때문입니다.

F : Unbelievable. Big changes should be made to Korean education system.
믿을 수 없군요. 한국 교육시스템에 큰 변화들이 있어야 되겠군요.

K : Have you ever lived in another country?
다른 나라에서 살아 본 적 있으세요?

F : No. Do you have any pet?
아뇨. 애완동물이 있으세요?

K : Yes, I have a cute little dog.
예. 작고 귀여운 개 한 마리가 있습니다.

F : A pet makes me forget about worries and stress.
애완동물은 걱정과 스트레스를 잊게 만들더군요.

K : When I was a child, I had a big dog.
    Were you born in New York here?

어렸을 적에는 큰 개를 키웠었어요.
당신은 이곳 뉴욕에서 태어나셨습니까?

F : No, I was born and grew up in Chicago.
Have you ever been to Chicago?
아뇨, 시카고에서 태어나고 자랐습니다.
시카고에 가보신 적이 있나요?

K : No, I've never been to Chicago. I heard that Chicago is windy city lies beside beautiful Lake Michigan.
아뇨. 시카고에는 간 적이 없습니다. 시카고는 아름다운 미시간 호수를 가진 바람의 도시라고 들었습니다.

F : Yes, Chicago gets its nickname, windy city.
Where is your hometown?
예. 시카고 별명은 바람의 도시죠. 고향이 어디시죠?

K : I was born and raised in Seoul.
저는 서울에서 태어나 자랐습니다.

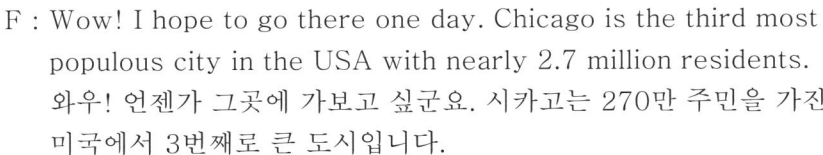

F : How big is Seoul?
서울은 얼마나 크죠?

K : About 10 million people live there.
약 1000만 명이 살고 있습니다.

F : Wow! I hope to go there one day. Chicago is the third most populous city in the USA with nearly 2.7 million residents.
와우! 언젠가 그곳에 가보고 싶군요. 시카고는 270만 주민을 가진 미국에서 3번째로 큰 도시입니다.

K : Yes. I know that.
예. 알고 있습니다.

F : What kind of work do you do?
무슨 일을 하시죠?

K : I work at business company in Seoul.
저는 서울에 있는 회사에서 일합니다.

F : I am a physician of the Northwestern Memorial Hospital in

Chicago.
저는 시카고에 있는 노스웨스트 메모리얼 병원의 의사입니다.

K : How long have you been worked there?
그곳에서 일한 지 얼마나 되셨습니까?

F : I've been more than 6 years.
6년 이상 되었습니다.

K : What do you spend time on your weekends?
주말에는 무엇을 하고 지내세요?

F : I spend my weekends for playing golf.
저는 주말에 골프로 보냅니다.

K : Does golf is your favorite sport?
골프를 좋아하시나요?

F : Yes. But I enjoy the beauty of a golf course.
예. 하지만 골프 코스의 아름다움을 즐깁니다.

K : As there are many beautiful mountains in Korea,
I love mountain climbing on weekend.
The mountain hiking is the national pastime.
한국에는 아름다운 산들이 많아 주말에 등산을 하길 좋아합니다.
등산은 전 국민들이 좋아하는 것입니다.

F : I also like to climb.
저도 등산을 좋아합니다.

K : What sports do you like besides golf?
골프 말고 어떤 스포츠를 좋아하시죠?

F : I like swimming and watching baseball.
저는 수영이나 야구를 보는 것을 좋아합니다.

K : Do you like to watch sports on TV? I also love watching sports.
TV에서 스포츠를 보는 것을 좋아하시나요? 저도 좋아합니다.

F : Is baseball popular in Korea?
야구도 한국에서 인기가 있나요?

K : Absolutely. Baseball and soccer are popular. There are Korean MLB players like Hyun-Jin Ryu, Shin-Soo Choo. Do you know them?
물론이죠. 야구와 축구가 인기가 있습니다. 류현진, 추신수 같은 메이저리그 한국인 선수가 있습니다. 그들을 아세요?

F : I definitely know. They are good players.
물론 압니다. 그들은 훌륭한 선수입니다.

K : Which team do you root for?
어느 팀을 응원하죠?

F : Naturally, I root for Chicago cubs.
당연히 시카고 컵스를 응원하죠.

K : How often do you go swimming?
얼마나 자주 수영장에 가시죠?

F : I usually go swimming three times a week.
항상 일주일에 3번 수영을 합니다.

K : When did you learn to swim?
언제 수영을 배웠나요?

F : I had learned when I was a child.
어렸을 때 수영을 배웠어요.

K : I envy you. I'm afraid of swimming.
당신이 부럽군요. 저는 수영이 무섭습니다.

F : If you're used to go swimming, you won't be afraid of it. By the way, what's your favorite winter activity?
수영을 자주 하다 보면 두려움이 없어질 것입니다.
그리고 겨울엔 어떤 활동을 좋아하시죠?

K : Nothing special.
특별한 것이 없습니다.

F : Have you ever been skiing?
스키를 타신 적이 있나요?

K : Absolutely. There are many attractive and excellent ski resorts in Korea.
당연하죠. 한국에는 멋지고 좋은 스키 리조트들이 많습니다.

F : How often do you ski?
얼마나 자주 가시나요?

K : I usually go skiing for a couple of days, once or twice a year. Are you a good skier?
일 년에 며칠, 한두 번 스키를 타러 갑니다. 스키를 잘 타시나요?

F : Yes. I love skiing.
예. 스키를 좋아합니다.

K : When did you learn how to ski?
언제 스키를 배우셨죠?

F : I learned when I was about 6. Have you ever tried snowboarding?
6살 때쯤 배웠습니다. 스노보드는 탄 적이 있으시나요?

K : Yes, I've tried snowboarding, but it's not easy.
예, 스노보드를 타봤는데 쉽지 않더군요.

F : We are approaching Cleveland. It was nice talking to you.
클리블랜드에 다 왔군요. 이야기 즐거웠습니다.

K : I enjoyed talking to you.
대화 즐거웠습니다.

The plane has landed at the Hopkins international airport.
비행기가 홉킨스 국제공항에 도착했다.

K : Hello.
여보세요.

F : This is Holiday Hotel. Can I help you?
홀리데이 호텔입니다.

K : I made a reservation under the name of Joonhyung Kim, but my flight is delayed. Will you postpone my check in time another hours?
김준형으로 예약을 했는데 비행기가 늦어져 체크인 타임을 늦추어도 될까요?

F : Just hold a moment. I'll check the reservation right now.
잠시만 기다려주세요. 예약을 지금 확인해 보겠습니다.

K : Okay.
알겠습니다.

F : Sorry for keeping you waiting, sir.
Your reservation is one single room.
Your stay is for 2days begining today. Is that correct?
기다리게 해서 죄송합니다. 싱글룸을 예약하셨고, 오늘부터 2박이죠?

K : Yes.
네.

F : What time shall we expect you, sir?
언제쯤 오실 것 같습니까?

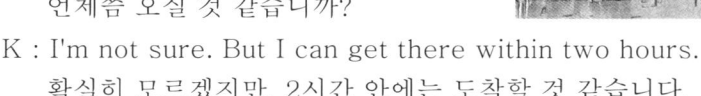

K : I'm not sure. But I can get there within two hours.
확실히 모르겠지만, 2시간 안에는 도착할 것 같습니다.

F : Thank you for calling, sir.
전화해 주셔서 감사합니다, 손님.

I get out of an airport to take a taxi.
나는 택시를 타기 위해 공항에서 나왔다.

K : Where can I get a taxi?
택시를 어디서 타죠?

F : The taxi stand is right over there.
택시 승강장이 저기입니다.

K : Would you happen to know how much it is to go to Holiday
    Hotel.
    혹시 홀리데이 호텔까지 가는데 얼마나 드는지 아세요?
F : It would be about 60 dollars.
    60달러 정도 입니다.
K : Okay, Thanks.
    알겠습니다.
    고맙습니다.

F : Where to, sir?
    어디로 가실래요?
K : Take me to Holiday Hotel.
    홀리데이 호텔로 가주세요.
F : All right.
    알았습니다.
K : How long does it take from here to hotel?
    여기서 호텔까지 얼마나 걸립니까?
F : It takes about 30 minutes.
    약 30분 걸립니다.

F : Here we are.
    다 왔습니다.
K : How much is the fare?
    요금이 얼마이지요?
F : It's 76 dollars.
    76달러입니다.
K : That's more than I thought. Here it is. Keep the change.
    제가 생각한 만큼보다는 많군요. 여기 있습니다. 잔돈은 가지세요.
F : Thanks. Have a nice day.
    감사합니다. 즐거운 하루 되세요.

The hotel is well accommodated. It's not fancy, but it's very good.
호텔 시설은 좋았다. 고급스럽지는 않았지만 꽤 좋았다.

K : Check in, please. My name is Joonhyung Kim.
체크인 하려는 데요? 김준형입니다.

F : OK. Are you staying for 2 nights, single room?
알겠습니다. 싱글 룸, 2박하실거죠?

K : Yes.
네.

F : Would you like a room facing the pool or the street?
수영장 또는 거리 어느 곳이 보이는 곳으로 하실래요?

K : Is there a difference in price between the two?
둘 사이에 가격에 차이가 있나요?

F : The rooms that face the pool are more $20 expensive per night.
수영장 보이는 곳이 하루에 20불 더 비쌉니다.

K : OK. I'll go with the one facing the pool.
수영장이 보이는 곳으로 하겠습니다.

F : Fill out this card.
이 카드를 작성해 주세요.

K : Do I have to pay upfront?
미리 선불로 계산해야 하나요?

F : When you check in, we ask for a credit card to guarantee extra charges.
체크인시 추가 금액을 보증하기 위해 신용카드를 필요로 합니다.

K : Okay. Here is my credit card.
여기 신용카드가 있습니다.

I make a call to Charlotte, she wants to pick me up for tomorrow party.
샬럿에게 전화를 걸었는데 그녀는 내일 파티에 나를 데리러 오길 원했다.

The next day, Charlotte comes in the lobby around 5 P.M. and takes me to her home.
다음날 샬럿은 오후 5시경 로비로 들려 나를 그녀의 집으로 데려갔다.
The house she lives in sits on the side of hill, overlooking the Lake Erie.
그녀가 사는 집은 이리호수를 볼 수 있는 언덕 옆에 있었다.

She leaves the car parked outside her house,
unlocks the front door and we walk inside.
그녀는 차를 그녀의 집 밖에 주차해두고 앞문을 열고 안으로 들어갔다.
I come in cautiously behind her and look around.
나는 조심스레 그녀의 뒤를 따라 들어가 주위를 둘러보았다.
The house has a perfect view of the lake from her living room.
그녀의 집은 거실에서 호수를 완벽히 바라볼 수 있는 곳이었다.
Wow! I make a tiny sound of surprise.
와우하고 나는 조용히 경탄을 했다.

K : It's a cozy place to live.
　　Your home looks nice.
　　살기에 아늑한 곳이군요. 집이 좋군요.
C : Thank you.
　　고마워요.
K : I think if I lived here, I'd never leave.

Thank you for inviting me here.
만약 이곳에 산다면 절대 떠나지 않을 것 같아요.
이곳으로 초대해줘서 고마워요.

C : My father has been one of the powerful men in the business,
and he assures me there is a place for me in his company,
but I have a desire to be free to do my business.
I don't want to be miserable in the rat race.
저의 아버지는 사업에 꽤나 힘이 있는데 저에게 그의 회사에 자리가
있다고 확신을 주지만, 저는 자유롭게 일을 하고 싶은 갈망이 있어요.
경쟁하는 것은 비참해서 싫어요.

K : You grew up in a good family background. James never told me
that. I also enjoy my life the way it is. Everybody thinks so.
좋은 가정환경에서 자랐군요. 제임스는 그런 말을 저에게 안 하더군요.
저 역시 인생을 있는 그대로 즐깁니다. 누구나 그렇게 생각할 것입니다.

C : By the time I am thirty five, I want to become the one of the
professional, talented journalist.
35세가 되기 전까지 유능한 전문 저널리스트가 되길 원해요.

K : I hope you will be like that.
그렇게 되길 바랄게요.

C : Have a seat. Can I get you coffee?
앉으세요. 커피를 좀 드릴까요?

K : No, thank you. I just drank coffee a little while ago.
아뇨 조금 전에 커피를 마셨어요.

C : I'll get you something to drink. I have orange juice, coke and
water. What would you like to drink?
마실 것 좀 가져올게요. 오렌지주스, 콜라, 물 중 무엇을 드실래요?

K : Just water would be fine. Thank you.
물이면 됩니다. 감사합니다.

K : Have you been lived here for a long time?

이곳에서 오래 살았나요?

C : I moved here 2 years ago.
2년 전에 이곳으로 이사를 왔어요.

K : It's a beautiful home.
아름다운 집이군요.

C : Thank you.
고마워요.

K : How do you spend your time?
시간을 어떻게 보내시죠?

C : I enjoy reading.
저는 독서를 즐겨요.

K : Reading? Which do you prefer to read? fiction or nonfiction?
독서요? 픽션과 논픽션 중 어느 것을 좋아하죠?

C : I personally like the kind of fiction.
저는 픽션 종류를 좋아해요.

K : Have you ever read a book that really changed the way you look at things?
당신의 생각을 바꾸게 만든 책이 있었습니까?

C : Yes, I have.
예, 있어요.

K : What was that book?
어떤 책이었죠?

C : Demian by Hermann Hesse. I read that book when I was a high school student. It's the story about a young boy's coming of age. And it gave me a great insight into what it's like going from child to teenager and then entering the adult world. I liked very much his thought-provoking phrases on life. He had impacted the standards and morals of past society. I think Demian is a must read book for juveniles who are searching for identity.
헤르만 헤세의 데미안이어요. 고등학교 때 그 책을 읽었어요. 소년이 성인되어가는 이야기죠. 그 책은 아이에서 십대가 되고 다시 어른이 되다는 것이 어떤 것인지에 대한 깊은 깨달음을 주었죠. 나는 생각을 자극하게 하는 그의 인생에 대한 글귀들을 무척 좋아해요. 그는 과거 사회의 표준이나 도덕에 충격을 주었었죠. 저는 데미안이 자아를 찾고자 하는 청소년들이 꼭 읽어보아야 할 책으로 생각해요.

K : Sure. Hermann Hesse is without a doubt one of the most intriguing writers. And he is also one of my favorite authors. Demian is very similar to his other works in that it shares certain philosophical views.
그렇습니다. 헤르만 헤세는 의심할 여지없이 가장 흥미로운 작가 중의 한 명입니다. 그 역시 제가 좋아하는 작가입니다. 데미안은 어떤 철학 사상을 공감하려는 면에서 그의 다른 작품들과 아주 비슷합니다.

C : He was far ahead of his times.
His books were my favorite novel of all-time in teenager.
그는 그 시대를 앞서갔어요. 그의 책들은 십대에 제가 항상 즐겨 읽는 소설들이었어요.

K : What was the last book you read?
가장 최근에 읽은 책이 어떤 것이죠?

C : Da Vinci Code. This book offers people of cool insight about the religion. It might be true that many people had taken part in Christ affairs for their own benefit.
다빈치 코드예요. 이 책은 사람들에게 종교에 대한 냉정한 통찰력을 주더군요. 예수님의 일들에 많은 사람들이 그들의 이익을 위해 관여되었다는 것은 사실일지도 모르죠.

K : I also read that book. I was astonished that something I have ever been told about Christianity may be a partially fabricated story for the political and social benefits.
저도 그 책을 읽었는데, 기독교에 대해 들었던 어떤 것들이 정치나 사회적 이익을 위해 부분적으로 조작될 수도 있었다는 것을 알고 무척 놀랐습니다.

C : But I think, for the most part, history was based on a true story.
하지만 대부분 역사는 진실에 기초를 두었다고 생각합니다.

K : Yes. There is a controversy about the truth until now. Therefore I like reading nonfiction books. I have great interest in self-help books or concepts like power of positive thinking. Have you ever read 'the secret' book?
예. 지금까지 진실에 대한 논란이 많습니다. 그래서 저는 논픽션 책들을 읽는 것을 좋아합니다. 저는 자신감이나 긍정적인 힘을 다루는 책에 아주 관심이 많습니다. 시크릿이란 책을 읽어 보셨나요?

C : No, I didn't.
아뇨. 읽어보지 못했어요.

K : 'The secret' tell us that anything in life like health, success, love and happiness could be achieved by positive thinking.
시크릿 책은 건강이나 성공, 사랑, 행복 같은 것들이 긍정적인 생각에서 얻을 수 있다고 말합니다.

C : I think it is true.
그것은 사실이라고 생각합니다.

K : I really like this phrase. Make a command to the universe. Let the universe know what you want. The universe responds to your thoughts. The universe will start to rearrange itself to make it happen for you.
저는 이 문구를 좋아하죠. 우주에 명령하여 당신이 무엇을 원하는지 알게 하라. 우주는 당신의 생각에 반응하고 당신에게 그러한 일들이 일어나게끔 할 것이다.

C : It's kind of a golden saying.
마치 금언 같군요.

K : But I don't know the entire universe cares so much about me.
하지만 우주가 얼마나 저에게 관심이 있는지 모르겠어요.

She looks at me with her bright blue eyes.
그녀는 밝은 푸른 눈빛으로 나를 쳐다보았다.
Quite unexpectedly, I feel suddenly some strange emotions,
a kind of the spark of connection.
뜻밖에도 나는 이상한 감정이 갑자기 들었는데
일종의 연대감 같은 것이었다.
She tries to refrain from talking about political stuff
or personal things which could make a disagreement.
그녀는 의견이 맞지 않을 정치적 또는
개인적은 것들에 대해서는 말하지 않았다.
And if she doesn't agree about things,
she just tries to leave it be, and doesn't talk about it anymore.
그리고 어떤 것에 대한 견해가 틀리면 그대로 듣기만 하고
더 이상 그것에 대해 말하지 않았다.

C : Are there any other hobbies you do?
다른 취미가 또 있나요?
K : When I have free time, I sometimes play electric guitar.
여유로운 시간이 되면 가끔 전자기타를 칩니다.
C : Oh, you actually do that?
아 정말로 할 줄 아시나요?
K : Yes, I do.
네. 할 줄 압니다.
C : How long have you known how to do that?
그것을 할 줄 아는지 얼마나 되셨죠?
K : I first learned how to play the guitar in university guitar group.
대학 기타 동아리에서 처음 배웠습니다.
C : Have you been practicing the guitar alone in your home?
집에서 혼자 기타를 연습하셨나요?

K : Yes. But sometimes I used to play guitar in amateur rock band.
예. 하지만 가끔 아마추어 록밴드에서 기타를 치곤 했습니다.

C : Well, you're so talented.
재능이 정말 많으시네요.

K : I appreciate your compliment.
칭찬 감사합니다.

C : Sometimes I travel around to see somewhere new and take photos of beautiful natural scenery and notable objects.
저는 가끔씩 새로운 곳들을 여행하며 아름다운 자연 경관이나 독특한 것들을 사진으로 찍어요.

K : It's a good hobby. By the way, do you like to watch movie?
좋은 취미를 가졌네요. 그런데 영화보기를 좋아하나요?

C : Yes. I love watching movie.
예. 영화보기를 좋아해요.

K : What are your favorite movies?
좋아하는 영화는 어떤 것들이죠?

C : My favorite movies are comic book hero movies. What kind of movies do you like to watch?
저는 만화에 나오는 영웅 영화를 좋아해요.
어떤 영화들을 보길 좋아하시나요?

K : I like science fiction.
저는 공상과학 영화를 좋아합니다.

C : What movie have impressed you the most?
어느 영화가 가장 인상 깊었나요?

K : Avatar. Have you seen it before?
아바타입니다. 아바타 보셨나요?

C : Yes. Avatar was a great film.
예. 아바타는 굉장한 영화였어요.

K : 3D computer animation is outstanding.
3차원 컴퓨터 애니메이션이 훌륭하더군요.

C : I saw that movie the first day it came out in theaters.
　　I had great fun through the whole movie.
　　극장에 나온 첫 날 봤습니다. 영화 내내 정말 재미있었습니다.
K : The visuals were lush, colorful and eye-pleasing.
　　 I got the movie when it came out on DVD.
　　화면이 생생하고 화려하고 눈을 즐겁게 하더군요.
　　 DVD가 나오자마자 샀어요.
C : It's far ahead of anything ever seen before.
　　이전에 본 어느 영화보다 앞서 있어요.
K : Avatar had made me realize what is really important in life.
　　What moved me was the meaning behind the story.
　　It delivered a powerful message of green and anti-war concept.
　　아바타는 저에게 인생에서 무엇이 중요한 지 깨닫게 해 주었습니다.
　　공감이 가는 것은 이야기에 담긴 뜻입니다.
　　환경 및 반전에 대한 강력한 메시지를 전하더군요.
C : Yes. The message of Avatar is clear.
　　All living things depend on each other.
　　예. 아바타 메시지는 확실해요.
　　모든 생물들은 서로 의지하고 있다는 것이죠.
K : We have to learn to live in harmony with the nature.
　　The networking of the nature in the movie is almost same as
　　the Gaia theory.
　　자연과 조화를 이루며 사는 법을 배워야 합니다.
　　영화 속 자연의 네트워크 연결은 가이아 이론과 흡사하더군요.
C : Gaia theory is an ecological hypothesis that the earth has self
　　regulating and interacting system.
　　가이아 이론은 지구 자체가 스스로 조절하고 상호 작용한다는
　　생태학적 이론이죠.

K : All living organisms on earth have been evolved together
　　as a single living system.
　　지구상의 모든 생명체들은 하나의 시스템에서 함께 진화하고 있습니다.
C : I have been worried about what we are doing to the earth.
　　지구에게 우리가 하고 있는 일들이 정말 걱정이 되어요.
K : We never forget that the nature will always win.
　　우리는 자연이 항상 이긴다는 점을 잊지 말아야 합니다.

　　　There is a ring at the door and three of her friends come into the house.
　　　현관에서 벨이 울리고, 그녀의 세 명의 친구들이 집으로 들어왔다.
　　　　　　　They bring some food and beverages.
　　　　　　　그들은 약간의 음식과 음료들을 가지고 왔다.
　　　　After exchanging bows, we prepare for party together.
　　　　우리는 서로 인사를 나눈 후, 함께 파티를 준비했다.
　　　　They sit around the kitchen table and make sandwiches
　from what they bring and some food from things left in the fridge,
　　　　　　　　I help Charlotte to make a salad.
　　그들은 부엌 식탁에 둘러 앉아 가져온 것들과 냉장고에 남은 것으로
　　샌드위치를 만들었고 나는 샬럿이 샐러드를 만드는 것을 도왔다.
　　　　　　　They are comfortable and familiar,
　　　　　so we become good friends quite quickly.
　　　편안하고 친숙한 성격들 때문에 우리는 금방 친구가 되었다.
　　　　　Half an hour later, we light the candles,
　　　sit down at the table and chatter all through dinner.
　　　　　30분 뒤쯤 우리는 촛불을 켜 놓고,
　　　식탁에 앉아 저녁을 먹으며 대화를 나누었다.

C : Do you use Instagram and twitter?
　　인스타그램과 트위터를 사용하나요?
K : I am now following on your instagram through James.
　　저는 지금 제임스를 통해서 당신의 인스타그램을 팔로우하고 있어요.
C : Do you? My feelings are always on Instagram or Twitter.
　　그래요? 제 감정들을 항상 인스타그램과 트위터에 올리고 있죠.

You can use it to find out what's going on in my life.
그것을 보면 제 생활이 어떤지 알 수 있을 거예요.
F1 : She has about 1,200 followers on Instagram. Very popular.
그녀는 인스타그램 팔로워가 1200명이나 됩니다. 아주 인기있죠.
F2 : Social Network Service(SNS) is the best way to discover what's new in the world.
SNS는 이 세계의 새로운 것들을 알 수 있는 아주 좋은 수단이죠.
And it helps me make new friends. I receive many text messages every week, inviting me to house parties.
새 친구들 사귀게 도움도 주는데 매주 많은 파티초대 메시지들을 받죠.
K : I use Facebook to keep up with my friends.
저는 친구들과 연락하고 지내는데 페이스북을 사용합니다.
F1 : We're going to check it out.
우리가 곧 살펴볼게요.
F3 : I am trying to promote my business on Facebook.
저는 페이스북으로는 저의 비즈니스를 알리려고 노력하죠.
F2 : The internet is changing our social life.
인터넷이 우리의 사회생활을 변화 시키고 있죠.
F3 : We are going through a major shift in social network.
우리는 사회적 교류에서 큰 변화를 겪고 있는 중이죠.
K : The internet will change the whole world in the future.
인터넷은 미래에 모든 세계를 변화시킬 것입니다
C : James told me that internet access is very easy in South Korea.
제임스가 한국에서는 인터넷 접속이 아주 쉽다고 하더군요.
K : Korea is the world's most wired country.
한국은 세계에서 가장 인터넷 연결망이 잘된 나라입니다.
F3 : How will the internet affect the future of business?
인터넷이 미래의 비즈니스에 어떻게 영향을 줄까요?
K : Cloud computing for business will go mainstream.
비즈니스에서 클라우드 컴퓨팅이 주류가 될 것입니다.

F3 : Company don't need a software or a server to use them and people would need is just an internet connection.
회사는 소프트웨어나 서버가 필요 없고 사람들은 그저 인터넷만 접속하면 그것들을 이용할 수 있겠죠.

K : Yes. People are working more and more from everywhere, therefore home and workspace will be rapidly merging.
예. 사람들이 일하는 곳이 점점 다양화되고 그래서 집과 직장이 급속도로 하나가 될 것입니다.

C : This technology is cost-efficient and unifying the business on a global basis. But security concern will be a big issue.
이 기술은 가격이 저렴하고 세계적으로 비즈니스를 단일화시키죠. 하지만 안정성이 큰 이슈가 될 것이에요.

K : But the cloud computing market will have grown enormously.
하지만 클라우드 컴퓨터 시장은 엄청나게 커질 것입니다.

F1 : You are so knowledgeable.
당신은 매우 아는 것이 많군요.

K : Thank you.
감사합니다.

F2 : I'm an English teacher.
저는 영어교사입니다.

K : Where do you teach?
어디서 가르치시죠?

F2 : Lakewood high school. And I taught Korean students English for 2 years in Seoul several years ago.
레이크우드 고등학교입니다. 그리고 몇 년 전 2년 동안 서울에서 한국의 학생들에게 영어를 가르쳤습니다.

K : Oh. Did you? You may be familiar with the Korean life style.
오 그래요? 한국인들의 생활에 익숙하시겠네요?

F2 : Yes. Koreans were very good to me.
예. 한국인들은 저에게 아주 잘해주었어요.

K : Did you enjoy teaching in Korea?
한국에서 가르친 것이 재미있었나요?

F2 : Absolutely yes. I had taught in both middle and high school. I have made nice Korean friends.
물론입니다. 중학교와 고등학교에서 같이 가르쳤습니다.
좋은 한국인 친구들을 사귀었습니다.

K : You may know well about Korean.
한국인에 대해 잘 알겠군요.

F2 : Absolutely. Do you frequently travel abroad for business?
그렇죠. 일 때문에 자주 해외로 나가시나요?

K : At least once or twice a year.
일 년에 한두 번 나갑니다.

C : What do you think the future will look like?
미래가 어떻게 될 거라 생각해요?

K : It's a tough question to me.
저에게 어려운 질문이군요.

C : I just want to know what you are thinking.
당신의 생각을 그저 알고 싶어요.

K : The future does not look good. Life will be worse considering what's going on in the world these days.
미래가 좋을 것 같진 않습니다. 요즘 세상이 돌아가는 것을 보면 삶이 더 나빠 질 것 같습니다.

F1 : Why do you think that?
왜 그렇게 생각하시죠?

K : Earth is gradually filled with pollution causing global warming and wealth is dominated by a small number of people or companies. And many wars are happening in the world right now and the conflicts between nations and races are likely to increase along with globalization. Besides, economic conflicts between countries have been spawned by the imbalance in global trades

and capital flows.
지구는 온난화를 일으키는 오염물질로 가득 차고 부유함도 소수의 사람이나 기업들에 의해 지배되고 있습니다. 그리고 지금도 많은 전쟁이 일어나고 있고 세계화 과정 중 국가와 민족들 간의 갈등이 증가되고 있습니다. 게다가 세계화된 무역과 자본의 불균등한 이동으로 국가 간의 경제적 갈등들도 커지고 있습니다.

C : The future of human being is uncertain.
But I think that is what makes a life to be a challenge.
인간들의 미래는 불분명하지요.
하지만 저는 그것이 바로 삶을 도전하게 만든다고 생각해요.

K : Yes. Future can be changed by continuous efforts of peoples.
그렇죠. 미래는 인간들의 노력에 의해 변화될 수 있겠죠.

F2 : I am sure there is a bright future for mankind if we can change the current situations.
저는 현재의 상황들을 변화시킬 수만 있다면 인류에게는 밝은 미래가 있다고 확신합니다.

K : I am worried about how long conflicts of the world is going to continue.
저는 세상의 갈등들이 얼마나 지속이 될 지 걱정입니다.

C : We should learn how to respect other different cultures and different social life.
서로 다른 문화나 생활에 대해 서로 존경하는 방법을 배워야 해요.

K : Yes. You are right. Conflicts of the religion and racism should be decreased. To achieve it, many politicians and executive business men have to play an important roles in the social harmony. Then there will be a turning point in human history.
네. 맞습니다. 종교나 인종간의 갈등이 줄어들어야 하고, 많은 정치가나 사업자들이 사회의 조화를 위해 중요한 역할들을 하여야 합니다. 그러면 인간들의 역사에 전환점이 생길 것입니다.

F3 : What's the meaning of the turning point?
전환점이란 무슨 의미를 말하는 것이죠?

K : It means the change by the social movement of ordinary people. Every people has a power to create new world. New minds for better world could have been continuously occurred through the active participation of ordinary peoples like you and me. And our efforts will impact on the butterfly effect of the whole life of the world. This is the start of the second evolution of human being.
그것은 일반인들의 사회적 운동에 의한 변화를 뜻합니다. 모든 사람들에게는 새로운 세계를 창조할 수 있는 힘이 있습니다. 더 나은 세계를 위한 새로운 마음가짐들이 당신과 나 같은 평범한 사람들의 능동적인 참여 하에 지속적으로 생겨날 수 있습니다. 그리고 우리들의 노력이 세상의 전체 생활을 변화시키는 나비효과를 일으킬 것입니다. 이것이 인간들의 2번째 진화의 시작이죠.

C : I agree. The empathy of the all human being as one species living on the earth is really important.
동의해요. 모든 인간들이 지구상에 사는 한 종으로써의 공감대 형성이 중요하다고 생각해요.

K : I am convinced that standardized global education could reduce the frequency of all the unreasonable affairs and discriminating occurrences.
저는 표준화된 지구적 교육이 불합리한 일들이나 차별을 줄일 것이라 확신합니다.

F2 : Yes. Systemic global education network should be needed for achieving goals.
네. 목표들을 이루기 위해서는 체계적인 지구적 교육망이 반드시 필요하죠.

K : Social network through internet will help people to know a better sense of what we do and how to do. There is a need for free, no-censorship worldwide internet access program.
인터넷을 통한 사회적 연결이 우리가 무엇을 하고 어떻게 해야 할 지에 좀 더 감각적으로 만들어 줄 것입니다. 무료이며 검열이 없는 세계적인 인터넷 접속 프로그램이 필요합니다.

F2 : It will probably be very important to influence positively on many peoples.
아마도 많은 사람들에게 긍정적으로 중요한 영양을 끼칠 겁니다.

K : I am sure that history will be rearranged in stable method by goodwill power.
역사는 좋은 의지의 힘에 의해 안정된 방법으로 재편될 것이라고 확신합니다.

F3 : I sincerely hope so. Korean seems to consider life from a philosophical point of view.
저도 그렇게 되길 진심으로 바랍니다. 한국인은 삶을 철학적 관점으로 보는 것 같군요.

F2 : May I take your picture with us?
우리와 함께 사진을 찍으실래요?

K : Sounds good.
좋습니다.

After dinner, we enjoy party till late at night.
우리는 밤늦게까지 파티를 즐겼다.
We eat, drink, talk, and have become buddies.
우리는 먹고 마시고 이야기를 나누었고 친구가 되었다.
At the front door, we say good bye with light hug and a cheek to cheek kiss.
정문 앞에서 우리는 가볍게 포옹하고 볼 인사를 나누고 작별을 했다.
There are thousands of stars shining brightly and a beautiful moon above us.
수천 개의 밝은 별들과 아름다운 달이 머리 위에 떠 있었다.

F2 : Well, it was a pleasure meeting you. I had fun today.
만나서 반가웠습니다. 즐거웠습니다.

K : Likewise. I had a great time talking to you. If you visit Korea, please let me know.
똑같이 저도 이야기가 즐거웠습니다. 만약 한국에 방문하면 저에게 알려주세요.

F2 : Absolutely. Give me your e-mail address. We'll keep in touch. Anyway, enjoy the rest of your trip.
물론이죠. 이 메일 주소를 주세요. 서로 연락을 하죠. 아무튼 남은 여행 즐겁게 보내세요.

F1 : Good bye.
잘 가세요.

F3 : Have a nice trip.
좋은 여행 되세요.

K : Thank you. Bye. Take care.
고맙습니다. 잘 가세요.

Charlotte takes me to the hotel after talking for another minutes.
샬럿은 나와 짧은 대화를 나눈 후 나를 호텔로 데려다 주었다.
She gives me warm hug in the lobby.
그녀는 로비에서 나에게 따듯한 포옹을 해주었다.

Today is my last day here and it's the perfect weekend.
오늘이 이곳에서의 나의 마지막 날인데, 완벽한 주말이었다.
Charlotte and I go to the Natural History Museum of Cleveland before I fly to Seoul.
샬럿과 나는 서울로 떠가기 전 클리블랜드의 자연사 박물관으로 갔다.
She wants to show me a Lucy,
the famous 3.2 million years old ancient human ancestor.
그녀는 320만 년 전의 고대 인간의 조상인
루시를 나에게 보여주고 싶어했다.

Lucy was discovered in 1974 in Ethiopia.
루시는 1974년 에티오피아에서 발견되었다.
Lucy provided valuable clues as to when and why
humans began to walk upright and develop larger brains.
루시는 인간들이 언제, 왜 서서 걷게 되고 뇌가 크게 발달이 되었는지
중요한 단서들을 주었다.

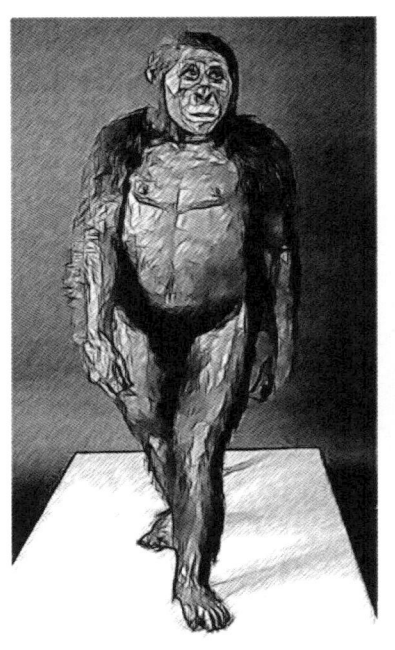 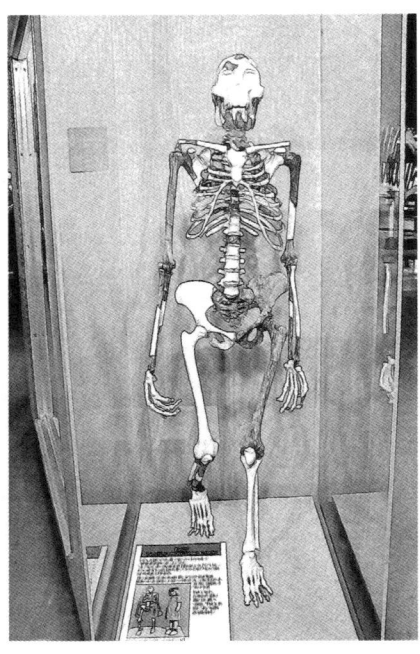

C : It sounds a little mystical, I think that our world exists because human consciousness is perceiving holographic universe having mass. In other words, this world is being created each moment at the speed of light.

조금 이상하게 들릴지 모르지만, 저는 인간들의 의식이 질량을 가진 홀로그램 우주를 인식하기 때문에 이 세상이 존재한다고 생각해요. 다시 말해 이 세상은 순간 순간 빛의 속도로 창조되고 있다는 것이죠.

K : I know about that universe may be a hologram. I have read many books on cosmic science and seen some great documentaries.
우주가 홀로그램일지 모른다는 것에 대해서는 알고 있어요.
우주 과학에 대한 책들을 읽고 훌륭한 다큐멘터리들을 보았습니다.

C : You are talking my language, as expected.
Universe is a holographic wave, so all is one.
When I watch a Lucy, human beings seem to have a long way to go.
역시 예상한 것처럼 당신과는 말이 통하는군요.
우주는 홀로그램 파동이므로 모두가 하나란 것이죠.
루시를 보고 있으면 인간들은 아직 갈 길이 먼 것 같아요.

I reply with a nod and add a word.
나는 고개를 끄덕이고 말을 덧붙였다.

K : The light contains the secret of the nature.
I am convinced that the universe is just continuous drawing picture with light speed.
I understand whole things are relative phenomena which making at every moment.
It explains Einstein theory vey well.
빛은 자연의 비밀을 담고 있습니다.
우주가 빛의 속도로 그려지는 것이라는 것을 확신합니다.
모든 것들이 매 순간 빛의 속도로 만들어지는 상대적 현상이라고
이해하고 있습니다. 이것은 아인슈타인의 이론을 잘 설명해 줍니다.

C : Yes. That's what I think, too.
예. 그게 바로 제가 생각하는 거에요.

K : The world is not good enough yet. Powers and techniques are still some private's or company's property. Unbalance of property among people makes still conflict. The most important thing in modern human species is the empathy and harmony mind connected with each other for making the all human mind.
아직은 좋은 세상이 아닙니다. 권력들과 기술들은 몇몇 개인이나 회사들의 전유물이죠. 사람들간의 부의 불균형은 갈등들을 야기시킵니다. 현대 인간들에게 가장 중요한 것은 모든 인간들의 마음을 만드는 연결된 개개인의 공감되고 조화된 마음입니다.

C : We need pure spirituality.
순수한 영혼이 필요한 것이죠.

K : Yes. Spirituality is a life-long learning process. Pure spirit is not a difficult feeling. It's just love and mercy.
맞습니다. 영혼이란 인생 전체를 걸쳐 만드는 것입니다. 순수한 영혼이란 어려운 감정이 아닙니다. 그것은 단지 사랑과 자비심입니다.

After conversation, I feel the odd mix of emotions about her.
대화 후 그녀에 대한 복잡하고 묘한 느낌이 들었다.
She is a really wonderful and good-hearted young woman.
그녀는 정말 멋지고 마음이 착한 젊은 여자였다.
I invite her to visit Korea.
나는 그녀에게 한국을 방문하라고 초대를 했다.

K : Be sure to come to Korea.
　　You have always been very generous toward me.
　　I have a lot of fun. I'll never forget you.
　　한국에 꼭 오세요. 당신은 항상 저에게 친절했어요.
　　정말 재미있게 보냈습니다.
　　결코 당신을 잊지 못할 것입니다.
C : Thank you. I have no fixed plans.
　　But I won't be disappointed by the things I didn't do than
　　by the ones I did do. I will surely visit you.
　　고마워요. 계획된 것은 없어요. 하지만 제가 한 일에 대한 후회보다
　　하지 않은 일에 대한 실망은 하고 싶지 않아요. 당신에게 꼭 갈게요.

　　　　She promises me to come to Korea and visit me on vacation.
　　　　그녀는 휴가 때 한국에 와서 나를 본다고 약속했다.
　　　　It's a relatively short drive from the museum to the airport.
　　　　박물관에서 공항까지는 비교적 짧은 거리였다.
　　　　Charlotte gives me a farewell hug and wishes me luck.
　　　　샬럿은 나에게 작별포옹을 해주고 행운을 빌어주었다.

PART II (제 2부)

Most Practical English Expressions for Travel
(여행에서 가장 실용적인 영어 표현들)

한국인의 감성과 예절이 담긴

해외여행 영어회화 책

1. 비행기 예약 (Booking Flight)

How can I help you?
무엇을 도와 드릴까요?

I would like to book a flight.
비행기를 예약하고 싶습니다.

Can I make a plane reservation?
비행기 예약을 할 수 있을까요?

Where are you traveling to?
어디로 가실 겁니까?

I'd like to make a reservation from Seoul to New York.
서울에서 뉴욕으로 가는 비행기를 예약하고 싶습니다.

I am going to go to New York.
뉴욕을 갈 예정입니다.

I will be traveling to New York.
뉴욕으로 여행을 갈 예정입니다.

Do you have a nonstop flight to New York from Seoul?
서울에서 뉴욕으로 가는 직항편이 있습니까?

We can do that for you.
예약해 드리겠습니다.

When would you like to go?
What date will you be traveling?
What is your travel date?
What date would you like to depart?
When do you want to depart?
언제 가시기를 원하시나요?

I want to fly on June 17th.
I need a flight on June 17th.
I would like to leave on June 17th.
I was hoping to reserve a seat for June 17th.
Can you check if June 17th is possible?
Is June 17th available?
6월 17일 비행기를 예약하고 싶습니다.

Hold on please. Let me check.
잠깐만 기다려주세요. 확인해 보겠습니다.

We have seats available for June 17th.
6월17일에 좌석이 있습니다.

Would you like me to reserve them?
예약을 하실 건가요?

How often do you have flights?
비행기가 얼마나 자주 있나요?

We have two flights departing on that date.
그 날 출발하는 비행기가 2대 있습니다.

What time does the first flight leave?
첫 비행기가 언제 출발하나요?

What time does the last flight leave?
마지막 비행기가 언제 출발하나요?

On June 17th, the departure times are 9A.M. and 7P.M.
6월 17일 아침 9시, 저녁 7시에 출발합니다.

Would you like to depart at 9A.M. or 7P.M?
아침 9시, 저녁 7시중 어느 것을 원하십니까?

I'd prefer a morning flight.
Is it possible?
아침 비행기를 타고 싶은데 가능한가요?

I'd like to take a morning flight.
아침 비행기를 타고 싶습니다.

I would prefer a morning departure.
아침 출발이 좋을 것 같습니다.

I need an afternoon flight.
오후 비행기가 필요합니다.

I need to leave in the evening.
저녁에 떠나야 합니다.

I can only take a flight that leaves in the evening.
저녁 비행기만 탈 수 있습니다.

All seats of evening flight are booked.
저녁 비행기는 모두 다 예약이 되었습니다.

We've got only morning flight.
Is that OK?
아침 비행기만 있습니다. 괜찮습니까?

I can leave at any time.
어느 시간이든 좋습니다.

I'll put you on morning flight.
아침 비행기에 예약을 하겠습니다.

We don't have any available seats on June 17th.
6월 17일에는 비행기 좌석이 없습니다.

June 17th is full.
There are no departures for June 17th.
6월 17일은 만석입니다.
6월 17일 비행기들은 없습니다.

Should I put you on the waiting list?
대기자 명단에 올려드릴까요?

The next available flight is on June 18th.
다음 가능한 비행기는 6월 18일입니다.

We have a flight leaving on June 18th.
6월 18일 비행기가 있습니다.

Is that OK for you?
Will that day work for you?
그 날은 괜찮으신가요?

Would you like me to reserve a seat on that date?
그날 좌석으로 예약해 드릴까요?

Would you like one way ticket or round trip ticket?
편도인가요? 왕복인가요?

On your return flight, would you prefer morning or afternoon?
돌아오실 때 아침 또는 오후 어느 비행기를 원하시나요?

I'll be returning on the 27th.
27일에 돌아 올 것입니다.

My return date is June 27th.
돌아올 날은 6월 27일입니다.

On return flight, I would prefer to come back in the morning.
돌아올 때 아침 비행기를 타고 싶습니다.

I'd like an afternoon return flight.
오는 비행기는 오후에 타고 싶습니다.

Do you want to go economy, business or first class?
이코노미, 비즈니스, 일등석 중 어디를 원하십니까?

How much is the flight?
비행기 요금은 얼마입니까?

What's the economic class round trip fare?
이코노미 석 왕복 요금이 얼마죠?

Is there anything special I can do to get the lowest price?
낮은 가격을 받을 수 있는 방법이 있나요?

Is that a non-stop flight?
논스톱 비행기죠?

Would you like to make a booking?
예약을 하시겠습니까?

How many people?
몇 명이죠?

Two people. My wife will be traveling with me.
두 명입니다. 제 아내가 함께 여행을 합니다.

May I have your name please?
성함이 어떻게 되시지요?

My first name is — last name is —.
이름은 — 이고 성은 —입니다.

My name is spelled —.
이름의 철자는 —입니다.

Tell me your mobile phone number.
휴대폰번호를 말씀해 주실래요?

Could you tell me my flight and reservation number?
비행기와 예약 번호를 말해 주시겠습니까?

Please confirm your reservation 3 days before your traveling date.
여행가기 3일 전 예약을 확인해주세요.

If I need to cancel, should I cancel at least 14 days before the date?
취소하려면 14일 이전에 취소하여야 하나요?

If you cancel your registration 14 or more days before departure, you will receive a full refund.
출발 14일 이전에 취소하면 전부 환불이 가능합니다.

I'm calling to confirm my flight.
비행기 탑승을 확정하려고 전화했습니다.

I would like to confirm my flight.
비행기 탑승을 확정하고 싶습니다.

I am scheduled to depart on June 17th at 9:00 A.M. And my flight number is —.
6월 17일 아침 9시에 예약이 되어 있습니다. 그리고 비행기 편명은 —입니다.

Can I get your ticket number? And your name?
Could you tell me ticket number and your name, Please?
May I have your name and ticket number?
비행기 티켓 번호와 성함이 어떻게 되지요?

My ticket number is —
My name is —.
비행기 예약 번호는 — 이고,
제 이름은 — 입니다.

Your reservation has been confirmed.
Your tickets have been confirmed.
Confirm is done.
확인되었습니다.

Can I confirm the other ticket?
다른 비행기 표도 확인할 수 있나요?

Is anybody traveling with you?
같이 가시는 분이 있나요?

Can we select our seats in advance?
미리 우리들 좌석을 선택할 수 있나요?

You can get the seat of your choice

133

online using the reservation number.
예약번호로 인터넷을 통해 좌석을 선택할 수 있습니다.

Do I have to arrive at the airport 3 hours before flight departure?
비행기 출발 3시간 전까지 공항에 도착해야 합니까?

I am calling to reconfirm your reservation.
예약을 재확인하기 위해 전화했습니다.

I am still going.
My schedule is unchanged.
예약대로 출발합니다.
변함이 없습니다.

2. 비행기 스케줄 변경 (Change of Flight Schedule)

I'd like to reschedule my flight.
비행기 예약을 변경하고 싶군요.

How would you like to change it?
어떻게 바꾸고 싶으십니까?

I have a ticket to depart on June 17th morning flight, to New York.
I made a reservation, June 17th, morning flight, to New York.
I am scheduled to fly on June 17th morning flight, to New York.
6월 17일 뉴욕으로 가는 아침 비행기가 예약되어 있습니다.

Can I change it to evening's flight?
I'd like to be rescheduled to the evening flight.
저녁 비행기로 변경했으면 합니다.

Can you change it for another day?
Can I change a schedule to another day?
다른 날로 변경할 수 있을까요?

Can I change it to a later date?
그 이후 날로 바꿀 수 있나요?

What day do you want?
What date would you like to change it to?
어느 날로 변경하실 건가요?

I'd like to change it to June 18th.
I'd like to book on June 18th flight instead.
대신 6월18일 가는 것으로 바꾸고 싶습니다.

Is there a change fee?
How much is change fee?
변경 비용이 있나요? 얼마이죠?

We will charge $75 fee for changes or cancellations prior to departure.
출발 전에 변경하거나 취소 시에는 75달러 비용을 청구합니다.

We booked a June 17th flight from Seoul to New York.
6월17일 서울에서 뉴욕으로 가는 비행기를 예약했습니다.

We were scheduled to fly on the 9:00 A.M. flight.
아침 9시 비행기로 예약되었습니다.

I would like to see if there is an earlier flight available.
더 빠른 비행기가 있을까요?

I would like to leave on June 16th. I would like to change it to a flight for June 16 th.
6월 16일 떠나고 싶습니다.

Is June 16th available?
6월 16일이 가능하나요?

Could you check if June 16th is possible?
6월 16일이 가능한 지 체크해 주실래요?

I'd like to cancel my reservation for the flight on June 17th, and book on June 16th instead, please.
6월17일 가는 비행기 예약을 취소하고 16일 가는 비행기로 바꾸고 싶습니다.

We have two flights on June 16th, but both flights were full booked.
6월 16일 2대의 비행편이 있는데 모두 다 예약이 되었습니다.

Can we put our names on the waiting list?
저희들을 대기자 명단에 올려주시겠습니까?

We'll place your names on a waiting list.
이름들을 대기자 명단에 올리겠습니다.

If your reservation is confirmed, we'll let you know.
만약 예약이 되면 알려드리겠습니다.

I expect to hear good news.
좋은 소식 기다리겠습니다.

I'm calling to change my destination from New York to San Francisco.
목적지를 뉴욕에서 샌프란시스코로 바꾸기 위해 전화했습니다.

I'd like to cancel my flight.
비행기 예약을 취소하고 싶습니다.

100$ cancellation fee will be charged if the ticket is cancelled.
예약을 취소하시면 100달러 취소 비용이 청구됩니다.

There is no fee to change or cancel a flight, if the reservation was made at least 7 days prior to departure.
예약이 만일 출발 7일 이전에 예약된 것이라면 변경이나 취소비용이 청구되지 않습니다.

Ticket can be exchanged for a credit for future use.
표는 다음에 사용할 수 있는 교환권으로 변경될 수 있습니다.

Refundable tickets can be cancelled without a fee at anytime.
환불 가능한 티켓은 언제든지 비용 없이 취소가 가능합니다.

Non-refundable tickets will be charged the full price of the original ticket as a fee.
환불 불가 티켓은 티켓비용만큼 전부 비용으로 처리가 됩니다.

Is there any chance flight can be cancelled due to bad weather condition?
기상 악화로 비행기가 취소될 가능성이 있나요?

Are all flights rescheduled to another day due to runway closure?
모든 비행기들이 활주로 폐쇄로 다른 날로 변경이 되었나요?

My flight has been cancelled due to bad weather. Can you reschedule me on the next available flight?
비행기가 기상 악화로 취소되었는데, 다음 가능한 비행기로 바꾸어줄 수 있나요?

I want to reserve a next flight as soon as possible.
가능한 빠르게 다음 비행기를 예약해 주세요.

Can I take an alternative flight?
대체 비행기를 탈 수 있나요?

Can you put me on the waiting list?
Please put me on the waiting list.
저를 대기자 명단에 올려주시겠습니까?

Is there any chance of getting the ticket?
티켓을 받을 가능성이 있나요?

If my reservation is confirmed, please let me know.
만약 예약이 완료되면 알려주세요.

I expect good news.
좋은 소식 기다리겠습니다.

I am calling to reschedule your reservation.
당신의 예약을 바꾸기 위해 전화했습니다.

Your flight has been cancelled due to bad weather.
당신의 비행기 편이 기상 악화로 취소되었습니다.

Do you want to reserve a later flight?
다음 비행기로 예약을 하실 건가요?

I'd like to take an alternative flight as soon as possible.
가능한 빠른 비행기로 대체해 주세요.

What's my rescheduled departing time?
변경된 출발시간이 언제인가요?

3. 비행기 연착 (Flight Delay)

My flight was delayed and I missed connecting flight. How can I do?
비행기가 연착되어 환승 비행기를 놓쳤습니다. 어떻게 해야 하나요?

What if there are no more connecting flights for today?
오늘 비행기 연결 편이 없으면 어떻게 해야 하나요?

My flight arrived late.
Can I check in now even though cut off time has passed?
Can I board a plane except baggage? And could you send it for me on the next flight? Please.
제 비행기가 늦게 도착했습니다. 마감 시간이 지났지만, 체크인 할 수 있나요? 짐은 놔두고 저 혼자만 타고 다음비행기로 보내주실래요?

Am I go-show passenger?
How long do I wait more?
If there are any seats available, would you please call me at this number. Please.
제가 대기승객이나요? 얼마나 더 기다려야하죠? 만약 자리가 생기면 이 번호로 전화를 해 주실래요? 부탁드립니다.

Can you see if there is connecting flight available?
이용할 수 있는 비행기 연결편이 있는 지 알아봐 주실래요?

Do you have any other flights available today?
오늘 이용할 수 있는 연결편이 있습니까?

Can you help me find an alternate flight?
대체 비행기 편을 찾아봐 주실래요?

Could you please check another flight for me?
다른 비행기를 알아봐 주실래요?

Can I take an alternative flight as soon as possible?
가능한 빨리 대체 비행기를 탈 수 있나요?

How long do I have to wait?
얼마나 오래 기다려야 하나요?

How long will I wait here?
이곳에서 얼마나 기다려야 하죠?

What's the best way if I want to book a flight?
비행기를 예약하려면 어떻게 하는게 최선의 방법일까요?

Am I just staying at the airport?
공항에서 머물러야 하나요?

Can you help me find transportation to a local hotel?
주변 호텔로 가는 교통편을 알아봐 주실래요?

Can I claim if the airline I flew has delayed?
제가 탄 비행기가 연착하면 보상을 청구할 수가 있나요?

My flight's been delayed.
How much will I get?
비행기가 지연되었는데 얼마나 보상받죠?

What can I do if I missed a connecting flight because of a cancellation?
비행기 취소 때문에 연결 편 비행기를 놓치면 어떻게 해야 하나요?

You're not entitled to compensation if the delay was due to severe weather condition.
만약 기상 악화로 지연된 경우에는 보상이 없습니다.

Am I entitled to compensation?
보상 받을 자격이 되나요?

Am I entitled to a refund of my fare?
제 요금을 반환 받을 자격이 되나요?

If your flight is delayed, you could be entitled to compensation or a refund.
비행기가 지연되면 보상이나 환불을 받을 자격이 됩니다.

Compensation for delayed flights depends on the reason for the delay.
항공기 지연에 대한 보상은 지연 이유에 따라 결정됩니다.

When can I claim for costs, and what can I claim?
비용을 언제 청구하고 무엇을 청구하죠?

What evidence do I need to submit?
어떤 증거들을 제출해야 하나요?

Do I need a boarding pass to claim?
청구할 때 비행기 표가 필요하나요?

Do I have to submit a flight claim to get compensation?
보상을 받으려면 비행지연 청구서를 신청해야 하나요?

Submit your flight number and the date of your flight.
비행기 편명과 비행 날짜를 제출하세요.

You may be entitled to compensation if your delay was more than two hours.
2시간 이상 비행기가 지연이 되면 보상 자격이 주어집니다.

What can I do if I am stuck at the airport?
공항에 갇혀있으면 어떻게 해야 하죠?

Will the airline pay for my hotel room if I have to spend the night?
밤을 보내게 되면 비행기회사에서 호텔 비용을 지불해 주나요?

Do I have to pay for a hotel room?
제가 호텔 비용을 지불해야 하나요?

The flight delay was your fault, so do you cover the cost of a hotel room?
비행기가 늦은 것이 당신들 잘못이니 호텔 비용을 부담하지 않나요?

You are entitled to free hotel accommodation and hotel transfers if an overnight stay is required.
만약 하룻밤 머물게 되면 호텔 이용과 이동 비용을 받을 수 있게 됩니다.

4. 공항 발권 (Airport Ticketing)

Is this check-in counter for Delta airline?
델타항공사인가요?

Isn't it too late?
The traffic was heavy everywhere.
너무 늦지는 않았나요?
모든 곳에서 길이 막히더군요.

May I see your ticket and passport?
티켓과 여권 좀 주실래요?

Here you are.
Here you go.
Here it is.
There you go.
여기 있습니다.

I have booked airline tickets online.
인터넷으로 비행기를 예약했습니다.

Do you prefer window or aisle?
창가나 복도 쪽 어느 좌석을 원하십니까?

Can I have a window seat, please?
창가 좌석이 있습니까?

We don't have any window seats remaining.
창가 좌석은 남은 게 없습니다.

There are only aisle seats available.
안쪽 좌석 밖에 남은 것이 없습니다.

Is an aisle seat ok with you?
복도 좌석도 괜찮으십니까?

Do you have a seat next to the emergency exit?
Can I have a seat closest to the emergency exit?
비상구 근처 좌석이 있습니까?

All the seats next to the exit have been taken.
비상구 근처 좌석은 다 찼습니다.

Can I have a seat closest to the lavatory?
화장실 근처 좌석을 가질 수 있나요?

Where can I check my luggage?
짐을 어디서 부치죠?

How many pieces of baggage?
How many bags are you checking in?
가방이 몇 개이지요?

I have these two suitcases.
여행가방 두 개가 있습니다.

You will be charged if you check in more than one bag.
가방 1개 이상일 경우 추가요금이 있습니다.

There are fragile items in my bag.
제 가방에 깨지기 쉬운 것들이 있습니다.

Could you attach fragile sticker on my bag?
파손주의 스티커를 제 가방에 붙여 주실래요?

How many luggages can I take on the plane with me?
How many baggages may I bring?
비행기에 몇 개의 가방을 가져갈 수 있죠?

Am I allowed just 1 carry-on bag?
Can I bring 2 carry-on bags onto a plane?
기내용 가방 하나만 허용되나요?
기내에 2개를 가져갈 수 있나요?

That suitcase is too large for carry-on.
You'll not be able to bring your bag onto the flight.
I am afraid you'll have to check it.
그 가방은 기내용으로는 너무 크군요.
기내로 가져갈 수가 없습니다.
체크인 해야 될 것 같습니다.

My bag is the right size.
제 가방 크기는 맞는 사이즈입니다.

Do you charge an additional fee for oversized baggage?
너무 큰 가방에 대한 추가요금을 매기나요?

Do I have to pay the extra charge?
추가요금을 내야 하나요?

Can you place your baggage up here?
가방을 이곳에 올려주실래요?

Put your baggage on the scale.
가방을 저울 위에 올려 주실래요?

Your luggage is 20 pounds over the limit.
20파운드 초과되었군요.

What's baggage allowance?
What's the baggage weight limits?
수하물 허용 중량이 얼마죠?

Over weight baggage charges should be applied if luggage is over 70 pounds limits.
수하물이 70 파운드가 넘으면 추가 수하물 금액이 적용되어야 합니다.

Do I have to pay additional charge for overweight baggage?
초과 중량 가방에 대해 추가로 돈을 더 지불해야 합니까?

Could you please let it go?
그냥 지나치면 안 될까요?

You have to pay extra.
초과 금액을 지불해야 합니다.

Are you carrying any food?
음식물을 가지고 계시나요?

Do you have any flammable items?
가연성 물질을 가지고 계시나요?

Do you have any illegal items?
불법적인 물품을 가지고 있나요?

Did someone you don't know ask you to take something on the plane with you?
모르는 사람이 당신에게 어떤 물건을 비행기에 같이 가져가 주라고 부탁한 것은 없나요?

Did you have possession of your luggage since you packed?
가방을 다 싼 후 직접 가지고 계셨나요?

Did you leave your luggage unattended at all in the airport?
공항에 가방을 보지 않고 놔둔 적이 있나요?

Here are your boarding pass and baggage claim tickets.
여기 탑승권과 수하물표가 있습니다.

You're in seat 17C
좌석은 17C입니다.

Flight will start boarding 20 minutes before the departure time.
출발 20분전에 탑승을 시작합니다.

Boarding will begin at A.M. 8:40.
탑승은 오전 8시40분에 시작됩니다.

I need to store my baggage.
가방을 맡기고 싶군요.

Can I leave my bags at the luggage storage service at terminal?
공항터미널에 있는 수하물 보관소에 가방을 맡길 수 있나요?

Is there any airport luggage storage facility available?
여기에 공항 수하물 보관소가 있나요?

Airport has luggage storage facility.
공항에 수하물 보관소가 있습니다.

Does the facility operate 24 hours?
이 시설이 24시간 운영하나요?

Should I pay more depending on the size of my bag?
수하물 크기에 따라 더 지불하나요?

The facility operates 24 hours, and charges $4 to $16 per day depending on the size of your luggage.
수하물 보관소는 24시간 운영하는데 수하물 크기에 따라 하루에 4-16불 받습니다.

Sorry for being late.
If I couldn't check in baggages, can I board a flight myself except my baggages. I must leave now.
Would you please send my baggages on the next flight?
늦어서 죄송합니다.
짐을 체크인 할 수가 없다면, 짐을 제외하고 저만 비행기에 타면 안되나요?
짐은 다음 비행기편으로 보내주실래요?

5. 공항 검색 및 탑승 수속
(Security Check & Boarding)

It's boarding time.
May I be excused to jump the line?
I ask for your understanding.
I can't wait till my turn comes.
탑승시간이네요.
줄을 건너 뛰어도 될까요?
이해를 해주시기를 부탁드립니다.
제 차례까지 기다릴 수가 없네요.

I can't miss my flight. I must go.
Can I skip the line?
비행기를 놓칠 수가 없습니다. 가야만 해요.
대기줄을 지나쳐도 될까요?

I have something very important to do. I never like to miss a flight.
Can I move to the head of the line?
아주 중요한 일이 있어 비행기를 놓치고 싶지 않습니다. 대기줄 앞으로 가도 될까요?

Should I take my shoes off?
Should I take my coat off?
Do I have to take off outerwear?
Should I take off my belt?
제 신발을 벗어야 하나요?
제 코트 (겉옷)를 벗어야하나요?
제 벨트를 풀어야 하나요?

Do I have to put these in the basket?
이것들을 바구니에 넣어야 하나요?

I emptied all my pockets.
주머니를 모두 비웠습니다.

Should I go through the gate one more time?
Do I have to walk through the gate again?
문을 한 번 더 통과해야 하나요?

Should I go through the body scanner?
몸 스캐너를 통과해야 하나요?

I am not carrying any restricted items.
금지 품목은 가지고 있지 않습니다.

I don't have any flammable material.
가연성 물질은 가지고 있지 않습니다.

I've removed all my metal objects.
금속 제품은 다 꺼내놨습니다.

I had an operation for bone fracture.
뼈가 골절되어 수술을 받았습니다.

So I have metal plate in my leg.
그래서 제 다리에 금속판이 있습니다.

My forearm bone was broken, so I had an operation.
팔이 부러져서 수술을 받았었습니다.

Metal plate and screws are fixated to my bone.
금속 핀들과 나사들이 제 뼈에 박혀있습니다.

Can you point me towards the gate?
탑승구가 어디인지 가르쳐 주실래요?

How do I get to the gate?
탑승구로 어떻게 가죠?

How can I take a connecting flight?
비행기 연결 편은 어떻게 타죠?

I am a transit passenger for New York.
I am in transit to New York.
뉴욕으로 가는 환승객입니다.

Where is the transit counter?
환승 카운터가 어디이죠?

Where do I take my connection flight?
환승 비행기를 어디에서 타죠?

Where can I transfer?
어디서 환승을 하죠?

Where can I connect with my next flight?
다음 비행기 연결 편을 어디서 탈 수 있나요?

Do you know what gate my plane is leaving from?
제 비행기가 어느 탑승구에서 출발하나요?

Which gate should I go to?
어느 탑승구로 가나요?

When does an airline start boarding?
언제 비행기 탑승을 시작하죠?

When does boarding begin?
탑승이 언제이죠?

Is the plane on schedule?
비행기가 예정대로 출발하나요?

I was wondering how to go through Customs.
세관을 어떻게 통과하는지 모르겠군요.

Where is the internet lounge?
인터넷 라운지가 어디죠?

Where can I use the WIFI?
와이파이는 어디에서 사용할 수 있죠?

Is there free WIFI place?
무료 와이파이 장소가 있나요?

Where is a convenience store?
편의점이 어디에 있나요?

Are there any cell phone charging services in this area?
이곳에 휴대폰 충전 서비스하는 곳이 있나요?

Excuse me. Where do I go?
죄송한데 어디로 가야 하죠?

Where are you going?
어디를 가시는데요?

Please get into that bus.
저 버스를 타세요.

Could you show me your boarding card?
탑승권 좀 보여 주실래요?

Go straight. Your seat is on the right.
좌석이 똑바로 가시면 오른쪽에 있습니다.

I won't be staying in the U.S. but is continuing on to Canada.
미국에 머물지 않고 계속 캐나다로 갑니다.

Go to the end of the walkway, down the stairs, and to the left.
복도 끝으로 가서 층계를 내려간 다음 왼쪽으로 가세요.

Travelers who are continuing on to another country will check in over there.
다른 나라로 연결 편으로 가시는 여행자들은 저곳에서 체크인 하시면 됩니다.

And you will be directed where you can connect with your next flight.
다음 비행기 타는 곳으로 안내 될 것입니다.

I was wondering if I have to go through Customs.
세관을 통과해야 되는지 궁금하군요.

6. 수하물 찾기 (Baggage Claim)

Where is the baggage claim area?
수하물 찾는 곳이 어디죠?

Where can I take my baggage from Seoul?
서울편 항공기 가방을 어디에서 찾지요?

You can get there by going down the escalator and following the signs.
에스컬레이터를 타고 내려가 표지판을 따라 가시면 됩니다.

Is the trolley free?
카트가 무료이나요?

My bag is a little bit damaged.
제 가방이 조금 손상이 되었네요.

I want to speak with someone who is responsible for damaged baggage.
I would like to speak to someone in charge of baggage service.
수하물 담당 책임자와 이야기하고 싶습니다.

Could your company repair my bag at your expense?
Does your company fix this for free?
가방을 항공사 부담으로 고쳐줄 수 있나요?

Is this your baggage?
이 짐은 당신것인가요?

My bags haven't come out yet.
제 가방들이 아직 나오지 않았거든요.

What does your bag look like?
가방이 어떻게 생겼지요?

My bag is black color trolley bag.
제 가방은 검은색 바퀴 달린 가방입니다.

My baggage seems to be missing.
가방을 잃어버린 것 같아요.

I've been waiting for 20 minutes.
20분이나 기다렸습니다.

My bag didn't arrive at this airport.
제 가방이 이 공항에 도착을 안 했네요.

My baggage had not yet arrived.
제 가방이 아직 도착을 안 했네요.

I have no idea where it is.
어디에 있는지 모르겠네요.

I can't find my bag anywhere.
어디에서도 제 가방을 찾지 못하겠어요.

Could you tell me how to get my baggages?
어떻게 제 가방들을 찾죠?

What should I do to get my lost baggage back?
잃어버린 가방을 찾으려면 어떻게 하죠?

What flight did you arrive on?
어느 비행기로 도착하셨죠?

I flew on Delta airlines.
델타 비행기를 타고 왔습니다.

I have been waiting until now, but it hasn't come out yet.
지금까지 기다렸는데 아직 안 나왔습니다.

Your baggage should be out by now.
당신의 짐이 벌써 나왔어야 됩니다.

Contact a staff of Delta Airlines.
델타 항공사 직원을 만나보세요.

You need to report to the baggage agents in the claim office.
수하물 담당자에게 보고해야 합니다.

7. 수하물 분실 신고 (Baggage Lost & Found)

Where is the Baggage Service Office?
(Baggage Claim Office)
(Baggage Handling Desk)
(Lost and Found Office)
수하물 담당 사무실이 어디 있지요?

Who is in charge of missing baggage?
누가 분실물 담당 책임자이죠?

I'd like to report to a baggage service agent about my missing baggage.
수하물 담당자에게 저의 잃어버린 짐에 대해 보고해야겠습니다.

I have lost my baggage.
제 가방을 잃어 버렸습니다.

My baggage didn't come out yet.
I didn't see my baggage there.
There was no similar baggage.
제 짐이 아직 안나왔습니다.
그곳에서 제 짐을 볼 수가 없었습니다.
비슷한 짐도 없습니다.

I've been waiting for 30 minutes.
30분이나 기다렸습니다.

Who should I talk to expedite this?
Whom should I ask to handle this?
이것을 빨리 처리하려면 누구에게 말하죠?

Do you have your baggage claim tag?
수하물표를 가지고 계십니까?

I have my baggage claim tag.
제 수하물표를 가지고 있습니다.

What happens if my baggage is lost?
가방을 잃어버리면 어떻게 하죠?

We're going to have to do an investigation. (We have to invesigate.)
조사를 해봐야겠군요.

Sometimes technical problems can lead to not arriving at the destination airport at the same time as the passenger.
때로 기술적 문제 때문에 승객과 동시에 수하물이 도착하지 않을 수 있습니다.

We will search for your baggage with the help of a world wide baggage tracing system.
세계 수하물 시스템을 이용하여 당신의 가방을 찾아볼 것입니다.

Should I fill out baggage claim form?
수하물 분실 신고서를 작성해야 하나요?

Fill out this baggage claim form.
이 수하물 분실 신고서에 기재해 주세요.

Should I describe the missing properties in my bags?
가방 안에 있는 것들을 다 기입해야 하나요?

Should I fill out the model, color and content of my baggage?
가방의 종류와 색깔, 내용물들을 기입해야 하나요?

Should I make an itemized list of what was in my bag?
가방 안에 있는 물건들의 항목들을 적어야 하나요?

You have to write item lists of what was in your bag.
당신 가방 안에 있었던 물건들의 항목들을 모두 적으셔야 합니다.

When does a missing bag become a lost bag if you can't find it?
만약 분실된 가방을 찾지 못하게 되면 언제 잃어버린 것으로 확정되나요?

It will take more than a week for your bag to be deemed lost.
일주일 이상이 지나면 당신의 가방은 완전히 분실 처리됩니다.

Can I claim on properties in my bag once it has been decided the bag has been lost?
일단 가방이 잃어버렸다고 결정되면 가방 안에 있는 것들을 청구할 수 있나요?

How long will it take?
얼마나 걸리죠?

As soon as your baggage is found, we will contact you to arrange delivery.
가방이 발견되면 바로 당신에게 연락하여 보내드리도록 하겠습니다.

Where are you going to stay at?
어느 곳에 계실 건가요?

Fill out your mobile number and email address.
핸드폰 번호와 이메일 주소도 기입해 주세요.

We will deliver it to you in a secure manner as soon as possible.
가능한 빨리 안전한 방법으로 보내드리겠습니다.

If you have any questions about your missing bag, please contact us on this number.
분실물에 대해 더 물어 보실 것이 있으면 이곳으로 전화를 하십시오.

Hello. What can I do for you?
여보세요. 무엇을 도와 드릴까요?

I want to speak with someone who is responsible for missing baggage.
분실된 수하물을 담당하는 사람과 이야기를 하고 싶습니다.

I arrived at JFK on Delta flight from Seoul last Saturday and my baggage had not arrived.
지난 토요일 JFK 공항에 델타항공으로 도착했는데 제 가방이 도착을 안 했습니다.

145

I spoke with the baggage officer and was told my baggage would be delivered as soon as possible.
수하물 담당자와 이야기를 했고 가능한 빨리 가방을 보내준다고 했습니다.

It has now been three days and I still don't have my baggage.
지금 3일이나 지났는데 아직 가방을 받지 못했습니다.

What would you suggest me to do?
제가 어떻게 해야 하지요?

Could I get information of the latest news about tracing my baggage?
제 가방에 대한 최근 추적 정보를 알 수 있을까요?

We apologize in advance and assure you of our entire support.
미리 죄송하다고 말씀을 드리며 저희들은 최선을 다하고 있습니다.

We will inform you of the latest news about tracing your baggage.
당신의 가방에 대한 최근 추적 정보를 알려 드리겠습니다.

I'd really like to get my baggage back. I was wondering how it went. Is that going to take long?
제 가방을 정말 돌려받고 싶습니다.
어떻게 되어 가는지 궁금하군요.
오래 걸리나요?

The search of your baggage has been processed.
당신의 가방은 계속 찾는 중입니다.

Will you deliver my baggage to my hotel as soon as you find?
찾는 즉시 제가 머무는 호텔로 가방을 보내주나요?

We will deliver your baggage to your hotel as soon as we find.
찾는 즉시 당신이 머무는 호텔로 보내드리겠습니다.

8. 비행기 기내에서 (On the Plane)

Someone is sitting in my seat.
누가 제 자리에 앉아있네요.

Could you see it for me?
확인해 주실래요?

Excuse me.
I believe you are in my seat.
실례합니다. 제 자리인 것 같은데요.

I am afraid. This is my seat.
이곳은 제 자리인 것 같습니다.

May I get through?
지나가도 될까요?

Could you help me find somewhere to put my luggage?
짐을 넣을 만한 곳을 찾아 주실래요?

Can I put my bag here?
이곳에 가방을 두어도 되나요?

Could you help me put my bag in the overhead bin?
가방을 선반에 넣는 것을 도와주실래요?

Would you mind not sitting here?
여기 앉지 말아주실래요?

I didn't realize this seat was taken.
죄송합니다. 자리가 있는 줄 몰랐습니다.

May I change seat with you?
저와 자리를 바꿀 수 있겠습니까?

Yes. But may I ask why?
예, 그런데 무슨 이유가 있습니까?

My wife and I would like to sit together.
집사람과 제가 함께 앉고 싶습니다.

Can I move over there?
저쪽으로 자리를 옮겨도 되나요?

Could you let me pass?
지나가도 될까요?

I'd like to go to the restroom.
화장실에 가려고 합니다.

May I recline my seat?
May I put my seat back?
Do you mind if I lean back?
의자를 뒤로 젖혀도 되나요?

Can I get something to drink?
I was wondering if I could order something to drink.
마실 것 좀 부탁합니다.

What would you like?
무엇을 드릴까요?

What do you have?
어떤 것들이 있나요?

Are the drinks free?
Are coffee and soda complimentary?
커피와 소다(음료수)는 무료인가요?

Drinks are free.
It's provided at no extra charge.
음료는 무료입니다. 추가 요금이 없습니다.

Can I have some water (coffee)?
물 (커피) 좀 주실래요?

Could I have some iced water?
얼음 물을 좀 주실래요?

Do you have any alcoholic drinks?
Is it provided free of charge?
주류는 있나요?
무료로 제공이 됩니까?

What's the price of alcoholic drinks?
주류는 가격이 얼마이죠?

How much should I pay for a beer?
How much? one can of beer?
맥주는 얼마이죠?

When will meals be served?
언제 식사가 제공되죠?

Will dinner be served soon?
저녁은 곧 나오나요?

I am a vegetarian.
I need a vegetarian meal.
저는 채식주의자라 채식 식사가 필요합니다.

Do vegetarian meals need to be requested before flight?
채식 식사는 탑승 전 미리 요청해야 하나요?

We are taking orders for dinner.
저녁 식사 주문을 받습니다.

Would you prefer chicken, fish or beef steak?
치킨과 생선, 비프스테이크 중 어느 것을 원하세요?

I'll have beef steak.
비프스테이크를 주세요.

Chicken, please.
치킨으로 주세요.

I'd like the fish.
생선으로 주세요.

I can't eat meat and fish.
고기나 생선은 먹지 않습니다.

Do you have vegetarian meal?
채식주의자 음식이 있나요?

Please put your tray down in front of you.
선반을 앞으로 내려 주실래요?

Would you like to have something to drink?
음료수는 무엇을 드릴까요?

Orange juice, please.
오렌지 주스 주세요.

Would you like some more orange juice?
오렌지 주스를 더 드릴까요?

Have you finished?
다 드셨나요?

Not yet.
아직이요.

I am having trouble with my seat.
의자에 문제가 있는데요.

How can I fasten this belt?
이 벨트를 어떻게 착용하지요?

Could I get an extra blanket?
담요 한 장 더 있으세요?

Do you have a pillow?
베개가 있으세요?

Could I have an earphone?
Will you get me a headset?
이어폰 (헤드폰) 좀 주실래요?

Get me an eye patch.
안대 좀 주세요.

My screen is not working.
스크린이 고장이 났네요.

This headphone is not working.
헤드폰이 고장 났네요.

Would you mind turning off the light?
불을 좀 꺼주실래요?

Would you mind speaking more quietly?
좀 조용히 말을 해주실래요?

Would you mind not putting your bag here?
여기에 가방을 놓지 말아주실래요?

Would you mind not kicking me?
Please, stop kicking.
Sir, Your child is kicking my seat.
의자를 차지 말아줄래요?
선생님, 당신의 아이가 의자를 차고있네요.

I can't endure your foot odor.
Do you mind moving your foot.
당신의 발 냄새를 더 이상 참을 수가 없네요.
당신의 발 좀 치워주실래요?

What seems to be the problem?
무슨 일이지요?

I'm feeling under the weather.
몸이 불편해요.

I want to lie down for a while.
잠깐 누워있고 싶습니다.

I feel dizzy.
어지럽군요.

I got airsick.
멀미를 하는 것 같아요.

I am feeling a little nauseous.
I feel nausea.
속이 메스껍네요.

My stomach doesn't feel good.
I have an upset stomach.
속이 좋질 않네요. 체한 것 같아요

I feel like vomiting.
I feel like throwing up.
I feel vomiting.
I am going to throw up.
토할 것 같습니다.

Where is an airsickness bag?
멀미 백이 어디에 있죠?

May I have an airsickness bag?
멀미 백 좀 주실래요?

I'll be right back.
곧 가져 오겠습니다.

Do you have any medicine?
(emergency or first-aid medicine)
약 (비상약, 구급약)이 있으세요?

I need some medicine for airsickness.
멀미 약이 필요합니다.

I'll get you airsickness medicine.
멀미 약을 드리지요.

My ears are popping.
귀가 먹먹하군요.

Flying seems to affect ear pressure.
비행이 귀압력에 영향을 주는것 같군요.

Swallowing and yawning helps relieve the pressure.
삼키거나 하품이 압력을 낮추는데 도움을 줄 것입니다.

Do you sell any duty-free goods on board?
기내에서 비과세 상품을 파나요?

Do you have any book I could read?
읽을 만한 책이 있나요?

Do you have any Korean newspaper?
한국 신문이 있나요?

Are the lavatories occupied?
화장실이 다 찼나요?

Is this a waiting line?
기다리는 줄인가요?

May I talk to you?
이야기해도 될까요?

Please fill out Visa Waiver Arrival Form and Customs Declaration.
비자 면제 입국 신고서와 세관 신고서를 작성해 주세요.

Can I borrow a pen?
펜 좀 빌릴 수 있을까요?

May I have Customs Declaration?
세관 신고서를 주실래요?

May I have another Disembarkation Card?
입국 신고서 한 장 더 주실래요?

May I have one more?
한 장 주실래요?

Could you help me to fill out this form?
이 신고서를 작성하는데 도와주실래요?

What should I write here?
이곳은 무엇을 쓰죠?

We will be landing shortly.
곧 착륙합니다.

149

9. 입국 수속
(Immigration Procedure)

I-94 W Visa Waiver Arrival Form
(I-94 비자 면제 입국 신고서)
& Disembarkation Card
(입국 신고서)

1. Family Name (Surname)
 - 성
2. First (Given) Name
 - 이름
3. Birth Date (Day/Mo/Yr)
 - 생년월일
4. Country of Citizenship
 (Nationality) - 국적
5 Sex (Male or Female)
 - 성별
6. Passport Number
 - 여권번호
7. Airline and Flight number
 - 비행기 편명
8. Country Where You Live
 - 거주 나라
9. City Where You Boarded
 (Port of Last Departure)
 - 탑승 도시
10. Address While
 in the United States
 (Number and Street)
 - 미국 체류 장소

11. City and State
 - 미국 체류 도시, 주 이름
12. City Where Visa Was Issued
 (Place of Issue)
 - 비자 발급 도시
13. Date Issued (Day/Mo/Yr)
 - 비자 발급 날짜
14. Main purpose of Travel
 - 방문 목적
15. Signature
 - 서명

How was your flight?
비행기 여행은 어땠어요?

Very comfortable.
좋았습니다.

May I see your passport and
immigration form?
여권과 입국신고서를 주실래요?

Here you go. (Here it is.)
여기 있습니다.

What's the purpose of your visit?
Why are you visiting United States?
방문 목적이 무엇이지요?

I am here for sightseeing.
For travel.
(For group tour with travel agency.)
관광차 왔습니다.
(여행사와 함께 단체관광하러 왔습니다.)

For study abroad program
해외 유학 프로그램 때문에 왔습니다.

I'll be attending the symposium.
심포지엄에 참석하러 왔습니다.

To visit my relatives.
친척들을 방문하러 왔습니다.

I am here on business.
일 때문에 왔습니다.

Who will you be visiting?
누구를 만날 예정이죠?

I have an appointment with the staff of trading company.
거래하는 회사 직원과 약속이 있습니다.

Have you ever been issued a US VISA?
미국비자를 발급받으신 적이 있습니까?

I have been issued VISA.
But it has expired a few years ago.
비자를 발급받은 적이 있지만,
몇 년 전 기간이 만료되었습니다.

I was previously permitted by ESTA (Electronic System for Travel Authorization, 전자여행 허가).
ESTA로 미리 여행 허가를 받았습니다.

Where are you going to stay here?
Where are you staying?
어디에서 머무르실 겁니까?

I am going to stay at A Hotel.
I will be staying with my relatives.
A 호텔에 머물 예정입니다.
친척과 같이 지낼 것입니다.

I haven't decided yet.
I plan to find cheap hotel or guest house in downtown.
아직 정하지 않았습니다. 시내에서 싼 호텔이나 게스트 하우스를 찾을 계획입니다.

How long will you stay?
How long will you be here?
How long are you going to stay?
얼마나 있으실 계획입니까?

I will stay for 2 weeks.
I'll be staying for 2 weeks.
I plan to stay for 2 weeks.
I plan on staying for 2 weeks.
2주 동안 머무를 예정입니다.

I'm going back to Korea next week.
다음 주에 한국으로 돌아갑니다.

Do you have a return ticket to Korea?
한국으로 돌아가는 비행기표가 있나요?

I made a reservation for returning flight. Here is my return ticket.
돌아가는 비행기 편을 예약했습니다. 여기에 귀국편 티켓이 있습니다.

How much money are you bringing?
현금은 얼마나 가져왔나요?

I will use my credit card and I have about $1,000 in cash.
신용카드를 사용할 것이고, 현금은 약 천불 정도 있습니다.

Have you visited U.S. before?
미국을 전에 방문한 적이 있나요?

I've been here once before. I visited as a traveler for sightseeing.
한번요. 관광 여행자로 방문한적이 있습니다.

Have you ever remained after your VISA expired?
비자기간 만료후에도 체류한 적이 있나요?

Look at the camera, please. OK.
Place the top of your finger over the fingerprint reader.
카메라를 봐주세요. 됐어요.
손가락 끝을 지문인식기에 올려주세요.

Put your fingers on a scanner.
Right hand. 4 fingers and thumb.
Next, left.
손가락들을 지문 스캐너에 올려주세요.
오른쪽 4손가락과 엄지. 다음은 왼쪽.

10. 세관 수속 (Customs Procedure)

Customs Declaration (세관 신고서)

1. Family Name (Surname)
   - 성
   First (Given) Name
   - 이름
2. Birth Date (Day/Month/Year)
   - 생년월일
3. Number of Family members traveling with you
   - 여행하는 가족 수
4. US Street address (hotel name/destination), City, State
   - 미국 체류 장소, 도시, 주
5. Passport issued by country
   - 여권 발급 나라
6. Passport Number
   - 여권번호
7. Country of Residence
   - 국적
8. Countries visited on this trip prior to US arrival
   - 미국 도착 전 방문한 나라들
9. Arriving Flight number
   - 도착 비행기 편명
10. The primary purpose of this trip is business
    - 입국 목적이 상업여부 (No)
11. I am (We are) bringing fruits, plants, food ⋯
    - 과일, 꽃, 식품 소지 여부 (No)
12. Closure proximity of livestock
    - 가축 근접 접촉 여부 (No)
13. Currency or monetary instruments over $10,000
    - 미화 만 불 이상 소지 여부 (No)
14. Commercial merchandise
    - 상업용 물품 여부 (No)
15. Total value of all articles
    - 모든 상품(선물)의 가치 금액 ( )

Over here.
Your customs declaration?
이곳으로 오세요. 세관신고서는요?

Here it is.
여기 있습니다.

Do you have anything to declare other than what you've got here?
이곳에 적은 것 말고 또 신고하실 것이 있으십니까?

No, I don't. I've nothing to declare.
없습니다. 신고할 것이 없습니다.

You are supposed to declare expensive items.
비싼 것은 세관에 신고해야 합니다.

I don't have anything to declare.
신고할 것이 없습니다.

Will you open your bag?
가방을 좀 열어 주실래요?

Are you bringing in fruits?
과일 같은 것은 없나요?

No. Just my personal belongings.
아닙니다. 개인적 물건들만 있습니다.

What's this?
이것은 무엇이죠?

That's my cold medicine.
Red pepper paste (= Chilli paste).
Seaweed Laver, Sea Mustard
It's something to eat.
감기약입니다.
고추장입니다. 김입니다. 미역입니다.
먹는 것입니다.

What do you have in this pack?
이 포장 안에는 무엇이 있죠?

This is Korean food, Kimchi.
이것은 한국의 김치입니다.

You are not allowed to bring this.
You must declare all food items.
이것은 가지고 갈 수 없습니다.
음식 품목은 모두 신고해야 합니다.

I put a check mark in food item.
음식반입 항목에 체크하였습니다.

They are my personal belongings.
그것들은 제 개인 용품들입니다.

I bought this at the duty free shop.
이것은 면세점에서 샀습니다.

I don't have any restricted items.
금지 품목은 가지고 있지 않습니다.

I bought just one bottle of liquor.
술은 한 병만 샀습니다.

It's present for my friend.
그것은 친구를 위한 선물입니다.

These are gifts for my relatives.
이것들은 친척들 선물입니다.

Ok. Everything is cleared.
됐습니다. 끝났습니다.

May I close my bag?
가방을 닫아도 될까요?

Yes, you may.
예, 좋습니다.

11. 호텔 예약 (Hotel Reservation)

I'd like to reserve a room.
방을 예약하고 싶습니다.

I'd like to make a reservation.
방을 예약하고 싶습니다.

For which dates are you going to stay in this hotel?
When do you need the room?
What days do you need that reservation?
What day will you be arriving?
What day are you coming in?
What day do you want to check in?
Which date do you want to reserve?
On what day will you be beginning your stay?
Please tell me the days you'll be here.
언제 머무르실 거죠?

I am planning to stay June 17th through(=till) June 27th.
I want a room from June 17th to June 27th.
6월 17일부터 27일까지 머무를 예정입니다.

I will be arriving on June 17th.
6월 17일 도착예정입니다.

My stay will be beginning on June 17th.
6월 17일부터 머무를 것입니다.

How long will you be staying?
When will you be checking out?
How many days would you like the room for?
며칠을 머무르실 거죠?

I am going to need the room until June 27th.
6월 27일까지 방이 필요합니다.

I need the room for 10 nights.
I will be staying for 10 nights.
I am going to stay for 10 days.
I would like to reserve the room for 10 days.
10박을 원합니다.

I'll check the reservation.
예약을 확인해 보겠습니다.

What kind of room do you want?
어떤 방을 원하세요?

I will be staying in the room alone.
혼자 머물 예정입니다.

I want a single room.
싱글 룸을 원합니다.

I'll be alone, so I need single room.
혼자여서 싱글 룸만 필요합니다.

Sorry, no single room is available for the period you have requested.
죄송합니다만 그 기간에는 싱글 룸이 없군요.

How about a double room, sir?
더블 룸은 어떠세요?

Do you prefer a smoking or non smoking room?
흡연 또는 금연 방중 어디를 원하시나요?

I would like a non smoking room.
금연 방을 원합니다.

How many people will be staying in the room?
몇 명이 머무르실 거죠?

A total of four. Two adults and two children.
모두 4명인데 성인 2명, 어린이 2명입니다.

How many rooms would you like to reserve?
How many rooms will you need?
방이 몇 개 필요하신가요?

I need a room for 3 people.
3명이 사용할 방이 필요합니다.

Would you like a double standard room?
더블 스탠더드 룸으로 하실래요?

I'd like to get a twin room.
트윈 룸을 예약하고 싶습니다.

We only have double rooms. Will that be ok?
더블 룸만 있습니다. 괜찮으십니까?

I want a suite room.
스위트 룸으로 주세요.

I'd like to book 2 rooms.
I am going to need two rooms.
방 2개를 예약하고 싶습니다.

I'd like to book a total of 4 rooms.
방 4개를 예약하고 싶습니다.

Is there a difference in price between the room facing the ocean or the street?
바다나 거리가 보이는 방 둘 사이에 가격에 차이가 있나요?

Are the rooms facing the ocean more expensive?
바다가 보이는 곳이 더 비싼가요?

I'd like to reserve a nonsmoking room facing the ocean.
금연실 바다가 보이는 방으로 해주세요.

What's the charge per night?
하루에 얼마이죠?

What's your rate?
가격이 얼마이죠?

The total comes to $1200 after tax.
세금을 포함하여 1200달러입니다.

Do you have anything cheaper?
더 싼 것은 없나요?

The price is acceptable.
가격이 괜찮군요.

I'll reserve it.
그 방을 예약할게요.

Do I have to pay upfront?
미리 선불로 계산해야 하나요?

Can I get a credit card number?
신용카드 번호를 말해주실래요?

Why are my credit card details needed?
왜 제 신용카드 정보가 필요하죠?

Your credit card details are required as a guarantee for the hotel in case you don't arrive or cancel too late.
신용카드 정보는 당신이 도착하지 않거나 너무 늦게 취소한 경우에 대한 보증으로 필요합니다.

Your credit card will not be charged if you cancel your room more than 3 days prior to check-in date.
체크인 3일 이전에 방을 취소하시면 카드 결제가 되지 않습니다.

When do you expect to arrive at the hotel, sir?
호텔에는 언제쯤 도착하실 예정이신가요?

I expect to get there by evening.
저녁까지 도착할 것입니다.

I'll arrive there at 7 P.M.
그곳에 저녁 7시쯤 도착합니다.

May I have your full name and telephone number?
당신의 이름과 전화번호를 알려 주실래요?

Your reservation is made.
We have booked a room for you.
Your room is booked.
We have reserved your room.
예약이 완료되었습니다.

Let me confirm your reservation.
예약을 확인해 드리겠습니다.

Please be sure to arrive before 7:00 P.M. on your check-in date.
체크인 하는 날 저녁 7시까지 와주시기 바랍니다.

If you have any change in your reservation, please let us know.
만약 예약 변경이 있으시면 연락을 주세요.

We look forward to seeing you in New York.
뉴욕에서 뵙기를 고대하겠습니다.

I'm calling to cancel my reservation.
예약을 취소하려고 전화했습니다.

My reservation was for June 17th through 27th.
6월 17일부터 27일까지 예약했습니다.

Is there any cancellation charge?
취소 수수료가 있습니까?

If you don't cancel your reservation by the day before your scheduled arrival, you'll be charged a penalty of one night's room rate.
호텔 도착 하루 전에 예약을 취소하지 않으면 하룻밤 페널티 비용이 청구됩니다.

12. 호텔 체크인 (Hotel Check In)

I'd like to check in, please.
체크인 하려는 데요?

I made a reservation online.
인터넷으로 예약을 했습니다.

I have a reservation under the name of -.
- 이란 이름으로 예약했습니다.

I don't have a reservation.
예약은 안 했습니다.

Do you have any rooms available?
Is there any rooms available?
Do you have any vacancies?
이용할 수 있는 방이 있나요?

What's the price per night?
How much do you charge per night?
How much is it per day?
What's the charge for a night?
How much are your rooms?
하룻밤에 방값이 얼마이죠?

Our rooms start at $150 for a standard room and go up to $400 for a suite.
스탠더드 룸 150불에서부터 스위트 룸 400불까지 있습니다.

Is there anything cheaper?
더 싼 것은 없습니까?

Could you recommend another hotel nearby?
근처 호텔을 추천해 주실래요?

Are there any other hotels nearby?
근처에 다른 호텔이 있나요?

I'd like a hotel near the beach.
해변 근처 호텔을 원합니다.

I'd like a hotel with ocean view.
바다 전망이 있는 호텔을 원합니다.

I want a room with ocean view.
바다 전망이 있는 방을 주세요.

How large is your party?
일행이 몇 분이죠?

There are three of us.
3명입니다.

I want one twin bedroom.
트윈 룸 한 개 주세요.

I'd like a quiet room facing the beach.
해변이 보이는 조용한 방으로 주세요.

Could you fill out this registration card?
이 등록카드를 작성해 주실래요?

Do I have to fill out all the items?
이 항목들을 전부 써야 하나요?

Is breakfast included in the price?
아침이 가격에 포함되어 있나요?

Does the room rate include break-fast?
숙박료에 아침이 포함되어 있나요?

What time does restaurant start serving breakfast?
식당이 아침을 언제부터 시작하나요?

What time does breakfast finish?
아침식사 시간이 언제 끝나나요?

Do I have to pay upfront?
선불로 지급해야 하나요?

Should I present the credit card at check in?
체크인 할때 신용카드를 제시해야 하나요?

Why do you take my credit card details?
왜 신용카드 정보가 필요하죠?

We take your card to guarantee payment of any incidental charges.
발생비용에 대한 보증으로 카드를 결재해 놓습니다.

Can I get one more room key?
방 키를 하나 더 주실래요?

What floor is the room on?
방이 몇 층이지요?

Do you need any help with your baggage?
Do you need a hotel porter?
가방을 들어줄 분이 필요한가요?

Could you take my baggage up to the room?
방으로 가방을 올려주실래요?

I need a porter to help me.
짐 운반을 도와줄 사람이 필요합니다.

Please take this big one.
이 큰 것을 들어주세요.

I'll take my bags myself.
가방들은 제가 가져갈게요.

There is one bag missing.
가방 하나가 안보이네요.

Where is the elevator?
엘리베이터가 어디죠?

Room key card is necessary to get the elevator to move.
엘리베이터 움직이는데 룸키가 필요합니다.

Where would you like your luggage?
짐을 어디에 놓을까요?

Just put it on the floor, please.
Here you are. This is a tip for you.
그냥 바닥에 두세요. 여기 팁입니다.

I am afraid I am running late.
My plane was delayed.
죄송하지만 늦겠는데요.
비행기가 연착했어요.

I'm now at the air port.
지금 공항에 있습니다.

Will you hold my reservation another hour?
예약 시간을 늦추어도 될까요?

What time shall we expect you, sir?
언제쯤 오실 것 같습니까?

I'll be there within two hours.
2시간 안에는 도착할 것 같습니다.

13. 호텔 체크아웃 (Hotel Check Out)

What's the check out time?
What time do we have to check out?
체크아웃 시간이 몇시죠?

I'd like to extend check out time till 3 P.M.
3시까지 체크아웃을 연장하고 싶습니다.

I'd like to stay another day.
하루 더 있겠습니다.

I'd like to check out a day earlier.
체크아웃을 하루 먼저 하겠습니다.

I'd like to check out.
체크아웃 하겠습니다.

How much is the bill?
얼마입니까?

What are all these charges?
이 요금들은 무엇이죠?

What's this charge for?
이 요금은 무엇이죠?

I think there is a mistake on my bill.
제 청구서에 잘못이 있는 것 같은데요.

There is a charge on my bill that I never made.
청구서에 제가 결제하지 않은 것이 청구되어 있네요.

I discover incorrect fee that I never ordered.
제가 주문하지 않은 잘못된 요금이 있군요.

That is absolutely incorrect.
잘못 되었습니다.

There must be some mistake.
무언가 잘못된 것 같습니다.

We didn't take anything from the mini bar.
미니바에서 아무 것도 먹지 않았습니다.

I didn't use the mini bar.
미니바를 사용하지 않았습니다.

I didn't see the movie on that night.
그날 밤 영화를 보지 않았습니다.

I didn't make an international call.
국제전화를 하지 않았습니다.

Why am I being charged for this that I never ordered?
왜 주문하지도 않은 이것이 청구되어 있죠?

I didn't get this service.
이 서비스는 받지 않았습니다.

I didn't get any room service.
룸 서비스를 받은 적이 없습니다.

I'd like to pay the bill by this credit card.
이 신용카드로 비용을 결제 하겠습니다.

I left something in my room.
방에 물건을 두고 나왔네요.

I'm going to spend some time exploring the city.
이 도시를 조금 더 구경하려 합니다.

Can I store my bags in this hotel?
제 가방을 이 호텔에 보관할 수 있나요?

Can I leave my baggage with you a little while longer?
당신에게 짐들을 조금 더 맡길 수 있나요?

Can I use storage facility?
물품보관소를 이용할 수 있나요?

Is there somewhere we can leave our bags until the evening?
저녁까지 짐을 맡길 곳이 있나요?

Can I leave a deposit?
보관료가 필요하나요?

Can you call a taxi?
택시 좀 불러 주실래요?

What time do we have to leave for the airport?
공항에 언제 출발해야 할까요?

Do we have to get there early?
미리 그곳으로 가야 하나요?

We plan on arriving there 3 hours before flight departure.
비행기 출발 3시간 전에 도착하려고 합니다.

Do you provide a limousine bus service from here to the airport?
이곳에서는 공항으로 가는 리무진 버스를 제공해 줍니까?

Which bus should I take to get to the airport?
공항까지 갈려면 어느 버스를 타야 하죠?

Can I have shuttle bus schedule information?
셔틀버스 스케줄 표를 받을 수 있나요?

How can I take airport shuttle bus?
공항으로 가는 셔틀버스를 어떻게 타지요?

What time does shuttle bus leave for the airport?
공항까지 가는 셔틀버스가 언제 있습니까?

14. 호텔 생활 영어
(Practical English at Hotel)

Where is the restaurant?
Which way is the restaurant?
식당이 어디에 있죠?

Which floor is the restaurant?
On what floor is the restaurant?
식당이 몇 층에 있지요?

Does this hotel have a fitness facility?
이 호텔에 피트니스 룸이 있나요?

What athletic facilities do you have in this hotel?
이 호텔에는 어떤 운동 시설이 있지요?

Would you tell me where it is?
어디에 있죠?

Do I have to pay extra?
비용을 따로 지불하나요?

Is a fitness facility free to guests?
숙박 손님에게 피트니스 룸이 무료이나요?

The gym is free to guests.
숙박 손님에게는 무료입니다.

What time does it close?
언제 문을 닫죠?

Which elevator should I take?
어느 승강기를 이용하죠?

Is room key card necessary to get the elevator to move?
엘리베이터 움직이는데 룸키가 필요하나요?

How can I use this air conditioner?
에어컨디셔너를 어떻게 사용하지요?

Could you explain about this?
이것 좀 설명해 주실래요?

Can I control by adjusting the temperature level?
온도 조절로 컨트롤 할 수 있나요?

Can I use electric outlet?
Is socket outlet working?
전기 콘센트를 쓸 수 있나요?

Can I drink the tap water?
물은 그냥 받아 마셔도 되나요?

Does the hotel provide free bottled waters?
무료 생수가 호텔에서 제공이 되나요?

Which floor has the ice?
얼음은 몇 층에 있나요?

Can I use internet in this room?
이방에서 인터넷을 사용할 수 있습니까?

Can I use wireless internet?
무선 인터넷을 사용할 수 있나요?

Guest room has a free internet.
객실은 무료 인터넷이 있습니다.

Just plug the Ethernet cable into your computer.
유선케이블을 컴퓨터에 꽂으시면 됩니다.

My laptop has no Ethernet port, it's wireless only.
제 노트북은 유선은 없고 무선만 됩니다.

Wireless internet access can be available in public area like lobby.
무선 인터넷은 이 호텔 로비와 같은 공공장소에서 사용할 수 있습니다.

You can use WiFi at anywhere. It's free.
와이파이는 어디에서든 됩니다. 무료입니다.

I can't log on.
Would you tell me ID and password?
로그인이 안 되는군요.
사용자 이름과 비밀번호를 말해주실래요?

It's asking me for a password.
비밀번호를 물어보는군요.

I need ID and password for access to internet.
인터넷에 접속하기 위한 사용자 이름과 비밀번호가 필요합니다.

Can I use the computer lab in the lobby?
로비의 컴퓨터실을 이용할 수 있나요?

Can I use your fax?
팩스를 이용할 수 있나요?

I need to make some copies.
복사할 것들이 있습니다.

What if I need to print something?
프린트 할 것이 있으면 어떻게 하지요?

Could you give me a wake-up call tomorrow morning?
내일 아침 모닝콜 좀 부탁합니다.

Can I have a wake-up call?
모닝콜 부탁합니다.

What time would you like your wake-up call?
모닝콜 몇 시로 해드릴까요?

I'd like to get up at 6:00.
6시에 일어나길 원합니다.

Can I get a wake-up call at 6 AM?
6시에 모닝콜 해주살래요?

Would you give me a wake-up call at 6 tomorrow morning.
내일 아침 6시에 모닝콜 해주실래요?

I'd like to change wake up call.
모닝콜을 바꾸고 싶습니다.

I'd like to cancel wake up call.
모닝콜을 취소하고 싶습니다.

Can I get an extra blanket?
담요를 더 얻을 수 있나요?

I have some valuables.
귀중품들이 있습니다.

Do you have a safe?
금고가 있나요?

How do I use the safe?
금고를 어떻게 쓰지요?

Can I deposit my valuables?
I'd like to deposit my valuables.
귀중품을 맡길 수 있을까요?

How long would you like us to keep it?
언제까지 맡겨 두실 건가요?

Until the day after tomorrow.
모레까지요.

Should I put my items in this box?
제 물건들을 이 박스에 넣어야 하나요?

Fill out this form, please.
이 서류를 작성해 주세요.

May I have my stuff back?
제 물건을 주실래요?

I need to get a taxi.
택시가 필요합니다.

May I leave my room key?
룸 키를 맡겨도 될까요?

Give me room key, please.
룸 키를 주시겠습니까?

I'm locked out of my room.
문이 잠겼습니다.

I left my key in my room.
방에 키를 두었네요.

I locked my key in my room.
방안에 키를 놓고 잠갔어요.

I can't find my key anywhere.
키를 찾을 수가 없네요.

I might have left it in my room.
방 안에 놔둔 것 같습니다.

Will you open my room?
문 좀 열어 주실래요?.

Do you have an extra key?
여분의 방 열쇠가 있습니까?

Could I get another towel and amenities like soap and shampoo?
수건과 비누, 샴푸를 더 주시겠어요?

I'd like to order a restock on mini bar.
미니바를 다시 채워주실래요?

Please, charge it to my room.
제 방에 청구하세요.

Please add the bill to my room.
제 방에 비용을 추가하세요.

I would like to ask for the laundry service.
세탁 서비스에 대해서 알고 싶습니다.

I have something to be laundered and pressed.
세탁과 다리미질 할 것이 있습니다.

I need to have some clothes cleaned.
세탁할 옷이 좀 있습니다.

Two dress shirts to be laundered and one suit to be pressed only.
셔츠 두 벌은 세탁해주고 양복 한 벌은 다리미질만 해주세요.

My shirts cleaned and my suit dry-cleaned.
셔츠는 세탁, 정장은 드라이클리닝 해주세요.

When will I get it back if I send it out now?
지금 세탁을 맡기면 언제 받을 수 있지요?

Can I get it back tomorrow morning?
내일 아침에 받을 수 있나요?

I want these cleaned by 8 A.M. tomorrow.
이것들을 내일 아침 8시까지 세탁해 주세요.

I still don't get my laundered clothes back.
아직 세탁맡긴 옷들을 돌려받지 못했습니다.

When will it be ready?
언제까지 되나요?

When can I have it back?
언제까지 돌려받을 수 있나요?

I want to make an international call to Korea.
한국에 국제 전화를 하고 싶은데요?

The line is busy.
Would you care to hold?
통화 중입니다. 기다리시겠습니까?

Is there somewhere I can exchange money around here?
이 주변에 환전 할 곳이 있나요?

Is this service free?
or do I have to pay for it?
이 서비스가 무료인가요?
계산을 해야 하나요?

Could you please make up my room?
제 방을 청소해 주실래요?

Please, make the bed.
침대를 정리해 주세요.

You don't need to clean our room.
우리들·방은 청소를 안서도 됩니다.

Is room service available now?
지금 룸 서비스가 가능한가요?

I'd like to order some breakfast.
아침을 주문하고 싶습니다.

What would you like to order?
무엇을 주문하실래요?

I'd like to order Continental breakfast.
콘티넨탈 식사를 주문하고 싶습니다.

I want sandwich and orange juice.
샌드위치과 오렌지 주스를 주세요.

When will my order be ready?
언제 주문이 준비가 되죠?

Can you rush my order?
주문한 것을 빨리 주실래요?

Would you speed up my order?
주문한 것을 빨리 주실래요?

We'll send up to you right away.
지금 바로 보내겠습니다.

Could you get my car?
제 차를 가져와 주실래요?

15. 호텔 불편 사항들
(Complaint details at Hotel)

I'm calling about a problem with my room.
방에 문제가 있어 전화했습니다.

This is Mr. Kim in room 701.
701호실 미스터 김입니다.

I have got a little problem with my room.
제 방에 문제가 있습니다.

Room key is not working.
방 키가 작동하지 않습니다.

Electric outlet is not working.
Socket outlet is not working.
전기 콘센트가 작동 안되는데요.

The power is out. (blackout)
전기가 나갔습니다. (정전)

When I turn on the switch, it starts sounding strange.
스위치를 켜면 이상한 소리가 납니다.

Room conditioner is out of order.
룸 조절기(에어컨)가 고장입니다.

My room is too cold.
방이 너무 추워요.

Air conditioner is broken.
에어컨이 고장이 났어요.

My room is too hot.
방이 너무 더워요.

The switch doesn't work.
스위치가 고장입니다.

The light is not working.
불이 안 켜집니다.

Light bulb has gone out.
전구가 나갔습니다.

Refrigerator doesn't work.
냉장고가 작동이 되지 않네요.

The coffee maker is not work.
커피메이커가 고장이 났어요.

I can't open the safe.
금고가 열리지 않습니다.

There is something wrong with the TV.
TV에 이상이 있습니다.

The television in our room was broken.
방 TV가 고장 나 있네요.

The TV is broken.
TV가 고장이 났습니다.

The wallpaper is peeling off.
벽지가 떨어졌어요.

It is too dark in here with so few windows.
창문이 없어 너무 어둡군요.

The room has very outdated electrical appliances.
이 방은 전자제품들이 아주 낡았군요.

Hot water is not coming out.
There is no hot water.
뜨거운 물이 안 나옵니다.

The water tap is leaking.
수도꼭지가 샙니다.

The faucet in the bathroom is leaking.
I have a leaky faucet in the bathroom.
욕실 수도꼭지에서 물이 샙니다.

The tap is broken.
수도꼭지가 고장 났습니다.

The toilet flushes really slowly.
화장실 물이 잘 안 내려갑니다.

The bathtub barely drains at all.
욕조에서 물이 잘 빠져 나가지 않습니다.

Bathroom plumbing is not working well.
욕조 배수가 잘 안됩니다.

The shower faucet is not working.
샤워기가 고장 났습니다.

The shower is not working well.
샤워기가 잘 작동하질 않습니다.

Too little water comes out from the shower.
샤워기에서 물이 너무 조금 나옵니다.

Toilet is blocked.
화장실이 막혔습니다.

Toilet won't flush.
화장실 물이 안 내려갑니다.

Toilet is overflowing.
화장실이 넘칩니다.

The sink is leaking.
세면대가 샙니다.

The bathtub is leaking.
욕조가 샙니다.

The drain is clogged.
하수구가 막혔습니다.

The water isn't running.
물이 안 나옵니다.

The water is cut off.
물이 안 나옵니다.

The water pressure is low.
물이 약하게 나옵니다.

The bathroom is out of toilet paper.
화장지가 다 떨어졌네요.

All the toilet paper is gone.
화장지가 다 떨어졌어요.

All the tissue paper is gone.
티슈가 다 떨어졌어요.

We don't have enough bath towels.
수건이 충분하지 않아요.

We need more towels.
수건이 더 필요합니다,

We need more bath towels.
목욕수건이 더 필요합니다.

I need more amenities like soap, lotion, and shampoo.
비누, 로션, 샴푸 같은 편의용품이 더 필요합니다.

There are molds on the walls.
벽에 곰팡이가 있습니다.

There is a spot of mildew on the ceiling.
천장에 곰팡이 자국이 있습니다.

There is a bad smell in the room.
방에서 나쁜 냄새가 납니다.

There is a smell of burning.
타는 냄새가 납니다.

There is water leaking in ceiling.
천장에서 물이 새는군요.

There is water leaking from ceiling and the carpet is wet.
천장에서 물이 새어 카펫이 젖었습니다.

I need hair dryer.
헤어드라이어가 필요합니다.

I need multifunctional plug adapter.
다기능 변환용 플러그 어댑터가 필요합니다.

I need plug, from round pin to flat pin.
둥근 핀을 평면 핀으로 바꾸는 플러그가 필요합니다.

I need 110-220 volt power converter.
(= adapter, voltage converter).
110볼트를 220볼트로 바꾸어주는 변압기가 필요합니다.

I need power transformer which converts the power from 110 volts to 220 volts.
110볼트를 220볼트로 바꾸어주는 변압기가 필요합니다.

I found cockroaches in my room.
제 방에 바퀴벌레들이 있습니다.

There are many insects.
I can't sleep.
곤충들이 많습니다. 잠을 못 자겠습니다.

Would you please send someone to check it?
확인하러 누군가를 좀 보내주실래요?

My room was robbed.
제 방이 도둑맞았습니다.

Can you send someone over?
누구 좀 보내주실래요?

Please, send anyone to fix it.
누구 좀 보내서 고쳐주세요.

When will you be able to fix it?
언제 고칠 수 있나요?

Why is this taking so long?
왜 이렇게 오래 걸리죠?

I hope you can replace it soon.
바로 교체해 주세요.

The elevator is not running.
엘리베이터가 작동이 안 되네요.

I am stuck in the elevator.
엘리베이터에서 갇혔습니다.

The room smells of smoke.
방에서 담배 냄새가 나네요.

The smell of smoke occurs suddenly.
갑자기 담배 냄새가 나네요.

The smell of smoke looks like coming from next door.
담배 냄새는 옆방에서 오는 것 같아요.

The next room is very noisy, and we can't get to sleep
옆방이 시끄러워 잠을 잘 수가 없네요.

There are really loud noises coming from the next door.
옆방이 너무 시끄럽습니다.

Could you tell the people in the next room to be quiet at night?
옆방에 밤에는 조용히 해주라고 말해주세요.

They are screaming all night and we can't sleep.
밤새 소리를 질러 잠을 잘 수가 없습니다.

Ask them to keep the noise down.
소음을 줄여주라고 말해주세요.

Have you spoken to them about the noise problem?
그들에게 소음 문제에 대해 말했나요?

They are still very noisy.
그들은 아직도 매우 시끄럽습니다.

The sound is coming through the wall. It's very annoying.
소리가 벽을 통해 옵니다. 아주 거슬리네요.

I hear them talking loudly and television is really loud.
그들이 말하는 소리가 들리고
TV 소리도 큽니다.

I couldn't sleep with the noise.
소음 때문에 잠을 못 잤습니다.

I'd like to complain to the hotel manager about that.
호텔 지배인에게 이의제기 하겠습니다.

I want to change room.
방을 바꾸어주세요.

Was it loud?
I didn't mean to be loud.
소리가 컸나요?
시끄럽게 할 의향은 없었습니다.

I apologize for being so loud.
시끄럽게 해서 죄송합니다.

I'll try to keep the noise down.
소음을 줄이도록 노력하겠습니다.

16. 버스 이용 (Taking a Bus)

Public Transportation

대중교통

Is there an airport bus to go to A?
A로 가는 공항버스가 있습니까?

Where can I take the airport bus?
공항버스를 어디서 타지요?

Where are the shuttle pick-up points?
셔틀버스를 탑승하는 곳이 어디죠?

There is a bus stop right in front of that building.
저 건물 앞에 정류장이 있습니다.

Do you have a bus route map?
버스 노선도가 있나요?

I'd like bus route map.
버스 노선도가 필요합니다.

Where do we take the bus?
버스를 어디서 타지요?

Is this where I catch the airport bus?
공항버스를 이곳에서 탑니까?

Is this where I catch the Shuttle Bus?
이곳이 셔틀 버스를 타는 곳인가요?

How often is it running?
얼마나 자주 오죠?

Buses run every 30 minutes.
30분마다 버스가 있습니다.

How long is the wait?
얼마나 기다려야 하죠?

Bus will be here shortly.
버스가 곧 올 것입니다.

Can I catch a bus bound for downtown? Which bus should I take?
시내까지 가는 버스를 탈 수 있나요?
어떤 버스를 타야하죠?

Do you know a bus that goes to the downtown?
시내로 가는 버스를 아나요?

Is there a bus that goes downtown?
시내로 가는 버스가 있나요?

You can take number －.
－번 버스를 타세요.

Get on the bus heading west.
서쪽으로 가는 버스를 타세요.

It will take you there.
당신을 그곳으로 데려다 줄 것입니다.

What street can I catch the bus?
어느 거리에서 버스를 타나요?

Has the bus left already?
버스가 이미 떠났나요?

It was supposed to be here
5 minutes ago.
5분 전에 왔어야 되는데요.

I think it's running late.
제 생각에 늦는 것 같은데요.

Bus doesn't come in time.
버스는 제 시간에 오지 않아요.

It should be coming soon.
곧 올 것입니다.

It gets always crowded during rush hour.
출퇴근 시간에는 붐빕니다.

There will be a lot of people on bus.
버스에는 사람이 많을 것입니다.

Is this bus going to Manhattan?
이 버스가 맨해튼까지 가나요?

Do you go to Manhattan?
맨해튼까지 가나요?

Where are you headed?
어디로 가시죠?

I am headed to Manhattan.
맨해튼으로 갑니다.

My destination is Manhattan.
제 목적지는 맨해튼입니다.

I am trying to get to Manhattan.
맨해튼으로 가려고 합니다.

This bus goes near the downtown.
이 버스는 시내 근처까지만 갑니다.

How long does bus stop here?
버스는 얼마 동안 이곳에 머무르지요?

How long does it take from here to Manhattan?
여기에서 맨해튼까지 얼마나 걸립니까?

Does this bus make a lot of stops?
이 버스는 정차할 곳이 많은가요?

What's the bus fare to Manhattan?
맨해튼까지 버스 요금은 얼마이지요?

How much is the fare?
요금이 얼마죠?

Do I have to drop money in the fare box?
요금 박스에 돈을 넣으면 되나요?

Should I swipe my pass card through the fare machine?
요금 정산기에 교통카드를 긁으면 되나요?

Hold the card name facing you.
카드 정면을 당신이 보이게 하세요.

Put the card into the slot of the fare box machine.
카드를 요금기계 구멍에 넣으세요.

Do I need to use exact change?
정확한 잔돈을 사용해야 하나요?

You have to give exact change.
정확한 잔돈을 지불해야 합니다.

If I have large bills, should I break them?
큰돈을 가지고 있으면 잔돈으로 바꾸어야 하나요?

I am sorry. I don't have any change.
죄송하지만 잔돈이 없습니다.

Can you break a 20 dollar?
20달러를 거슬러 줄 수 있나요?

How can I use traffic card?
교통카드를 어떻게 사용하죠?

Can I bring my bags on the bus?
버스로 가방들을 가져가도 되나요?

I'm not sure where to get off.
어디에서 내릴 지 잘 모르겠군요.

Would you let me know where to get off?
내려야 할 곳에서 말씀해 주실래요?

Please, tell me when we get there.
그곳에 도착하면 말해주세요.

Where do I get off at?
어디서 내려야 하죠?

Did I miss my stop?
제가 내릴 곳을 지나쳤나요?

How much further do I have to go?
얼마나 더 가야 하죠?

Which stop do I get off?
어느 정류소에서 내리나요?

Are we supposed to get off right here?
이곳에서 우리가 내리나요?

My destination is A.
Do you know where I get off at?
목적지가 A인데, 어디서 내리는지 아세요?

Are we almost there?
거의 다 왔나요?

I'll let you know.
제가 알려드리겠습니다.

You still have more to go.
좀 더 가야 합니다.

We've arrived. Get off the bus.
도착했습니다. 버스에서 내리세요.

If you tell the bus driver where you're going, he'll announce to you when to get off.
버스 기사에게 어디를 가는 지 말하면 내릴 때 말해 줄 것입니다.

Where is the stop bell?
정차 벨이 어디에 있나요?

Should I push the signal strip to get off?
내리려면 신호 선을 눌러야 하나요?

Do I have to pull the cord on the side of the bus before my desired stop?
원하는 곳에 정차하기 전 버스 옆에 있는 선을 잡아당겨야 하나요?

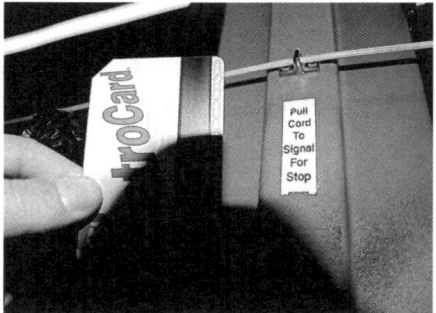

Let me get off here.
이곳에서 내릴게요.

Please, open the door.
문 좀 열어주세요.

Are there any buses going to A?
A로 가는 버스들이 있나요?

Do buses run hourly?
매 시간 버스가 가나요?

Can I have a discount if I buy ticket in advance?
미리 표를 사면 할인이 되나요?

How long is the trip to Boston?
보스턴까지는 얼마나 걸리죠?

Can I bring my baggage on the bus with me?
버스에 제 가방을 같이 가져가도 되나요?

17. 지하철 이용 (Taking a Subway)

How do we get there on public transportation?
대중교통으로 어떻게 가죠?

Is there a subway to go there?
그곳으로 가는 지하철이 있나요?

Where do I take a subway?
지하철을 어디서 타죠?

Are there any subway stations around here?
이 주변에 지하철역이 있나요?

Do you have a subway map?
지하철 노선도가 있나요?

I'd like subway map.
지하철 노선도가 필요합니다.

Is there a pass card?
교통카드가 있나요?

You can buy pass card that offers unlimited subway and bus rides at subway stations with cash or credit.
지하철역에서 지하철과 버스를 제한 없이 탈 수 있는 교통카드를 현금이나 신용카드로 살 수 있습니다.

Which subway will I have to take?
어느 지하철을 타야 하죠?

Where are you trying to go?
어디를 가려고 하시는데요?

Is this subway going to the Manhattan?
이 지하철이 맨해튼까지 가나요?

Do I have to ride on the other side?
반대편에서 타야 하나요?

You actually need to take two subways to get there.
그곳에 가려면 지하철을 2번 타야 됩니다.

How often does the subway run?
지하철이 얼마나 자주 있지요?

It runs every several minutes.
수분마다 있습니다.

How long will it take to get there?
얼마나 걸리죠?

Is there an express?
급행이 있습니까?

Do I have to transfer?
갈아타야 하나요?

What station do I transfer at?
어느 역에서 갈아타죠?

Where should I transfer?
어디서 갈아타지요?

Am I on the wrong line?
잘못된 노선을 탔나요?

Which station should I get off at?
어느 역에서 내려야 하죠?

Did I miss my station?
제가 내릴 역을 지나쳤나요?

Am I supposed to get off right here?
이곳에서 제가 내리나요?

How much further is it?
얼마나 더 가야 하죠?

What's the cheapest way to get to Penn station?
펜역까지 가는 가장 싼 방법이 무엇이죠?

The cheapest is by subway.
가장 싼 것은 지하철입니다.

How do I get there?
그곳까지 어떻게 가죠?

Take Airtrain from terminal to Jamaica Station and transfer there to the E subway.
에어트레인을 타고 자마이카역까지 간 후 지하철 E 라인으로 갈아타세요.

Airtrain is $5 and subway is $2.75.
에어트레인은 5불, 지하철은 2.75불입니다.

But the best way to go there is to take Long Island Railroad (LIRR) train.
하지만 그곳으로 가는 가장 좋은 방법은 LIRR 기차를 타는 것입니다.

LIRR is the fastest ride to Manhattan. It's $7.25.
LIRR은 맨하탄으로 가는 가장 빠른 교통편입니다. 가격은 7.25불입니다.

Transfer to LIRR at Jamaica Station.
자마이카역에서 LIRR 기차를 타세요.

How often does the train run?
기차가 얼마나 자주 있지요?

It runs about every half hour.
약 30분마다 있습니다.

Thanks for letting me know.
가르쳐 주셔서 감사합니다.

18. 택시 이용 (Taking a Taxi)

Where can I get a taxi?
Where can I catch a cab?
택시를 어디서 타죠?

Where is the taxi stand?
택시 승강장이 어디죠?

The taxi stand is right over there.
택시 승강장이 저기입니다.

How much will it cost if I take a taxi from here to A hotel?
Would you happen to know how much it is to go to A hotel?
혹시 A호텔까지 가는데 얼마인지 아세요?

How much is the basic fare?
기본 요금이 얼마이죠?

How much to A hotel?
How much will it cost to go to A hotel?
A 호텔까지 택시비가 얼마나 하죠?

Where to, sir?
어디로 가실래요?

Take me to A hotel, please.
I'd like to go to A hotel.
A 호텔로 가주세요.

This is the map. There is a mark on the map. Take me there.
지도에 표시되어 있는 곳으로 데려다 주세요.

Can you open the trunk?
트렁크 좀 열어주실래요?

Would you help me put my bag into the car?
가방을 차에 싣는 것 좀 도와주실래요?

Coffee is spilled on the car seat.
커피가 차 시트에 엎질러져 있네요.

There is a stuff I don't know.
제가 모르는 물건이 있네요.

Would you clear these stuffs?
이 물건들을 치워 주실래요?

How long will it take to get there?
그곳까지는 얼마나 걸리지요?

I am late for an appointment.
약속시간에 늦었습니다.

I am in a hurry.
Please, take the fatest way.
Please take a short cut.
지금 바쁘군요. 빠른 길로 가 주세요.

173

Could you hurry a little, please?
Could you please step on it?
Can you speed up a little?
조금 빨리 가주실래요?

I'll do my best.
최선을 다 하죠.

Please, drive more slowly.
좀 더 천천히 운전해 주세요.

Are we almost there?
거의 다 왔나요?

Here we are.
다 왔습니다.

Let me get off here.
Pull over here.
Stop here, please.
이곳에서 내릴게요.

How much is the fare?
What's the fare?
요금이 얼마이지요?

That's more than I thought.
제가 생각한 만큼보다는 많군요.

Why do you charge me more?
왜 돈을 더 많이 받나요?

You are overcharging me.
비용이 너무 많이 나왔네요.

I feel like I am getting ripped off.
바가지 쓰는 기분이네요.

Don't you try to rip me off.
나에게 바가지를 씌우려고 하지마세요.

Please, bring down the price.
가격을 내려주세요.

Can I see the fare table for taxi?
택시 요금표를 볼 수 있을까요?

Is it customary to tip taxi driver in this country?
이 나라에서는 보통 택시 운전사에게 팁을 주나요?

20% tipping is customary for good service.
좋은 서비스에는 보통 20% 봉사료를 줍니다.

I need a receipt.
영수증이 필요합니다.

Do you give me back my change?
잔돈을 주실래요?

Here it is. Keep the change.
여기 있습니다. 잔돈은 가지세요.

I left my bag in the taxi.
택시에 가방을 두고 내렸습니다.

Could you wait for me?
잠깐 기다려 주실래요?

Would you wait for me here?
I'll pay you more.
이곳에서 기다려 주실래요?
돈을 더 지불하겠습니다.

I'll be back in a few minutes after doing business.
일을 마치고 금방 올게요.

19. 기차 이용 (Taking a Train)

Are there any trains for A?
A로 가는 기차가 있습니까?

Where is the train station?
기차역이 어디입니까?

Where is the ticket office?
매표소가 어디에 있나요?

How can I use ticket machine?
자동매표기를 어떻게 사용하나요?

Where will you be going?
어디로 가실 건가요?

I'd like to buy ticket to A.
A로 가는 티켓을 사고 싶습니다.

What time would you like?
언제를 원하시나요?

How often does the train run?
기차가 얼마나 자주 있지요?

Where is the time table?
시간표가 어디에 있나요?

What time does the train leave?
기차가 언제 떠나죠?

What time is the earliest (last) train to A?
A로 가는 빠른 (마지막) 기차가 언제이죠?

I'd like to buy a sleeper seat.
침대칸을 사고 싶습니다.

I've got a discount coupon for tourist.
관광객을 위한 할인 쿠폰을 가지고 있습니다.

Can I use this discount coupon?
이 할인 쿠폰을 사용할 수 있나요?

I just want one way ticket.
편도 티켓만 주세요.

First class, one way ticket to Boston at 10 A.M.
오전 10시 보스턴 1등석 티켓을 주세요.

I want round trip ticket.
왕복 티켓을 주세요.

One first class.
일등석 하나 주세요.

One coach class.
일반석 하나 주세요.

175

Sleeper seat, round trip ticket to Boston at 10 A.M. and 8 P.M.
오전 10시, 오후 8시 보스턴 침대칸 왕복표를 주세요.

Is there one day pass ticket?
일일 자유 티켓이 있나요?

I don't have any cash.
현금이 없네요.

Can I pay by credit card?
신용카드로 지불해도 되나요?

Are infants under 2 years old free of charge?
2세 이하 유아들은 무료인가요?

How much is the ticket for my 3 years old child?
3살 어린이 티켓은 얼마입니까?

Could children under 12 years old receive a 50% discount?
12세 이하 어린이는 50% 할인이 되나요?

Where is the platform?
승강장이 어디죠?

From which track does train start?
어느 트랙에서 기차가 출발하나요?

How long does it take to get to Boston?
보스턴까지 얼마나 걸리죠?

I got on the wrong train.
기차를 잘못 탔네요.

Is this seat taken?
이 자리는 사람이 있습니까?

May I sit here?
여기 앉아도 되나요?

May I open the window?
창문을 열어도 되나요?

The window can't close completely.
창문이 완전히 닫히지 않네요.

Is there a restaurant car on this train?
이 기차에 식당차가 있습니까?

Where is the dining car?
식당차가 어디에 있나요?

Stand clear of the door.
문 앞에 서있지 마세요.

Don't lean on me like that.
그렇게 저에게 기대지 마세요.

Would you watch my bag when I use the toilet?
화장실 가는 동안 가방을 좀 봐주실래요?

Could you keep an eye on my bag when I am sleeping?
자는 동안 가방 좀 지켜봐 주실래요?

Do I get off here?
이곳에서 내리나요?

Should I take train from terminal to A station and transfer there to the subway?
기차를 타고 A역까지 간 후, 지하철로 갈아타야 하나요?

20. 렌터카 이용 (Rent a Car)

Where can I rent a car?
어디서 차를 렌트하죠?

Could you tell me how I get to rental car area?
렌터카 있는 곳까지 어떻게 가죠?

Should I take a shuttle from terminal to airport car rental area?
렌터카 회사까지 공항에서 셔틀을 타나요?

I'd like to rent a car.
차를 렌트하고 싶습니다.

Do you have any cars available?
사용할 수 있는 차가 있나요?

Did you make a reservation?
Do you have a reservation?
예약을 하셨나요?

Do I need to make a reservation?
예약이 필요한가요?

We don't have any cars available today.
오늘은 빈 차가 없습니다.

What kind of car would you like?
무슨 차를 원하세요?

Do you have any convertibles?
오픈카는 있나요?

What size would you like?
What size are you looking for?
어떤 크기를 원하시나요?

What sizes do you have?
어느 사이즈가 있나요?

We have compact, medium, full, SUV.
소형, 중형, 대형, SUV가 있습니다.

I want a midsize automatic sedan.
오토 중형차를 원합니다.

I'll take an automatic SUV.
오토인 SUV를 렌트하고 싶습니다.

How long will you have it for?
How long will you be needing the car?
How long will you be renting the car?
얼마나 사용하실 거죠?

I need it for 10 days.
10일 필요합니다.

What's the rental rate?
대여료가 얼마죠?

How much per day?
What's the rate per day?
How much is the rate per day?
하루에 대여료가 얼마죠?

177

What does the rental price include?
대여료에 무엇이 포함되죠?

The rental price includes limited mileage and tax.
가격에는 제한된 거리와 세금이 포함되어 있습니다.

Do you have anything cheaper?
더 싼 것은 없나요?

I'd like the unlimited miles for one week.
1주일간 거리 무제한으로 하겠어요.

Do I use regular gasoline?
보통 휘발유를 넣으면 되나요?

Does the price include insurance?
가격에 보험이 포함되어 있나요?

Would you like to have car insurance?
Would you like insurance on the car?
차 보험에 드실래요?

I'd like to be insured.
I'd like to get insurance.
보험에 들겠습니다.

What kind of car insurance do you have?
차 보험은 어떤 것들이 있나요?

I'd like compare rates and services available.
요금과 서비스를 비교하고 싶습니다.

How much is insurance?
보험은 얼마이죠?

Who is going to be the driver?
누가 운전을 하죠?

How many people are going to drive?
How many people will be driving the car?
몇 명이 운전을 하나요?

Are all the drivers at least 25 years old?
모든 운전자가 25세 이상인가요?

I'd like to take just minimum insurance coverage. Liability insurance like as bodily injury, property damage and in addition, roadside service.
최소한의 책임 보험만 들게요. 대인, 대물 배상과 추가로 긴급차량 서비스 같은 것만요.

I'd like to have just Collision Damage Waiver(CDW) Insurance.
자기차량 손해보험만 들겠습니다.

Don't you want comprehensive coverage, uninsured motorist protection or personal injury protection?
자연재해에 의한 보험이나, 무보험차량, 대인 배상 보험은 원치 않나요?

I'd like to have full coverage.
종합보험으로 들겠습니다.

When you have an accident, car insurance company will pay for damages and you will only need to pay your auto deductible.
사고가 나면 보험회사가 손상에 대해 보상을 하고 당신은 본인 부담금만 지불하면 됩니다.

What is car insurance deductible?
교통사고 자기 부담금이 무엇이지요?

A deductible is the amount of money that you are required to pay if your car gets damaged.
자기부담금은 차가 파손되었을 경우 당신이 지불해야 할 비용입니다.

If you are in an accident and you have $5,000 of damage to your vehicle, $500 deductible, you will pay $500 and car insurance company will pay the remaining $4,500.
만약 사고가 나서 차량 손상이 5000불이라면, 당신이 500불 지급하고 나머지 4500불은 보험회사에서 지급하는 것을 말합니다.

How much altogether?
전부 얼마이죠?

The total will be $ 1500.
전부 1500불입니다.

I need a GPS navigation.
네비게이션이 필요합니다.

Can I see your international driver's license?
국제 운전 면허증 좀 볼까요?

Do you need my international driver's license?
국제 운전 면허증이 필요하나요?

Is there a space wheel in the car?
예비 타이어가 있나요?

How do I return the car?
어떻게 차를 돌려주죠?

Should I fill it up before returning the car?
차를 돌려주기 전에 기름을 가득 채워야 하나요?

The gas tank is full.
연료는 가득 차 있습니다.

You should fill it up before you return the car.
돌려주기 전에 연료를 가득 채워야 합니다.

If the car is not returned with a full tank of fuel, then should I pay for the fuel service fee?
연료를 가득 채워 반환하지 않으면 연료서비스 비용을 지급해야 하나요?

If you don't fill up the tank, you have to pay extra charge.
연료를 채우지 않으면 추가 비용을 냅니다.

Can I use fuel up front option?
연료비 선지급 옵션을 이용할 수 있나요?

Where can I drop off the car?
차를 어디에 반납하죠?

Return it to the same place you picked up the car.
차를 가져간 같은 장소로 반납해야 합니다.

You will need to return it by 2P.M. on the 26th.
26일 오후 2시까지 반납해 주세요.

How much do you charge if I am late?
늦으면 얼마나 내야 하죠?

We charge an additional $10 for every four hours that you are late.
늦으면 매 4시간당 10불씩 추가합니다.

Should I drop off the car at this area?
차를 이곳으로 꼭 돌려주어야 하나요?

Can I return it to another location?
다른 곳에 반환해도 되나요?

Should I pay drop-off charge?
반환 서비스료를 지불해야 하나요?

You can return it to another location if you intend to pay drop-off charge.
인도비용을 지급할 의향이 있으면 다른 곳에 반환 하셔도 됩니다.

Show them this invoice at pick up area and they will have your car ready for you.
이 계약서를 픽업장소로 가져가 보여주면 차를 준비해줄 것입니다.

There are scratches on the outside of this car.
이 차 외부에 긁힌 자국들이 있네요.

This car is dented on the side.
이 차 옆이 찌그러져 있네요.

There is a dent in the front bumper.
앞 범퍼가 찌그러졌네요.

There are some cracks on the rear bumper.
뒤 범퍼가 조금 깨져 있네요.

Please keep this invoice in the car.
이 계약서를 차 안에 보관해 두세요.

Bring this invoice with you when you return the car.
차를 반환할 때 이것을 가지고 오셔야 합니다.

21. 자가 운전 (Car Driving)

Where's the nearest gas station?
Can you direct me to the nearest gas station?
Is there a gas station near me?
이 근처에 주유소가 있나요?

Can you show me where it's on the map?
이 지도에 표시를 해주실래요?

Pump number 3, regular, $30.
주유펌프 3번, 보통 휘발유, 30불어치요.

$30 on gas pump 3, regular(87), Credit card (Debit)
주유펌프 3번, 보통휘발유(옥탄가 87), 신용카드요 (직불카드, 체크카드).

Gas pump couldn't read my credit card. I swiped twice.
It failed to read.
주유펌프가 제 신용카드를 읽지를 못하네요.
2번이나 긁었는데, 읽지를 못해요.

Pin code(number)암호. ZIP code 우편번호

I am a tourist. I don't have ZIP code.
Should I pay at cashier's office?
여행자라서 우편번호가 없는데 계산대에서 계산원에게 지급해야 하나요?

Fill it up with regular unleaded.
무연 보통으로 가득 채워 주세요.

Is this the road to A?
이 길이 A로 가는 길인가요?

Am I going the right way?
Am I going in the right direction?
올바른 방향으로 가고 있나요?

Do I keep going straight?
똑바로 가면 되나요?

Where is the on-ramp?
고속도로 진입로가 어디인가요?

Do I take the next exit on this highway?
이 고속도로에서 다음 출구로 나가면 되나요?

Is there a parking lot nearby?
근처에 주차장이 있나요?

I need to find somewhere to park.
주차할 곳이 필요합니다.

Do you know if the parking area is full or not?
주차지역이 가득 찼는지 아세요?

Do you think it'll be full now?
Would it be full now?
지금은 가득 찼을까요?

Is overnight parking permitted?
밤에도 주차가 되나요?

I got a flat tire on the way.
도중에 타이어에 펑크가 났습니다.

I have a flat tire.
타이어가 펑크 났습니다.

The brake doesn't work.
브레이크가 듣지 않습니다.

I locked my key in my car.
차에 열쇠를 두고 잠갔습니다.

I ran out of gas.
휘발유가 떨어졌네요.

My battery is dead.
배터리가 방전되었습니다.

My car doesn't start.
시동이 걸리지 않습니다.

I need to call roadside service.
긴급출동 서비스에 연락해야겠네요.

Can you fix it?
고칠 수 있나요?

Can you help me recharge my battery?
배터리를 재충전하게 도와주실래요?

My car is running rough.
제 차가 덜컥거립니다.

I need a car tune up.
차 정비가 필요합니다.

Should I change the fuel and air filter?
연료필터나 에어필터를 바꾸어야 할까요?

How much does an average tune up cost?
자동차 일반적인 검사는 얼마이죠?

I'd like my car washed.
세차해 주세요.

22. 교통사고 (Traffic Accident)

Hello, you hit my car.
제 차를 받으셨네요.

My car is damaged.
제 차가 손상을 입었네요.

My rear bumper is scratched and smashed in. (dented, got a dent)
뒤 범퍼가 긁히고 들어갔잖아요.

I want to make the call to 911.
I'll call 911. (Ambulance + police)
911(앰블런스+경찰)을 부르겠습니다.

Do you have some identification?
신분증이 있나요?

Please, give me your name, address, car number and phone number.
당신의 이름, 주소, 차 번호, 전화번호를 알려주세요.

Hello, I got into an accident.
여보세요. 사고가 났습니다.

I want to report a traffic accident.
교통사고를 신고하려고 합니다.

Car accident happens on the road.
길에서 차 사고가 있었습니다.

Someone ran into my car.
누가 제 차를 받았습니다.

It was his fault. I recorded witness's name and account of the accident using my cell phone.
그 사람 잘못입니다. 제 핸드폰으로 목격자의 이름과 사고에 대한 진술을 녹음했습니다.

I didn't break any laws.
저는 교통법규를 위반하지 않았습니다.

I was at a red light, but a car hit me from behind. I am the victim.
빨간 신호등에 서 있는데 차가 뒤에서 내 차를 받았습니다. 제가 피해자입니다.

Officer. I need police report for submitting to insurance company.
경관님. 보험회사에 줄 경찰조사서를 주세요.

I have taken accident scene photos.
나는 교통사고 현장을 촬영하였습니다.

I am immediately reporting the car accident to the rental company.
렌터카 회사에 차 사고에 대한 보고를 바로 하고 있습니다.

I need a tow truck.
견인차가 필요합니다.

That was my fault. I'm sorry.
제 잘못이군요. 미안합니다.

Your bumper looks exactly the same.
범퍼는 이상이 없는 것 같군요.

I'll take care of it. Trust me.
제가 처리해 드리겠습니다. 믿어주세요.

I have insurance to cover it.
비용처리 할 보험을 들었습니다.

I just need your information and insurance.
당신의 정보와 보험이 필요합니다.

23. 교통신호 위반
(Traffic Violation)

Is there a problem, officer?
Did I do anything wrong?
무슨 문제가 있나요 경관님?
제가 잘못한 것이 있습니까?

Why do you pull me over?
왜 저를 세우셨나요?

I didn't see the stop sign.
정지 신호를 못 보았습니다.

I'm sorry for running it.
지나쳐서 죄송합니다.

I honestly see it yellow light.
솔직히 노란색으로 보았습니다.

I didn't mean to run it.
지나치려는 생각은 없었습니다.

I didn't know I was speeding.
과속한지 몰랐습니다.

I was obeying the speed limit.
속도를 지켰는데요.

I think I was going about 50mph.
50마일로 달린 것 같은데요.

I am really sorry.
I was not aware of that.
죄송합니다. 모르고 있었습니다.

I apologize, but I didn't realize that.
죄송합니다. 알지 못했습니다.

I have no excuse.
변명의 여지가 없습니다.

Am I getting a ticket for this?
교통위반 딱지를 받아야 하나요?

Could you let me go with warning?
경고만 하고 보내주시면 안될까요?

I am a foreign tourist.
저는 외국인 관광객입니다.

I am not familiar with this road.
이 길에 익숙하지 않습니다.

Thanks for being so understanding.
이해해 주셔서 감사합니다.

I will pay closer attention to traffic signal.
교통신호에 주의를 기울이겠습니다.

24. 길 묻기 (Asking for Directions)

Hello, May I ask for some help?
I need to get to A.
How can I go there?
잠깐만요. A까지 가려는데 어떻게 가죠?

Excuse me.
Do you know where A is?
죄송한데 A가 어디에 있는지 아세요?

I'm looking for A.
Will you show me the way to A?
A를 찾고 있는데 어디 있는지 아세요?

Can you direct me to the nearest convenience store?
가장 가까운 편의점 좀 가르쳐 주실래요?

Go down the street for 2 blocks and turn left at the next intersection.
2블록 더 가 다음 교차로에서 좌회전하세요.

How do I get to the downtown from here?
이곳에서 시내까지 어떻게 가죠?

Go down along this street and you'll see an entrance to the freeway.
이 길을 따라 쭉 가면 고속도로 입구를 볼 수 있을 것입니다.

I seem to be lost.
길을 잃은 것 같습니다.

Do you know how to get to A from here?
이곳에서 A로 어떻게 가는지 아세요?

When you pass the traffic light, turn right. It's right there.
신호등을 지나 우회전하면 그곳에 있습니다.

Could you show me on this map?
이 지도로 좀 가르쳐 주실래요?

How do I go to this address?
이 주소로 어떻게 가지요?

Go straight down the road.
길을 따라 쭉 가세요.

How do I get there?
Can you tell me how to get there?
그곳에 어떻게 가죠?

It's far from here.
이곳에서 멉니다.

Could you tell me in more details?
좀 더 자세하게 설명해 주실래요?

Which way should I go?
어디로 가야 하죠?

Keep going straight on this street for 1 mile.
이 길을 따라 1마일 정도 가야 합니다.

Could you direct me the way?
가는 길을 가르쳐 주실래요?

Is this road to downtown?
이 길이 시내로 가는 길인가요?

I am not from around here.
저는 이 근처 사람이 아닙니다.

Can you direct me to A?
A까지 어떻게 가는 지 말해 주실래요?

Cross the road and go 2 blocks east.
길을 건너서 동쪽으로 2 블록 가세요.

What's the best route?
어느 경로가 좋죠?

How far is it to A?
A까지는 얼마나 먼가요?

Is it close by?
가깝나요?

Is it far from here?
여기서 머나요?

It is a couple of miles away.
2마일 정도 거리에 있어요.

Can I go there on foot?
걸어서 갈 수 있나요?

How long does it take on foot?
걸어서 얼마나 걸리죠?

It's around the corner over there.
바로 저곳 근처에 있어요.

Should I walk a little bit?
약간 걸어야 하나요?

You have to walk a little bit.
약간 걸으셔야 합니다.

It's near here. I'll show you.
가까운 곳에 있습니다. 안내해 드릴게요.

It will probably be over there.
아마도 저곳에 있을 것입니다.

Is this the right direction?
이 방향이 맞나요?

Should I go through the alley?
골목길을 지나가야 하나요?

Can you tell me where I am?
여기가 어디죠?

Show me where I am on the map.
지도상에 제가 어디 있는 지 가르쳐 주세요.

185

25. 관광지 정보
(Tourist & Sightseeing Information)

Where is the tourist information center?
관광안내소가 어디인가요?

May I have free map or brochure?
무료 지도나 안내 책자를 얻을 수 있나요?

Do you have some free tourist map?
무료 관광지도가 있나요?

I am interested in seeing scenic areas and need some information.
경관이 좋은 곳들을 보고 싶은데 자료가 필요합니다.

Can I take these brochures?
이 책자들을 가져도 되나요?

May I take this?
이것을 가져가도 되나요?

Can I get any discount coupon?
할인 쿠폰을 받을 수 있나요?

This is my first time visiting this city. (It's my first time here.)
이 도시는 처음 방문하는 것입니다.

I'm planning to go sightseeing, so I'd like to get your advice.
관광하려는데 도움말 좀 주실래요?

Could you recommend any tourist attractions?
가 볼만한 곳들 좀 추천해 주실래요?

Where is the scenic area?
경치 좋은 곳이 어디죠?

Where can I enjoy nice view?
어디에서 경치 좋은 곳을 즐길 수 있죠?

Is that place worth a visit?
저곳은 가 볼만 한가요?

Is there any place that I should go first?
먼저 가봐야 할 만한 곳이 있나요?

Is there anything special I must to see in this city?
이 도시에서 꼭 보아야 할 특별한 것들이 있나요?

Could you tell me the most popular tourist attractions?
가장 인기 있는 관광지들 좀 말해 주실래요?

Can you help me figure out how to book tickets online?
인터넷으로 티켓을 예약하는 데 어떻게 하는지 도와주실래요?

What do I need to know to book a ticket online?
인터넷으로 티켓 예약하는데 무엇을 알아야 하죠?

What is the best way to get a cheap ticket?
싼 표를 살 수 있는 좋은 방법이 있나요?

How do I get the best price?
더 좋은 가격으로 어떻게 구하나요?

Do I need to take any special precautions in this city?
이 도시에서 주의해야 될 것들이 있나요?

What should I watch out for?
무엇을 조심해야 하나요?

Do I need to abstain from drinking any water that isn't bottled?
병에 든 물이 아니면 마시면 안되나요?

Do I need to avoid street foods?
가판대 음식을 먹지 말아야 하나요?

26. 관광지 생활 영어 (Practical English at Tourist Attractions)

What's that over there?
저것은 무엇이죠?

How old is it?
얼마나 오래되었죠?

Is the admission free?
입장료가 공짜인가요?

What show is playing down there?
저곳에서 무슨 쇼를 하고 있죠?

How long does it take to see?
보는데 얼마나 걸리죠?

What time does it begin?
언제 시작하죠?

Where is the ticket line?
표 사는 줄이 어디죠?

Are there going to be long lines?
기다리는 줄이 길까요?

Don't cut in line.
끼어들지 마세요.

You have to stand in line.
줄을 서야 합니다.

187

Take a number, wait for your turn.
번호표를 뽑고, 당신 차례를 기다리세요.

How long is this going to take?
How long will I have to wait?
얼마나 걸리죠? (기다려야 하죠?)

How much is the admission fee?
입장료가 얼마이죠?

Can I get a discount?
할인을 받을 수 있나요?

Is there any discount?
할인은 없나요?

Do children get discounts?
어린이들은 할인이 있나요?

Do you have discounts for group?
단체를 위한 할인도 있나요?

How many people do we need to get the group rate?
단체 할인요금은 몇 사람이 모여야 되나요?

Can I get a ticket right now?
지금 표를 받을 수 있나요?

I want to buy ticket in advance.
미리 표를 사고 싶습니다.

I would like to buy two advance tickets.
예매권을 2장을 사고 싶습니다.

I've got 10% discount coupon.
10% 할인 쿠폰을 가지고 있습니다.

Is it sold out?
매진되었나요?

What time (When) is the next?
다음은 언제 하죠?

Are there any seats left?
남은 자리가 있나요?

Which seat do you want?
어느 좌석을 원하세요?

Get me the front seat.
앞 좌석으로 주세요.

I want middle row seat.
중간 자리로 주세요.

Please give me the cheapest seat.
가장 싼 자리로 주세요.

Where is the entrance?
입구가 어디입니까?

Excuse me, coming through.
May I get through?
죄송합니다, 지나갈게요.

Where is the exit?
출구가 어디입니까?

What time does the show start?
쇼가 언제 시작하죠?

Is this seat vacant?
Is this seat unoccupied?
이 자리가 비었나요?

Do we have to sit separately?
따로 떨어져 앉아야 하나요?

Are you coming together?
같이 오셨나요?

Can I change seat with you?
당신과 자리를 바꿀 수 있을까요?

Would you mind not sitting here?
여기에 앉지 말아주실래요?

I didn't know this seat was taken.
자리가 있는 줄 몰랐습니다.

What time does the show finish?
쇼가 언제 끝나죠?

How long is the performance?
공연이 얼마나 하죠?

It's a fantastic performance.
환상적인 공연이군요.

Can I get a refund for an unused ticket?
사용하지 않은 티켓은 환불이 되나요?

How long will you be here?
이곳에 얼마나 있으실 건가요?

I will be here for 2 weeks.
저는 2주일 있을 겁니다.

Is this your first staying in this city?
이 도시는 처음 머무르는 건가요?

Are you enjoying yor trip?
What sights did you visit?
여행을 즐기고 있으시나요?
어디를 구경하셨어요?

Have you ever visited Korea before?
한국에 전에 와 본적이 있으신가요?

Where do you plan on going for your next vacation?
다음 휴가는 어디로 가려고 하세요?

If you could live anywhere in the world, where would it be?
만약 다른 곳에서 살 수 있다면 어디에서 살고 싶으세요?

What countries have you traveled?
Which countries did you visit?
어느 나라들을 여행하셨어요?

Where will you be traveling?
어디를 여행 하실 건가요?

Do you want to travel to every corner of the world?
세계 곳곳을 여행하길 원하세요?

Would you like to go somewhere?
어딘가를 가고 싶으세요?

I would like to travel to everywhere.
저는 모든 곳을 다 여행하고 싶습니다.

What are you planning to do?
무엇을 할 계획입니까?

That sounds like fun.
재미있을 것 같군요.

Don't get your hopes up.
너무 기대를 하지 마세요.

Have you been there?
그곳에 가보셨어요?

It will take 2 hours at the most, depending on your walking pace.
걷는 속도에 따라 2시간 정도 걸릴 것입니다.

I'm sure you'll have a good time.
즐거운 시간을 보낼 수 있을 것입니다.

I want to go there someday.
언젠가 그곳에 가보고 싶어요.

Can you help me figure out the best place to buy a little souvenir?
조그만 기념품을 사려고 하는데 어디가 가장 좋은 지 가르쳐 주실래요?

Let's look at the souvenirs at the street stand.
거리 가판대에서 기념품들을 보도록 하죠.

Let's go across the street and see what they have over there.
길을 건너 저곳에 무엇이 있는지 보죠.

I am looking for something unique.
뭔가 특별한 것을 찾고 있습니다.

I feel like this stuff is too expensive, kind of overpriced.
이것들이 너무 비싸다고 느껴지는군요.

Things seem to be expensive at this stand.
이 가판대는 좀 비싼 것 같군요.

Let's walk some more and see what the prices are like there.
좀 더 걸어가서 저곳의 가격은 얼마인지 보도록 하죠.

Do I need to get a visa to cross the border for sightseeing?
관광을 위해 국경을 지나려면 비자를 발급받아야 하나요?

Can I make an appointment online?
인터넷으로 미리 예약을 할 수 있나요?

Are there any fees involved?
지불 비용이 있을까요?

How much money will I have to pay?
얼마나 지불하게 되나요?

What else do I need to bring?
무엇을 가져가야 하죠?

I am afraid that they will decline.
그들이 거절할까 걱정되는군요.

There isn't anything else to do right now except wait.
지금은 기다릴 수밖에 없습니다.

27. 선택 관광 및 야외 활동 (Optional Tours & Outdoor Activities)

I was wondering if you could help me take a few tours.
몇 가지 관광을 하는데 도와주실래요?

I need help planning my tour schedule.
관광 스케줄 짜는데 도와주실래요?

I haven't decided yet where to go.
어디로 갈 지 아직 결정하지 않았어요.

I'd like to have travel brochure about the tour package.
관광 패키지가 적힌 여행책자를 얻고 싶군요.

I am only staying for two days.
이틀 정도 밖에 머무르질 않습니다.

I will be here for a week. I'd like to look around slowly.
1주일 있을 건데 천천히 둘러보고 싶군요

Do you have a city tour?
시티투어 상품이 있나요?

Do you have a quick tour where I can get an overview of this city?
이 도시 전체를 빠르게 돌아볼 수 있는 투어가 있나요?

Is there any way that I can take a quick tour?
빠르게 투어를 하는 방법이 있나요?

Do you have a half day tour? I am short of time.
반일관광 상품이 있나요? 시간이 부족합니다.

Do you have any sightseeing tour?
탐방관광 상품이 있나요?

I am open to suggestions.
어떤 의견이든 좋습니다.

Could you suggest me the best places?
좋은 곳들 좀 추천해 주실래요?

Could you recommend must-see places?
반드시 보아야 할 곳들을 추천해 주실래요?

What would be a good place to go at night?
밤에는 어느 곳을 가는 게 좋을까요?

Do you have a tour to A?
A로 가는 여행상품이 있나요?

Is it a day trip or 2 days trip?
하루 여행이나요 이틀 여행인가요?

What kind of one day tour do you have?
하루 관광상품으로 어떤 것들이 있나요?

Are any meals included?
식사가 포함되어 있나요?

Do you have any evening tours?
저녁관광 상품이 있나요?

This is my first visit.
이곳은 처음 방문하는 것입니다.

I have been here before on a business trip.
일 때문에 이곳에 출장을 온 적이 있습니다.

I'd like to get a feel for the local culture.
지역 문화에 대해 느끼고 싶군요.

I love to spend some time at the beach.
해안에서 시간을 좀 보내고 싶습니다.

Do you have any water sports package?
해양스포츠 패키지가 있나요?

How much is this tour package?
이 관광 패키지는 얼마이죠?

Which courses are available now?
지금 어느 코스를 이용할 수 있죠?

What else do I need to consider?
무엇을 고려해야 할까요?

Does the price include the admission fee and meal?
가격에 입장료와 식사가 포함된 것인가요?

I think I can spend 100 dollars in my budget for one day trip.
하루 여행에 100달러 정도 쓰려고 생각하고 있습니다.

I am not rich. Could I get a discount?
저는 부자가 아닌데 할인 받을 수 있을까요?

How much will the half day tour cost?
반나절 관광은 얼마나 하나요?

Do I need a reservation for tour package?
관광 패키지는 예약해야 하나요?

When are we leaving for our package tour?
패키지 관광을 언제 떠나나요?

Does the tour start here?
이곳에서 관광을 출발하나요?

Do I have to come here half an hour early?
30분 전에 와야 하나요?

I will be here on time.
제시간에 올게요.

What should we bring with us?
무엇을 가져와야 되나요?

How long does it take?
얼마나 걸리죠?

What time do you pick us up?
언제 픽업하러 오시죠?

When does the tour begin?
언제 관광이 시작되나요?

What time are we leaving?
언제 출발하죠?

Where do we wait?
어디에서 기다리죠?

Do we wait in front of the lobby?
로비 앞에서 기다리나요?

Has the tour bus come yet?
Is the tour bus here yet?
버스가 아직 안 왔나요?

Tour company doesn't seem to have a tight schedule.
여행사가 꽉 짜인 스케줄이 없는 것 같네요.

Do we have to pay more if there are any changes in itinerary?
여행 일정이 변경되면 추가 요금을 지불해야 하나요?

That will add an extra charge.
추가 요금이 붙게됩니다.

What time does it finish?
When will it be over?
When will it end?
언제 끝나죠?

Do we come back to this hotel?
이 호텔까지 돌아오나요?

How long do we take a rest here?
이곳에서 얼마 동안 쉬나요?

How long do we stay at the rest area?
휴게소에서 얼마나 머무를 것인가요?

Can I go to the rest room?
May I leave my bag here?
화장실 가도 되나요? 가방을 두어도 되나요?

Do you mind opening the window?
창문을 열어도 되나요?

My dress got stuck in the door.
제 옷이 문에 끼었네요.

I want to go snorkeling.
스노클링을 하고 싶습니다.

I'd like to enroll in scuba diving course.
스쿠버 다이빙 코스에 들어가고 싶습니다.

May I choose anything?
아무거나 고르면 되나요?

I need help figuring out how to use.
이것을 어떻게 사용하는지 알고 싶습니다.

Could you take a few minutes and
see if there are any problems?
잠깐 시간을 내 주셔서 무슨 문제가 있는 지
봐주실래요?

That was so much fun.
Let me try one more time.
정말 재미있네요. 한 번 더 해 볼게요.

I need a little more practice.
Please, give me some more time.
더 연습이 필요합니다. 시간을 좀 더 주세요.

By what time should I come back?
언제까지 돌아와야 하나요?

Where do I return this?
이것을 어디에 돌려주나요?

I had so much fun.
I enjoyed every minute(moment).
정말 재미있었습니다.
순간 순간이 즐거웠습니다.

28. 사진 촬영 (Taking Pictures)

What a lovely view!
아름다운 경치이군요!

Landscape is wonderful!
경치가 훌륭하군요!

It's so beautiful and nice scenic
view! It's spectacular.
정말 아름답고 좋은 경치이군요! 장관이네요.

Can I take a photo here?
이곳에서 사진을 찍어도 되나요?

May I take pictures here?
이곳에서 사진을 찍어도 되나요?

May I use a flash?
플래시를 사용해도 되나요?

Would you please take a picture?
사진 좀 찍어 주실래요?

Will you take my picture in front of
this place, please?
이곳에서 사진을 좀 찍어 주실래요?

Could you make sure that building is
in the background?
저 빌딩이 뒤에 나오게 해주실래요?

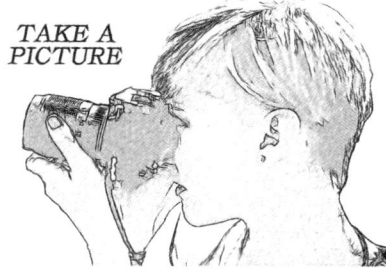
TAKE A PICTURE

Would you please take a picture of
us? (Could you take a photo for us?)
우리들 사진을 좀 찍어주실래요?

Can I take a picture of you?
당신 사진을 찍어도 되겠습니까?

Can I take a picture with you?
당신과 사진을 같이 찍어도 될까요?

May I take your picture with us?
우리와 함께 사진을 찍으실래요?

Shall I take a picture of all of you?
당신들의 사진을 찍어 드릴까요?

Please, move(go) back one step.
한 발 뒤로 물러서 주세요.

Move a little to the left.
좌측으로 조금 옮겨주세요.

Say, Cheese.
치즈 하세요.

The flash is not working.
플래시가 안 터지네요.

How does this work?
어떻게 작동시키죠?

Let me take one more.
한 장 더 찍을게요.

I hope photos come out good(well).
사진들이 잘 나왔으면 좋겠습니다.

29. 쇼핑 (Shopping)

Can I help you?
May I help you?
어서 오세요.

I am just browsing.
그냥 구경만 합니다.

I am just looking around.
그냥 둘러보고 있습니다.

What are you looking for?
당신이 찾고 있는 것이 무엇이죠?

I don't want to put you any trouble.
귀찮게 하고 싶지 않습니다.

Are you being helped?
도와드릴까요?

I'd like to look around by myself.
혼자서 둘러보고 싶습니다.

Is there anything else you would like?
맘에 드시는 것이 있나요?

I don't need it.
필요하지 않습니다.

Let me know when you need something.
필요한 것이 있으면 알려주세요.

Have you found anything that you like?
마음에 드는 것을 찾으셨어요?

What's that for?
무엇에 쓰는 것이죠?

What's inside?
안에 뭐가 있죠?

How can I help you?
무엇을 도와드릴까요?

What are you going to look for?
무엇을 찾으세요?

I am looking for some souvenirs.
기념품을 찾고 있습니다.

I'd like to buy something for my friends.
친구들에게 줄 선물을 사고 싶습니다.

Can you help me pick out a gift?
선물 고르는데 도와주실래요?

Would you like to take a look at these?
이것들 좀 보실래요?

Can you recommend an inexpensive gift?
비싸지 않은 선물을 추천해 주실래요?

Can I see some perfumes?
향수 좀 볼까요?

Do you have free samples of this perfume?
이 향수의 무료 샘플 없나요?

Can I get complimentary samples?
무료 샘플을 얻을 수 있을까요?

Show me one, please.
하나 보여 주세요.

Let me have one.
하나 주세요.

I've got a discount coupon.
할인 쿠폰을 가지고 있습니다.

Can I use this discount coupon?
이 할인 쿠폰을 사용할 수 있나요?

Are all of those on sale?
저것들 모두 세일하나요?

Are they on sale?
세일하나요?

Some of them are on sale and some of them aren't.
어떤 것은 세일하고 어떤 것은 안 합니다.

Is this dress on sale?
이 옷 세일하나요?

It's not on sale at the moment.
지금은 세일이 아닙니다.

Is there anything on sale today?
오늘 세일하는 것이 있나요?

There are no sales today.
오늘은 세일이 없습니다.

Everything's going to be on sale next month.
다음 달부터 세일입니다.

We are having a clearance sale on everything.
지금 모두 재고정리 할인을 하고 있습니다.

I don't see anything I want.
제가 원하는 것이 없네요.

The price range is affordable.
가격이 저렴합니다.

Would you like anything else?
맘에 드는 것이 있나요?

Is there anything you have in mind?
정하신 물건이 있나요?

I want a more attractive one.
좀 더 좋은 것을 원합니다.

I like that style over there.
저 스타일이 좋군요.

Do you have any other color?
다른 색깔은 없습니까?

It's too dark.
Don't you have any bright one?
너무 어둡군요. 더 밝은 것은 없습니까?

I don't like this color.
Are there any other colors?
이 색이 마음에 들지 않군요.
다른 색은 없나요?

Please show me another one.
다른 것을 보여 주세요.

Are there any similar ones?
다른 비슷한 것들은 없나요?

Can you show me different ones?
다른 것들을 보여 주실래요?

Come this way.
이곳으로 오세요.

Do you have this style in yellow?
이런 스타일의 노란색은 없나요?

How do you like this one?
이것은 어떠세요?

I can't make up mind.
결정할 수가 없군요.

Do you have any other style?
다른 스타일은 없나요?

I like this. This is much better.
이것이 좋습니다. 훨씬 좋군요.

How does it look?
잘 맞나요?

Can I try it on?
입어 봐도 될까요?

What size do you wear?
어느 사이즈를 입으세요?

Can you guess my size?
제 사이즈를 아시겠습니까?

Which one is my size?
어느 것이 제 사이즈일까요?

I don't know what my size is.
제 사이즈를 모르겠습니다.

Can you take my measurements?
제 치수를 재 주실래요?

Will you please measure me?
치수를 재어 주실래요?

What size is this?
이 사이즈가 몇이죠?

Can I try this again?
이것을 다시 입어보아도 되겠습니까?

Where is the fitting room?
피팅 룸이 어디죠?

You can try it on in the fitting room over there.
저곳 탈의실에서 입어보세요.

Do you have a mirror?
Where is the mirror?
거울은 없나요? 어디에 있죠?

The dressing room is right over there. Just around the corner.
드레싱 룸이 저곳 모퉁이에 있습니다.

How do I look?
이 옷이 어떤가요?

It looks like it's a perfect fit.
아주 잘 맞는 것 같습니다.

Does it look too big?
너무 크지 않나요?

It's too small.
너무 작네요.

Does this come in a larger size?
더 큰 것이 있나요?

We have all sizes available.
모든 사이즈가 있습니다.

It's a little big.
조금 크네요.

Try on it.
입어보세요.

It's too loose.
너무 헐렁하네요.

Do you have a smaller one?
더 작은 것은 없나요?

Let me try a smaller size.
작은 것을 입어볼게요.

It suits you.
잘 어울립니다.

I like it. I'll get it.
좋습니다. 살게요.

I'd like to have two, the same as this.
이것과 같은 것 2개를 가지고 싶습니다.

Is there anything else you'd like to get?
맘에 드시는 것이 또 있으신가요?

This will be fine.
이것이면 됩니다.

How much is this?
얼마죠?

How much are they?
저것들은 얼마죠?

Will it be expensive?
비쌀까요?

Let's talk price.
가격에 대해 말해보죠.

Are these the same price?
이것들은 가격이 동일한가요?

You can't be serious.
진짜요?

That's too expensive for me.
제겐 너무 비싸군요.

This is of very high quality.
이것은 질이 아주 좋습니다.

Could you lower the price a little?
가격을 좀 낮추어줄 수 없나요?

197

I can't go down on the price.
가격을 내릴 수는 없습니다.

The price is unreasonable.
가격이 너무 터무니없군요.

Too expensive.
Could you make a discount?
너무 비쌉니다. 할인해 주실래요?

I will give you 10 percent off.
10% 할인해 드리겠습니다.

I can't afford that.
그럴 여유가 없군요.

I am short of money.
I don't have enough money.
돈이 부족합니다.

Thank you for your time.
시간 내 주서서 감사합니다.

How much are you talking?
얼마를 말하시나요?

I want something inexpensive.
저는 싼 것을 원합니다.

Are there any cheaper one?
Do you have anything cheaper?
Do you have something a little cheaper?
좀 더 싼 것은 없나요?

Can't you give me a better price?
좀 더 좋은 가격에 줄 수 없나요?

Can you lower the price a little?
Can you come down a little?
가격을 좀 낮추어 주실래요?

I will buy it if the price is reasonable. (satisfactory)
가격이 적당하면(만족스러우면) 살게요.

Would you like gift-wrapping?
Would you like that gift wrapped?
포장을 해드릴까요?

Please wrap them separately.
따로 따로 포장해 주세요.

Could you gift-wrap it?
Please wrap it as a gift.
Please gift-wrap it.
선물용으로 포장해 주세요.

Is there any extra charge for gift-
wrapping?
선물용 포장은 추가비용이 있나요?

How much altogether?
모두 얼마죠?

How would you like to pay for it?
어떻게 지불하시겠습니까?

Will that be cash or charge?
현금이나요 카드이나요?

Do you accept VISA card?
비자카드로 되나요?

Don't you allow discount for cash?
현금이면 할인이 안 되나요?

I will be paying with cash.
현금으로 계산할게요.

Can I pay with US dollars?
미국 달러로 계산해도 되나요?

How much is that in US dollars?
미국 달러로는 얼마이죠?

I need your signature here, please.
여기 사인해 주세요.

Here's your receipt.
여기 영수증이 있습니다.

There is a mistake on the bill.
계산이 틀리는데요.

Please check the bill again.
계산서를 다시 체크해 주세요.

Did you give me a receipt?
저에게 영수증을 주셨나요?

Can you send these things to my address in Korea?
이것들을 한국 주소로 보내줄 수 있나요?

Can I change this at a later date?
나중에 이것을 교환해도 되나요?

I bought this a little while ago.
조금 전에 이것을 샀습니다.

Can I exchange this dress?
I want to exchange this dress.
I'd like to exchange this dress.
이 옷을 바꾸어도 될까요?

You can exchange it with anything of the same price.
같은 가격 어느 것이든 바꿀 수 있습니다.

Sorry to bother you, but I was wondering if you could make a refund?
죄송합니다만 환불해줄 수 있나요?

I want to get a refund.
I'd just like a refund.
I'd like to return this.
I want to return.
환불하길 원합니다.

I purchased this yesterday.
어제 이것을 샀습니다.

Is there something wrong with it?
무슨 문제가 있나요?

There is a stain on this clothes.
이 옷에 얼룩이 있어요.

This is damaged.
이것은 손상되어 있어요.

The zipper is broken.
It doesn't work.
지퍼가 고장 났어요. 작동이 안 되네요.

It's defective.
결함이 있어요.

I changed my mind because I don't like the color.
색깔이 마음에 안 들어 생각을 바꾸었습니다.

Do I need to pay for the damage?
손상된 부분은 보상해야 하나요?

Do you have the receipt?
영수증을 가지고 계시나요?

I lost my receipt.
영수증을 잃어버렸습니다.

You need a receipt for a refund.
환불하기 위해서는 영수증이 필요합니다.

I'd like to talk to customer service.
소비자센터에 말하고 싶습니다.

30. 편의점, 식료품점에서
(At Convenience, Grocery Store)

Excuse me. Do you know where the convenience store is?
편의점이 어디 있는지 아세요?

Is there any supermarket or grocery store around here?
이 근처에 슈퍼마켓이나 상점이 있습니까?

I'm looking for batteries.
건전지를 찾고 있습니다.

Where would I find soap and laundry detergent?
비누와 세탁세제가 어디에 있죠?

I want to buy a toothbrush and toothpaste.
칫솔과 치약을 사고 싶습니다.

Do you sell mineral water here?
생수를 이곳에서 파나요?

This mineral water is warm. Do you have a cold one?
생수가 따뜻한데 찬 것 없나요?

Is this milk fresh?
It's sour. This milk has gone bad.
이 우유가 신선하나요?
신데요. 이 우유가 상했어요.

It smells as if it has gone bad.
상한 것 같은 냄새가 나네요.

This milk has passed the expiration date.
이 우유가 유통 기한이 지났습니다.

The expiration date on this milk was last week.
이 우유 유효 기간이 지난 주까지였어요.

Where can I find beer?
맥주가 어디에 있죠?

Where is the produce section?
농산물코너가 어디죠?

Are there any organic fruits?
유기농 과일이 있나요?

Are there any fresh tomatoes?
신선한 토마토가 있나요?

Where can I find the tomatoes?
토마토가 어디에 있죠?

I'm looking for some apples.
사과를 찾고 있습니다.

There aren't any ripe apples.
잘 익은 사과가 없네요.

How much is this organic apple?
이 유기농 사과는 얼마죠?

This apple tastes a bit sour.
이 사과가 떫은데요.

Are oranges on sale today?
오렌지는 오늘 세일인가요?

The flyer says that it's on sale.
전단지에 세일이라고 되어있던데요.

I'll take these. I'll pay cash.
이것들을 사겠습니다. 현금으로 할게요.

Can you break a 100 dollar?
100달러인데 괜찮겠습니까?

Where is the vending machine?
자동판매기가 어디 있죠?

Is there any vending machine in this area?
이곳에 자판기가 있나요?

It's at the end of hallway.
복도 끝에 있습니다.

I put money in, but it doesn't work. Please, check it.
돈을 넣었는데 작동이 안 되네요. 확인을 해 주세요.

31. 식당에서 (At Restaurant)

I would like to make a reservation for tomorrow night.
내일 저녁을 예약하고 싶습니다.

I would like to make a dinner reservation for this Friday night.
이번 주 금요일 저녁을 예약하고 싶습니다.

What time would you like the reservation for?
몇 시에 예약해 드릴까요?

We will be coming at 7 o'clock.
Can I have a table for 4 at 7 o'clock?
7시에 갈게요. (7시에 4명 좌석 부탁합니다.)

How many people in your party?
How many company do you have?
몇 명이나 되지요?

There will be four of us. (4 people)
4명입니다.

7 P.M. A party of four. Nonsmoking.
저녁 7시에 4명입니다. 금연석으로 주세요.

May I have your name?
성함이 어떻게 되시지요?

Do you have a dress code?
복장을 갖추어야 하나요?

The dress code is a casual elegance.
(Smart casual)
단정한 평상복(정장 평상복)이면 됩니다.

Men are required to wear jackets,
but ties are optional.
남자들은 재킷을 걸쳐야 하고 넥타이는 자유입니다.

Come as you are.
있는 그대로 오세요.

Do you have a reservation?
예약하셨습니까?

I've a reservation at 7:00 for Kim -.
7시 김-으로 예약하였습니다.

We have a reservation at 7:00 under
the name of Kim - for 4 people.
김-으로 7시에 4명 예약했습니다.

We don't have a reservation.
예약을 안 했습니다.

Would it be possible for us to have
a dinner?
저녁을 먹을 수 있을까요?

Is there any table available for us?
빈 테이블이 있나요?

Do you have a table for three?
3명 앉을 곳이 있나요?

How many people?
몇 명이죠?

A party of 7.
7명입니다.

All tables are occupied.
You need to wait for a while.
테이블이 다 차서 잠시 기다려야합니다.

Could you put my name on the list?
대기자 명단에 올려주실래요?

Please, wait in the lounge area.
Please wait to be seated.
대기실에서(안내될 때까지)기다려 주십시오.

How long do you think it will be?
How long do we have to wait?
얼마나 기다려야 하죠?

We'll take whatever comes up first.
자리가 먼저 나면 아무거나 주세요.

Would it be possible to be seated
out there (outside)?
저 바깥 테이블에 앉을 수 있나요?

Could we have a table on the
terrace?
테라스에 있는 테이블에 앉을 수 있나요?

We are expecting two more friends.
After a while (A little while later),
2 more people are coming.
2 more people will come soon.
2 more people will be here.
잠시 후, 일행 두 명이 곧 올 것입니다.

We are expecting someone.
We are waiting for someone.
누구를 기다리고 있습니다.

The outside table looks really nice.
바깥 테이블들이 멋있게 보이는군요.

Can we move over there?
저곳으로 옮길 수 있을까요?

Can we sit here?
이곳에 앉아도 되나요?

This table is reserved.
이 테이블은 예약이 되어있습니다.

What's that smell?
저 냄새가 뭐죠?

It smells good.
냄새가 좋군요.

May I have your order?
Would you like to order now?
지금 주문하실래요?

Could I get a menu?
메뉴판 좀 주실래요?

There are so many different dishes listed that it's hard to decide.
결정하기 힘들 정도로 많은 종류가 있군요.

Could you give us a few minutes to decide?
결정하기까지 잠시만 시간 좀 주실래요?

We'll call you when we're ready to order.
주문 준비가 되면 다시 부를게요.

Could you take my order, please?
주문을 받으실래요?

Can you tell me what this is?
이것이 무엇이지요?

Is there a set menu?
세트 메뉴가 있습니까?

I'd like to order prix fixe menu.
정식(프리 픽스)을 주문하고 싶습니다.

What can be served quickly?
어떤 것이 빨리 나오죠?

Choose whatever you like.
Pick whatever you want.
원하는 것을 고르세요.

I am not sure what to get(order).
무엇을 시킬 지 모르겠네요.

Do you have a special menu?
특별한 메뉴가 있나요?

What kind of dish is this?
이것은 무슨 요리인가요?

I'd like to order filet mignon.
필레미뇽을 주문하고 싶군요.

I want to order this.
이것을 주문하고 싶습니다.

The same for me.
I'll have the same.
Make it two.
같은 것으로 해주세요.

Could I change my order?
주문을 바꾸어도 될까요?

Medium-Well done please.
약간 익혀주세요.

Could you make it less salty?
짜지 않게 해주세요.

What kind of soup would you like?
수프는 어떤 것으로 하시겠습니까?

I'll have mushroom soup.
버섯 수프로 주세요.

What kind of dressing would you like?
드레싱은 어떤 것으로 하시겠습니까?

French, Italian, Honey mustard, Thousand island.
프렌치, 이탈리안, 하니 머스타드, 싸우즌 아일랜드가 있습니다.

203

I'll have salad with honey mustard dressing.
허니 머스타드 드레싱 샐러드를 먹겠습니다.

It looks delicious.
맛있게 보이네요.

It tastes so good.
This meat is very tender.
맛이 좋네요. 고기가 아주 부드러워요.

My steak isn't done enough.
스테이크가 충분히 익질 않았어요.

Steak is too tough and hard to chew.
스테이크가 너무 질기고 씹기 힘드네요.

I ordered it medium-well done.
약간 구워주라고 했는데요.

This doesn't smell fresh.
냄새가 신선하지 않습니다.

I can't possibly eat this.
이것을 먹을 수가 없군요.

I am afraid this is stale.
이것은 상한 것 같군요.

This meat is burnt. (burned)
고기가 다 탔네요.

Something is wrong with it.
It's too salty.
뭔가 잘못되었는데요. 너무 짜군요.

This is not my order.
이건 제 주문이 아닌데요.

My order hasn't come out yet.
제 주문이 아직 안 나왔습니다.

Could you hurry the orders?
음식 좀 빨리 주실래요?

What's taking so long?
왜 이렇게 오래 걸리죠?

May I have more bread and butter?
빵과 버터를 좀 더 주실래요?

May I have more water?
물 좀 더 주실래요?

I need some salt and pepper.
소금과 후추 좀 주세요.

Can I have some napkins?
냅킨 좀 주실래요?

Would you take dishes away?
접시들을 치워 주실래요?

I dropped a fork.
I need another fork.
포크를 떨어뜨렸네요. 하나 더 주세요.

Will you get me a cup of coffee?
커피 한 잔 주실래요?

Will you get us three beers?
맥주 3병 주실래요?

Can I get the free refill on coffee?
커피 무료 리필 되나요?

I'd like to have a refill.
리필 해주세요.

May I have a refill on my coffee?
제 커피 리필 해주실래요?

I'll pass on dessert.
디저트는 사양하겠습니다.

I'll skip the dessert.
디저트는 안 먹을게요.

There are no empty tables.
Would you mind sharing a table?
빈 자리가 없는데 합석해도 되나요?

Could you please put our leftover in a box to take home?
남은 음식을 집에 가져가게 포장해 주실래요?

I would like to get a doggy bag for the leftover.
남은 것을 가져가고 싶습니다.

Could I have a doggy bag?
남은 것 좀 포장해 주실래요?

That was a good meal. I'm satisfied.
좋은 식사였습니다. 만족합니다.

May I have the check, please?
계산서를 주실래요?

Put them all on one check, please.
모두 같이 계산해 주세요.

I'll treat you.
I want to treat you.
It's my treat.
I'll pay it all. (I'll get the bill.)
Be my guest.
It's on me
제가 대접할게요. 제가 낼게요.

You don't have to.
그럴 필요없어요.

Let's share the bill.
Let's go Dutch.
각자 부담합시다.

How much is my share?
제가 부담할 돈이 얼마이죠?

I'll pay for mine.
Let me pay for my share.
제 몫은 제가 계산할게요.

Separate bills, please.
나누어진 계산서를 주세요.

I'll pay for it this time.
이번엔 제가 계산할게요.

I think this bill is incorrect.
There is a mistake on this bill.
이 청구서가 틀린 것 같군요.

What's this amount on the bill?
계산서의 이 비용은 어떤 것이죠?

I never ordered this.
이것은 안 시켰는데요.

The amount seems to be wrong.
I think you charged the wrong amount.
금액이 잘못된 것 같습니다.

Do we pay you at the table?
테이블에서 당신에게 계산하나요?

How much should I tip?
팁을 얼마나 주나요?

The tip amount is added onto the bill.
팁은 계산서에 청구되어 있습니다.

I want to tip just 15%.
15%만 팁을 주고 싶습니다.

I tip 20%.
20% 팁을 줄게요.

Do you accept credit card?
카드로 되나요?

Can I have the receipt?
영수증을 주실래요?

32 패스트푸드점에서
(At Fast Food Restaurant)

Could you help me find a place where I have lunch?
점심 먹을 만한 곳을 가르쳐 주실래요?

Do you know a good place to have lunch?
점심 먹을 만한 좋은 곳을 아나요?

Do you know of a great restaurant somewhere?
좋은 식당 혹시 알고 있나요?

Fast food or Chinese food would be great.
패스트푸드나 중국음식이면 좋겠습니다.

Let's have lunch together.
같이 점심을 드시죠.

Let's grab a bite somewhere close.
가까운 곳에서 뭐 좀 먹죠.

If you didn't have breakfast yet, let's grab a bite to eat together.
아직 아침을 드시지 않았으면 같이 간단히 뭐 좀 먹도록 하죠.

Are there any cafeterias or restaurants around here?
이 근처에 카페나 식당들이 있습니까?

Let's grab a quick bite.
간단히 먹읍시다.

What would you like to order?
무엇을 주문하실래요?

What's the most delicious food in here?
이곳에서 가장 맛있는 음식이 어떤 것이죠?

Would you like some chicken curry?
닭고기 카레를 드실래요?

That's a good suggestion.
좋습니다.

What about something to drink?
What would you like to drink?
Would you like to order a drink?
음료는 뭐로 하실래요?

I'll have one hot(iced) Americano.
뜨거운(차가운) 아메리카노를 마실게요.

With milk or syrup?
밀크나 시럽은요?

Black please.
블랙으로요.

Can I get you a drink?
마실 것을 드릴까요?

I'll have a large sprite.
With plenty of ice.
얼음 많이, 스프라이트 큰 사이즈로 주세요.

I'll have a glass of water(Ice water).
물 (얼음물) 한잔 마실게요.

Would you clear the table, please?
테이블 좀 치워줄래요?

Here are your orders.
주문하신 것들 나왔습니다.

Where is a straw?
빨대가 어디 있나요?

Can I have a refill?
리필 되나요?

May I take your order?
무엇을 드실래요?

I'll have one hamburger and one medium coke.
햄버거 하나와 콜라 중간 사이즈로 주세요.

Combo number 3 please.
콤보 3번으로 주세요.

Here or to go?
여기서 드실래요? 아니면 가져 가실래요?

For here. (To go)
여기서 먹을게요. (가져 갈게요.)

What kind of sauce do you have?
어떤 종류의 햄버거 소스가 있나요?

I'll have Ketchup sauce.
(Mustard, Chili)
케첩 (머스타드, 칠리) 소스로 주세요.

Two double cheeseburgers to go.
치즈버거 2개 포장해 주세요.

With everything on it?
토핑은 전부할까요?

Would you like fries with that?
감자튀김도 드실래요?

No, thanks. (Let me get some fries.)
아닙니다. (감자튀김도 주세요.)

Will that be all?
Is that everything?
그것이 전부인가요?

Yes, that's all. (That's it.)
예, 그것이 전부입니다.

Can it be done right now?
지금 바로 되나요?

Please serve us quickly.
Please hurry.
빨리 주실래요?

I(We) don't have much time.
시간이 없어요.

Your total is (comes to) $11.
That'll be $11.
모두 11달러입니다.

May I help you?
무엇을 드실래요?

I'll take number 2.
2번 세트를 주세요.

Can I have a coffee instead of coke?
콜라 대신 커피로 되나요?

One small pizza and a cup of coffee to go.
작은 피자와 커피 한 잔 가져가도록 주세요.

What kind of toppings would you like?
토핑을 어떤 것으로 하실래요?

I'd like pineapple and pepperoni.
파인애플과 페퍼로니로 주세요.

Can I have it right away?
곧 가져갈 수 있습니까?

33. 화장실 (Restroom, Toilet)

May I be excused?
실례해야 되겠네요.

Nature calls.
I have to go to the restroom.
I need to go to the bathroom.
(lavatory, toilet)
화장실에 가야 합니다.

Where can I wash my hands?
Where is the bathroom?
Where is the restroom?
화장실이 어디 있습니까?

Is there a public restroom around here?
이 주변에 공중화장실이 있나요?

Is this a pay toilet?
유료화장실입니까?

Can I use the restroom?
May I use the bathroom?
화장실을 사용해도 되나요?

I'm looking for the restroom.
Is it on this floor?
화장실을 찾고 있는데 이층에 있나요?

It's on the second floor.
2층에 있습니다.

It's down the corridor on the right.
복도 끝 오른쪽에 있습니다.

Excuse me. Where is the rest room?
I took too many wrong turns.
화장실이 어디 있습니까?
너무 자주 길을 잘 못 들었어요.

It's straight down the hallway, then turn right.
이 복도로 쭉 가서서 오른 쪽으로 도세요.

Is there a toilet sign?
Is there a restroom sign?
화장실 안내판이 있나요?

There are signs directing you.
길을 알려 줄 표지판들이 있습니다.

The restroom is locked.
화장실 문이 잠겨져 있네요.

I have a shy bladder.
사람이 있으면 소변을 못 봐요.

I'd like to have bowel movement.
대변을 보고 싶습니다.

I have a shy bowel syndrome.
사람이 있으면 용변을 못 봐요.

It's really crowded.
정말 붐비네요.

Is anybody inside? I am in a hurry.
안에 누가 있나요? 저 급해요.

Is there someone in the toilet?
화장실에 사람이 있나요?

Hello. Is anybody in there?
안에 누구 있나요?

How long do I have to wait?
얼마나 기다려야 하죠?

There is no toilet paper.
화장지가 없네요.

Where could I get a toilet paper?
어디서 화장지를 구하지요?

Would you please get a toilet paper?
화장지 좀 가져다가 주실래요?

Please wait a minute.
기다려 주세요.

I am on the toilet.
화장실 사용 중입니다.

Sorry, give me a little more time.
조금만 더 기다려 주세요.

I have no bowel movements.
변비입니다.

34. 미용실, 이발소에서 (At Beauty Shop, Barbershop)

Where can I get a haircut?
Is there a beauty shop around here?
어디서 머리를 자르죠?
이 근처에 미용실이 있나요?

I'd like hair cut.
Where did you go to get it cut?
머리를 자르려고 합니다.
당신은 어디로 가서 자르세요?

Will I need an appointment?
예약이 필요하나요?

How much do they charge?
가격이 얼마나 하죠?

I want a haircut.
머리를 잘라주세요.

How would you like your haircut?
머리를 어떻게 해드릴까요?

What can I do for you?
어떻게 해드릴까요?

I would like a trim.
조금만 잘라주세요.

I'd like cutting off moderately.
적당히 잘라주세요.

Cut my hair short. please.
짧게 잘라주세요.

I would like a buzz cut.
아주 짧게 잘라주세요.

I want to cut it short all over.
전체적으로 짧게 잘라 주세요.

Don't cut it too short.
너무 짧게 자르지 마세요.

I would like to get short bangs.
앞머리를 짧게 잘라주세요.

I want the bangs to be a little longer.
앞머리는 좀 길게 해주세요.

How do you part your hair?
가르마를 어느 쪽으로 타세요?

Part my hair on the right.
가르마는 우측으로 해주세요.

My hair is very thick.
Could you thin my hair out?
머리숱이 많아요. 머리숱을 조금 쳐주실래요?

How much do you want to cut off your hair?
머리를 얼마나 자르길 원하세요?

Can you cut off about 7cm?
7cm 길이만 잘라 주실래요?

Please cut side hair off short, but not too much off the top.
옆머리는 짧게 잘라주시고, 윗머리는 너무 자르지 마세요.

Do you want any layering?
층을 지게 할까요?

Would you like your hair shampooed?
머리 샴푸를 하실래요?

Do you want to get your hair colored?
머리 염색을 원하세요?

I would like to dye my hair.
염색을 하고 싶습니다.

What color were you thinking for your hair today?
무슨 색을 생각하셨어요?

Can you color my hair to brown?
브라운으로 해주실래요?

Do you want to book a massage?
마사지도 예약 하실래요?

What type of massage do you like?
어떤 마사지를 원하세요?

Do you prefer male or female for your massage?
마사지는 남자로 할까요? 여자로 할까요?

I would like a straight perm.
스트레이트 파마를 해주세요.

I want to get a perm.
파마를 하고 싶습니다.

35. 환전 및 은행
(Currency Exchange & Bank)

Where is the Currency Exchange office?
환전소가 어디에 있나요?

Where can I exchange money?
어디서 돈을 바꾸지요?

I'd like to exchange some money.
돈을 좀 바꾸고 싶습니다.

Do you exchange foreign currency?
외국 돈을 환전해주나요?

What currencies do you want to exchange?
어떤 돈으로 바꾸시길 원하시죠?

I'd like to change Korean money into U.S. dollars.
한국 돈을 미 달러로 바꾸고 싶습니다.

Can you exchange Korean money for U.S. dollars?
한국 돈을 미국 달러로 바꿀 수 있습니까?

What's your exchange rate for the Korean Won?
What's the exchange rate today?
한국 원에 대한 환율이 얼마이죠?

How much do you want?
얼마를 원하죠?

I want exchange this money for dollar.
이 돈을 달러로 바꾸어 주세요.

Do you have change for 100 dollar?
Would you change a $100 bill?
100 달러를 잔돈으로 바꾸어 주실래요?

Can I change this bill into coins?
이 지폐를 동전으로 바꿀 수 있습니까?

How would you like it?
How do you like your money?
어떻게 가져가시겠습니까?

Three twenties, three tens and the rest in ones.
20달러 3장, 10달러 3장, 나머지는 1달러로 주세요.

All tens, please.
모두 10달러로 주세요.

Excuse me. Is there a bank nearby?
실례합니다. 근처에 은행이 있나요?

I'm looking for Bank.
Do you know where it is?
은행을 찾고 있는데 어디인지 아세요?

Can I cash my traveler's check?
I'd like to cash this traveler's check.
May I exchange this traveler's check for cash?
여행자 수표를 현금으로 바꿀 수 있나요?

Would you show me your passport?
여권 좀 보여주실래요?

Sign your name here, please.
이곳에 사인을 해주세요.

Is there a cash (an ATM) machine?
현금 지급기가 있을까요?

I'd like to send money to this number.
이 계좌로 송금하고 싶습니다.

I'd like to withdraw (take out) money from my account.
제 계좌에서 돈을 인출하고 싶습니다.

Do you need my identification or passport?
제 신분증이나 여권이 필요하나요?

I'd like to open a bank account.
은행계좌를 만들고 싶습니다.

I want to open a savings account.
예금계좌를 개설하고 싶습니다.

I'd like to open a savings and checking account.
일반 통장과 수표통장을 만들고 싶습니다.

In order to open accounts, do I need to deposit a minimum of $100.
계좌들을 만들려면 최소 100달러 입금이 필요합니까?

I want to deposit $500 in account.
계좌에 500달러를 입금하겠습니다.

Do I need to keep a minimum balance in checking account.
수표통장에 최소 금액을 유지하여야 합니까?

Do I have to maintain at least $100 in my account?
제 계좌에 최소한 100달러를 유지하여야 합니까?

What happens if I can't meet that requirement?
만약 그 조건이 유지가 안 되면 어떤가요?

Will I get a fine?
벌금이 나오나요?

Can I set up my accounts right now?
지금 바로 제 계좌들을 만들 수 있나요?

Can I use my account right away?
바로 지금 제 계좌를 사용할 수 있나요?

I want to make a deposit into my checking account.
수표통장에 입금을 하겠습니다.

I will be depositing cash.
현금으로 입금하겠습니다.

I am depositing a check $1000.
1000달러 수표를 입금하겠습니다.

And I'd like to cash back $500.
그리고 500달러를 현금으로 받을게요.

Should I sign the back of the check?
수표 뒷면에 사인을 해야 하나요?

I would like to order checks.
수표용지를 받고 싶군요.

Do I need to fill out this application?
이 요청서에 기재를 해야 하나요?

Will I receive my checks in the mail a few days later?
며칠 뒤 우편으로 수표용지를 받게 되나요?

I would like to transfer some money from savings account into checking account.
제 일반통장에서 수표통장으로 돈을 송금하고 싶습니다.

I need to transfer $500.
500달러를 송금하겠습니다.

I want to take some money out of my savings account.
일반통장에서 현금을 인출하고 싶습니다.

Let me get $500.
500달러를 주세요.

Cash machine ate my credit card.
현금인출기가 신용카드를 먹었습니다.

What can I do now?
어떻게 하죠?

36. 우체국 (Post Office)

Excuse me. I'm looking for the post office. Do you know where it is?
우체국을 찾고 있는데 어디인지 아세요?

Pardon me. Is there the post office around here?
이 근처에 우체국이 있나요?

Do I have to keep walking straight along this street?
이 길을 따라 쭉 가면 되나요?

I need to send this by mail.
우편으로 이것을 보내고 싶습니다.

I want to send this by parcel post.
이것을 소포로 부치고 싶습니다.

How much does it cost to send this through regular airmail?
일반 소포로 이것을 부치면 얼마이죠?

What is the fastest way to send this parcel?
소포를 보내는 가장 빠른 방법이 무엇이죠?

I want to send this by express mail service.
이것을 빠른 우편으로 보내고 싶습니다.

I'd like to send this package by sea mail.
이 상자를 선박우편으로 보내고 싶습니다.

How much does it cost to send this by sea mail?
이것을 선박우편으로 보낼 경우 얼마이죠?

How much will it cost by air mail?
항공 우편으로 보내면 얼마인가요?

How much is the postage on it?
얼마짜리 우표를 붙여야 하나요?

What's the postage for this?
이것은 얼마짜리 우표를 붙이나요?

Price for parcel depends on the size as well as weight.
소포의 가격은 크기와 무게에 따라 정해집니다.

Container box should be strong enough for the contents.
포장 박스는 내용물에 충분하도록 강해야 합니다.

Is there anything fragile?
깨지기 쉬운 것들이 있나요?

Fragile items should be protected from breaking.
깨지기 쉬운 것들은 깨지지 않게 보호를 해야 합니다.

When you are packing your items, you have to use bubble wrap.
포장할 때 반드시 버블랩을 사용해야 합니다.

Fragile items never touch each other, so you have to fill out your box with cushioning material.
깨지기 쉬운 것들은 같이 부딪히면 안 되므로, 박스 안에 쿠션 물질들을 넣어야 합니다.

213

Please attach a fragile sticker.
파손 조심 스티커를 붙이세요.

Would you like to insure the parcel?
소포를 보험에 들겠습니까?

Do I have to seal mail box with nylon or vinyl tape?
소포를 나일론이나 테이프로 봉해야 하나요?

How long will it take?
얼마나 걸리죠?

37. 도둑 및 범죄
(Getting stolen & Crime)

I was robbed.
강도를 당했습니다.

He is a robber.
그는 강도입니다.

He robbed my wallet. Arrest him.
그가 지갑을 빼앗았어요. 체포하세요.

She is a thief. Pickpocket. Get her!
그녀는 도둑입니다. 소매치기예요. 잡아라!

Help! Thief! Stop him! Get him!
도와주세요. 도둑이야! 잡아요! 잡아라!

Over there. Stop thief!
저기입니다. 도둑 잡아라!

My wallet is gone.
지갑이 없어졌어요.

I think that someone stole my purse.
누가 지갑을 훔쳐간 것 같습니다.

I got my wallet stolen.
I had my wallet stolen.
지갑을 도둑맞았어요.

Someone stole my passport.
누가 여권을 훔쳐갔습니다.

Have you seen anyone suspicious?
의심될만한 사람을 보았나요?

I didn't notice anyone unusual or stranger.
이상한 사람은 보지 못했습니다.

I don't want to accuse you.
당신을 고소하고 싶지 않습니다.

I want to find the best solution.
가장 좋은 해결법을 찾고 싶습니다.

Give me my bag.
제 가방을 돌려주세요.

I don't have expensive items.
비싼 것은 가지고 있지 않습니다.

I'd like to take an action against you.
당신을 고소하겠습니다.

Don't bother me. Leave me alone.
귀찮게 하지 마세요. 내버려 두세요.

I'm going to call the police.
경찰을 부르겠습니다.

I am going to yell.
소리 지를 겁니다.

You'd better go away.
저리 가는 게 좋을 겁니다.

Please, call the police.
경찰 좀 불러주세요.

Thank you for coming, officer.
와 주셔서 감사합니다. 경찰관.

Officer, could you help me, please?
경찰관, 저 좀 도와주세요.

Robber was gone already.
강도는 이미 가버렸습니다.

Someone is following me.
누가 나를 따라오고 있어요.

Someone suspicious is hanging around.
수상한 사람이 서성거리고 있습니다.

Someone hit me and threatened me.
누가 나를 치고 위협했어요.

Would you help me?
I am really scared.
저를 도와주실래요? 정말 무서워요.

I need you are here with me.
저와 같이 있어 주시면 고맙겠습니다.

Would you protect me?
저를 보호해 주실래요?

Will you take me to the safe area?
안전한 곳까지 데려다 주실래요?

I feel relieved.
I feel safe (with you).
안심이 됩니다. (당신과 함께 있으니)

You need to keep in mind that there are thieves in this country.
이 도시에 도둑이 많다는 것을 명심하세요.

Be careful anytime you are in a crowded place.
사람이 붐비는 곳에서는 항상 조심하세요.

Tourist sites are favorite spots for pickpockets.
관광지는 소매치기가 많은 곳입니다.

If you have seen children on the street begging, it's best not to give money.
거리에서 어린이들이 구걸하면 돈을 주지 않는 것이 좋습니다.

You have to take a taxi to your hotel at night.
밤에는 호텔까지 택시를 타고 가세요.

I wouldn't suggest walking around and seeing the sights at night.
밤에 돌아다니거나 구경하는 것은 권하고 싶지 않군요.

Don't walk down the street alone at night. Don't go out after dark.
길을 밤에 혼자 걸어가지 마세요.
어두워지면 나가지 마세요.

Try to stay in well lit areas at night.
밤에 불이 밝은 곳에 있도록 하세요.

You need to keep in mind that crime can happen anywhere.
범죄는 언제든지 발생될 수 있다는 것을 항상 명심하세요.

I'll keep that in mind.
명심할게요.

Officer. Can I make a call to you if I feel scared?
경관님, 무서우면 전화해도 되나요?

38. 분실 (Missing and Loss)

LOST & FOUND

My bag is gone.
제 가방이 없어졌어요.

My bag seems to be missing.
가방을 잃어버린 것 같아요.

I've lost my bag.
가방을 잃어버렸습니다.

I can't find my bag anywhere.
제 가방을 어디에서도 찾을 수 없어요.

I forgot to take my bag with me when I got off the bus.
버스에서 내리면서 가방을 가지고 내리는 것을 잊어 버렸습니다.

I left my bag in the bus.
가방을 버스에 두고 내렸습니다.

I left my wallet in the taxi.
택시에 지갑을 두고 내렸습니다.

Is there any way to find my bag?
제 가방을 찾을 방법이 있나요?

Where is the lost and found center?
분실물 센터가 어디에 있나요?

I've lost my wallet.
지갑을 분실했습니다.

I noticed that my purse was missing a little while ago.
지갑이 없어진 것을 조금 전에 알았습니다.

Hello. Is this the police station?
여보세요. 경찰서이죠?

I would like to report the loss of my bag.
제 가방에 대한 분실을 신고하고 싶습니다.

It contained my wallet and passport.
그곳에는 지갑과 여권이 있었습니다.

There was about $1000 in my wallet, and I had cell phone in there.
지갑에는 천 달러가 있었고 가방에는 핸드폰도 있었습니다.

I've lost my passport.
여권을 분실했습니다.

Where should I report that my passport is missing?
제 여권을 잃어버렸다고 어디에 신고를 하죠?

I'd like to contact Korean embassy.
한국대사관에 연락하고 싶습니다.

I need to go to the Korean embassy to report that right away.
지금 대사관에 신고하기 위해 가야 합니다.

I'd like to make a call to Korean embassy right now.
지금 한국 대사관에 전화하고 싶습니다.

The embassy will be able to help me replace my passport.
대사관에서 여권을 재발급하는데 도와줄 것입니다.

I'd like to get my passport reissued.
제 여권을 다시 발급받고 싶습니다.

How long will it take to reissue?
재발급하는데 얼마나 걸리죠?

39. 여행 중 공감 대화
(Empathy Conversation while Traveling)

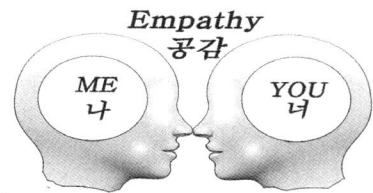

Thank you for all your kindness.
친절에 감사드립니다.

I appreciate all your care.
당신의 후의에 감사드립니다.

I'm very grateful for everything you have done for me.
저에게 베풀어 주신 모든 것에 감사드립니다.

It has been a great help.
큰 도움이 되었습니다.

That would be a great help.
큰 도움이 될 것 같군요.

I'll never forget your kindness.
당신의 친절을 결코 잊지 않겠습니다.

I am happy to help.
도움이 돼서 기쁩니다.

I'll return your kindness one day.
언젠가 보답하겠습니다.

It's my pleasure.
You are welcome.
Not at all.
No trouble at all.
Don't mention it.
괜찮아요. 천만에요.

It's been a good time over here.
이곳에서 좋은 시간을 보냈습니다.

Everyone here seems very friendly.
모두가 매우 친절한 것 같습니다.

Everyone that I've met seems so helpful.
만난 모든 사람들이 도움이 되었습니다.

I have a nice rememberance to my stay. It'll be a nice memory.
지내면서 좋은 추억이 되었습니다.

You seem to be a nice person.
You look like a good person
당신은 좋은 사람인 것 같습니다.

I hope we will be friends.
I hope we can be friends.
친구가 되길 원합니다.

When will(would) you be leaving?
언제 떠나시나요?

Are you interested in joining us?
Would you like to come along with us?
How about going together?
우리랑 같이 가실래요?

Do you want me to go with you?
제가 같이 가길 원하세요?

That would be great.
Sounds good to me.
좋습니다.

I am glad you asked me to join you.
같이 가자고 하니 좋군요.

I'll be happy to come along with you.
같이 가는 것이 저는 정말 기쁠 겁니다.

Thank you for letting me go with you.
당신과 같이 가게 해주어 고맙습니다.

I am happy to meet new people during the travel.
여행중 새로운 사람을 만나면 즐거워요.

I've met various people from all over the world.
세계 여러나라의 사람들을 만났습니다.

I feel refreshed when I travel.
여행을 하면 기분전환이 되는 것 같아요.

You look like so tired.
피곤해 보이는군요.

You look sick. What's the matter?
아파 보이는군요. 무슨 일이죠?

You look a bit under the weather.
Is there something the matter?
Why are you so down?
Is anything the matter?
안 좋아보이시군요. 무슨 일 있나요?

It's been a long day.
I'm just tired.
힘든 하루였습니다. 그저 피곤합니다.

I didn't sleep well last night.
I stayed up all night.
어젯밤 잠을 못 잤어요. 꼬박 새었네요.

It's nothing.
There wasn't much to share.
아닙니다. 별거 없어요.

I'll be alright after some rest.
좀 쉬면 좋아질 것입니다.

You look concerned.
What's the problem?
걱정이 있나 보군요. 무슨 문제죠?

It's not serious, it's minor.
심각한 것이 아닙니다. 단순한 것입니다.

That sort of thing could happen to anyone. You need to calm down.
그런 일들은 누구에게나 일어납니다. 진정할 필요가 있습니다.

Don't take it so seriously.
너무 심각하게 받아들이지 마세요.

Life is much too short to be angry.
인생은 화내기에는 너무 짧아요.

Is there anything I can help you with?
제가 도움이 될 만한 게 있을까요?

I hope all goes well with that.
그것이 잘되기를 바랄게요.

Things are not looking good.
상황이 좋질 않군요.

Things will get better soon.
상황이 곧 좋아질 것입니다.

I've had a very memorable experience while traveling.
여행중 아주 추억이 될 만한 경험을 했네요.

I've had a great time.
I hope we can get together again.
좋은 시간이었습니다. 또 같이하길 바랄게요.

I was having so much fun.
I hope you enjoy the trip.
즐거웠습니다. 즐거운 여행 되세요.

It's been a pleasure traveling with you. I hope you have a safe journey.
It's been fun. Travel safely.
여행 즐거웠습니다. 안전한 여행 되세요.

40. 질병 및 응급상황
(Disease & Emergency Situation)

I need some help. Help.
도움이 필요합니다. 도와주세요.

Something is wrong with my friend.
친구에게 문제가 생겼습니다.

He just collapsed on the floor.
He fell to the ground in a faint.
그가 의식을 잃고 바닥에 쓰러졌습니다.

Call 911.
911를 불러주세요.

Hurry up, please.
서둘러주세요.

Where are you now?
지금 어디에 계시죠?

We are on A Street near B.
B 근처 A 거리에 있습니다.

We will be there right away.
지금 곧 가겠습니다.

Would you help me?
도와주실래요?

I feel car sickness.
I am getting motion sickness.
차멀미가 났어요.

I feel sick.
I am not feeling well.
I'm feeling under the weather.
몸이 좋지 않습니다.

I haven't been feeling well for a few days. I feel achy all over.
며칠간 몸이 좋지 않았어요. 온 몸이 아파요.

I seem to be coming down with a bad cold. I ache all over.
독감에 걸린 것 같습니다. 온 몸이 아프군요.

I have a fever and headache.
열이 나고 두통이 있어요.

I have a cough and runny nose.
기침을 하고 콧물이 납니다.

I have a cold.
I catch a cold.
I am coming down with a cold.
감기에 걸렸습니다.

I have a sore throat.
목안이 아픕니다.

I am running a fever.
열이 납니다.

I have chills.
오한이 납니다.

It looks like I have the flu.
독감에 걸린 것 같습니다.

Headache and the pain really got bad.
두통과 통증이 더 심해졌습니다.

Headache is bothering me.
두통이 저를 괴롭히는군요.

Could I get some Tylenol?
타이레놀 좀 얻을 수 있나요?

Do you have any cold medicine or cough syrup?
감기약이나 기침약 같은 것 있으세요?

I have indigestion.
I think I am suffering indigestion.
소화불량인 것 같아요.

I have an upset stomach.
배탈이 난 것 같아요.

Could I have some medicine for indigestion (an upset stomach)?
소화불량 약이 있나요?

Do you have any medicine to aid digestion?
소화제가 있나요?

I feel nausea.
I feel like vomiting.
메스꺼워요. 토할 것 같아요.

I have been throwing up.
계속 토해요.

A few people from our group get an upset stomach, and everyone thinks it's from the bad meal that we ate. People get food poisoning.
우리 그룹 중에 몇 명이 아픈데, 우리가 먹은 상한 음식 때문이라고 모두 생각합니다. 그들은 식중독에 걸렸습니다.

I am sick to my stomach.
I have a stomachache.
I've got a tummy ache.
My tummy hurts.
My stomach hurts.
배가 아파요.

I have diarrhea.
I've got diarrhea.
설사를 해요.

I ate some rotten food.
I've had diarrhea all night.
상한 음식을 먹고 밤새 설사를 했습니다.

I haven't had a bite since yesterday.
어제부터 아무 것도 먹지 못했습니다.

I have no bowel movements.
I have constipation.
변비가 있습니다.

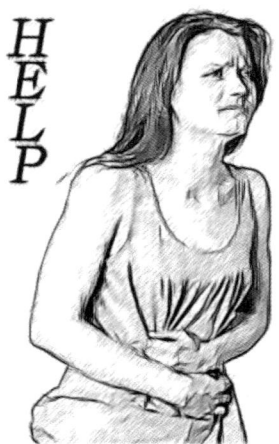

I got sunburn.
햇볕에 화상을 입었습니다.

I have been coughing all day.
하루 종일 기침을 했습니다.

I sprained my ankle.
발목을 삐었습니다.

I think my ankle is broken.
제 생각에 발목이 골절된 것 같습니다.

I think my wrist is sprained or broken.
제 생각에 손목 인대가 늘어났거나 골절된 것 같습니다.

Could I get some painkillers?
진통제를 좀 주실래요?

I am allergic to peanuts.
땅콩에 알러지가 있습니다.

I got a rash and urticaria on my body. I am itching.
몸에 발진과 두드러기가 났는데 간지러워요.

Do you have antihistamines? (allergy pills, allergy medicines)
항히스타민제(알러지 약이)가 있나요?

I got scratched on my face.
얼굴에 찰과상을 입었습니다.

I got a cut on my finger with a knife.
칼로 손을 베었습니다.

Could I have some band aids or plaster?
밴드나 반창고 있나요?

Bleeding is not stopping.
피가 멈추질 않네요.

Could I get some disinfectant?
소독약 좀 주실래요?

My tooth got broken.
치아가 깨졌네요.

I will ask for help if I get any worse.
만약 더 좋지 않으면 도움을 청하겠습니다.

It seems to be getting worse.
점점 더 나빠지는 것 같습니다.

My body aches all over.
온 몸이 아프네요.

I think I need to go to a doctor.
의사에게 가봐야 할 것 같군요.

How do we find a doctor in this country?
이 나라에서는 의사를 어떻게 찾죠?

Do you know how to find a doctor?
의사를 어떻게 찾는지 아세요?

Could you possibly help me get to the hospital?
병원 가는데 도와줄 수 있나요?

I should get checked out at the hospital.
아마도 병원에서 검사해봐야 될 것 같군요.

Where is the nearest hospital?
가장 가까운 병원이 어디죠?

Please, take me to the hospital.
저를 병원에 데려다 주세요.

Where is the nearest pharmacy?
가장 가까운 약국이 어디죠?

I have travel insurance.
여행 보험이 있습니다.

I hope you feel better.
좋아지시길 바랍니다.

I hope it's not serious.
별거 아니길 바랍니다.

I hope you are feeling better soon.
당신이 곧 좋아지길 바랍니다.

We'll take care of you.
우리가 당신을 돌봐드릴 것입니다.

I hope you will get well soon.
곧 좋아지길 바랍니다.

I understand what you're going through.
당신이 당하는 고통을 이해합니다.

You'll be fine.
곧 좋아질 것입니다.

We will do everything we can.
우리가 할 수 있는 것은 다 할 것입니다.

Hello, Is this emergency service center?
응급구조 센터인가요?

We've got a patient.
환자가 있어요.

Patient is extremely ill.
환자는 매우 아픈 상황입니다.

We can't be sure that the patient will pull through.
환자가 이겨낼지 확실하지 않습니다.

Patient is in serious condition.
환자가 심각한 상황입니다.

The patient is dying.
환자는 죽어가고 있습니다.

We need emergency treatment.
긴급치료가 필요합니다.

Could you tell me about the simple method of emergency treatment?
응급조치를 할 수 있는 간단한 방법을 말씀해 주시겠습니까?

Keep the patient warm and elevate the feet.
환자를 따뜻하게 해주고, 다리를 올려주세요.

Apply direct pressure to the wound for several minutes.
상처 부위를 수 분간 눌러 주세요.

Tie the wound with any bandage.
붕대로 묶어주세요.

Anaphylaxis is a life threatening emergency.
과민반응은 생명이 위험한 응급상황입니다.

Take an antihistamine medicine.
항히스타민제를 복용하세요.

Get to the nearest hospital as fast as you can.
가능한 빨리 가장 가까운 병원으로 가세요.

Call 911 for help.
911에 도움을 요청해 주세요.

He(She) seems to be suffering from some medical emergency.
응급상황인 것 같습니다.

Call an ambulance.
앰뷸런스를 불러주세요.

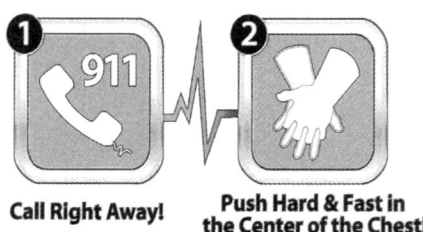

Let's start cardiopulmonary resuscitation (CPR).
심폐소생술을 시작합시다.

He(She) is unconscious.
Shake his(her) shoulders.
의식이 없네요.
어깨를 흔들어 보세요.

Are you OK? Can you hear me?
괜찮으세요? 제 말 들리세요?

He(She) makes no response.
Call emergency center(911).
반응이 없네요. 911 응급센터에 전화하세요.

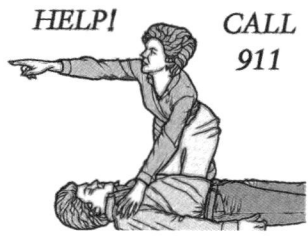

This is American Heart Associa-
tion's Guidelines.
이것이 미국 심장학회 가이드라인입니다.

The order of CPR step is CAB
(Compressions, Airway, Breathing).
심폐소생술 단계는 심장 압박, 기도 확보,
숨 불어넣기 순서입니다.

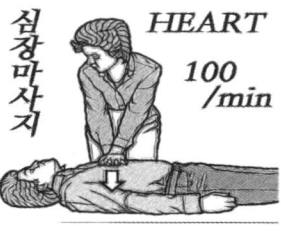

Place two hands over the center of
the chest between the nipples.
양손을 젖꼭지 사이 가슴 중앙에 놓습니다.

Push straight down on the chest at
least 5cm.
가슴을 곧바로 최소 5cm 아래까지 내려가도
록 누릅니다.

Push at a rate of about 100
compressions a minute.
분당 100회 정도의 속도로 누릅니다.

Tilt the head back and lift the chin
forward to open the airway.
머리를 뒤로 하고 턱을 앞으로 하여 기도를
엽니다.

Begin mouth-to-mouth breathing
with pinching the nostrils shut.
코를 잡고 막은 후, 입과 입으로 호흡을 불어
줍니다.

Give two breaths after every 30
chest compressions.
30회 가슴압박, 호흡 2번 식으로 반복합니다.

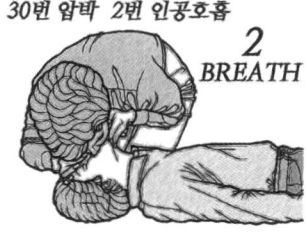

PART III (제 3부)

Basic Practical English for Daily Life

기본적인 일상생활 영어

(41) 인사 (Greetings & Farewell)

Nice to meet you.
Good to see you.
Pleasure to meet you.
Great meeting you.
I am pleased to meet you.
만나서 반갑습니다.

How do you do? (First Meeting)
How are you?
How are you doing?
How have you been?
How is it going?
How are things going?
How are things with you?
안녕하세요.

I am fine. How about you?
I am good. How about yourself?
I've been great. What about you?
I'm doing well. And you?
Not bad. How have you been?
Things are going well. How are you?
Everything is good. How are things with you?
좋습니다. 당신은요?

How are you these days?
How(What) have you been up to?
How is your day going?
What are you up to these days?
How are things these days?
What's new?
What's up? (What's happening?)
요즘 어떠세요?

Everything is great.
Things are going good.
Things are fine with me.
Things have been going well.
모든 것이 좋습니다.

Nothing much.
Pretty much the same.
별일 없어요. 똑같아요.

I've heard a lot about you.
I've frequently heard your name.
당신에 대해서 많이 들었습니다.

I've been wanting to meet you.
I was looking forward to meeting you.
만나 뵙고 싶었습니다.

It's been a long time.
It's been a while.
I haven't seen you in a long time.
Long time no see.
It's been so long.
오랜만이네요.

How long has it been?
얼마만이죠?

It seems like more than 5 years.
5년 이상인 것 같군요.

Good(nice, happy) to see you again.
How have you been?
다시 만나서 반갑네요. 어떠세요?

I've been doing well.
Not too bad.
좋아요.

I've been busy these days.
I've been busy working.
요즘 (일하느라) 바빴습니다.

How is your work these days?
일은 좀 어떠세요?

My business is brisk.
My business is doing well.
일은 잘되고 있습니다.

So-so.
I have a slump in business.
그저 그래요.
사업이 잘 안되네요.

225

It was nice talking to you.
I enjoyed talking to you.
I had fun talking to you.
I've enjoyed conversing with you.
이야기 즐거웠습니다.

It was great to meet you.
It was nice meeting you.
It was nice seeing you.
It was good to see you.
It was a pleasure meeting you.
It was nice to have met you.
만나서 반가웠습니다.

Good bye.
Take care.

Have a good (nice, great) day.
안녕히 가세요.

Good luck and be happy.
행운을 빌어요. 행복하세요.

See you again(later, next time).
다시 만나요.

(42) 대화 및 자기소개
(Conversation & Self Introduction)

Could you speak more slowly?
Would you mind speaking a bit more slowly?
천천히 말씀해 주실래요?

Pardon me?
Come again?
Excuse me?
Say again?
I beg your pardon.
Would you say it again?
What was that again?
뭐라고요? 다시 말해 주실래요?

I can speak a bit of English.
I can speak a little (bit) English.
저는 영어를 조금만 할 줄 압니다.

I can't speak English well.
영어를 잘 하지 못합니다.

I can't express myself very well in English.
영어로 잘 표현하질 못합니다

I can't understand very well in English.
영어를 잘 이해하지 못합니다.

I don't get it.
I don't follow you.
I don't understand.
못 알아들었습니다.

I understand.
I see.
I got it
All right.
알겠습니다.

I don't know
I have no idea.
I am not sure.
모르겠습니다.

It's on the tip of my tongue.
I can't recall it right now.
I can't think of it at the moment.
지금은 생각이 잘 안 나네요.

I think you misunderstood what I said.
제가 말한 것을 오해하신 듯합니다.

I am afraid you don't understand me.
제 말을 이해하지 못하신 것 같군요.

Don't get me wrong.
오해하지 마세요.

I can't remember what it's called in English.
영어로 무엇이라 하는 지 기억이 안 납니다.

What's this called in English?
이것은 영어로 무엇이라고 합니까?

What's the meaning of A.
A의 뜻이 무엇이지요?

Let me introduce myself.
제 소개를 하겠습니다.

My name is －. My family name is － and given name is －.
제 이름은 － 입니다. 성은 － 이고 이름은 － 입니다.

Kim is one of the most common family names in Korea.
김씨 성은 한국에서 흔한 성씨의 하나입니다.

Here is my business card.
여기 제 명함이 있습니다.

I've run out of business cards.
죄송한데 명함이 떨어졌습니다.

I don't have any left.
남은 것이 없습니다.

How do you spell your name?
이름 철자가 어떻게 되시나요?

My name is spelt as －.
제 이름의 철자는 －입니다.

You can call me －.
저를 －로 부르십시오.

Do you mind if I ask your age?
나이를 물어봐도 되겠습니까?

How old are you?
몇 살이시죠?

You look much younger.
나이에 비해 젊어 보이시네요.

How old do you think I am?
제가 몇 살인 것 같아요?

I was bone in Seoul in 1980.
저는 1980년 서울에서 태어났습니다.

I am going to be 36 next month.
다음 달이면 36이 됩니다.

Where are you from?
어디 출신이세요?

I am from Seoul.
저는 서울 출신입니다.

Where did you grow up?
어디서 자라셨어요?

I left my hometown when I was a child.
어렸을 때 고향을 떠났습니다.

Where do you live?
어디에 사시죠?

I am living in Seoul.
서울에서 살고 있습니다.

I've lived most of my life in Seoul.
대부분 서울에서 살았습니다.

I live on the ninth floor of a 15 story apartment.
15층 아파트의 9층에 삽니다.

227

Are you married or single?
결혼 했나요 미혼인가요?

How long have you been married?
결혼을 한지 얼마나 되셨어요?

How large is your family?
가족이 몇 분이세요?

Do you have any children?
아이들이 있나요?

I got married at the age of 29.
29에 결혼을 했습니다.

There are four people in my family.
가족이 모두 4명입니다.

I have a son in elementary school and a baby girl.
초등학교 다니는 아들과 딸이 있습니다.

Are your parents in good health?
부모님들은 건강하신가요?

Are your parents alive and well?
부모님들은 살아계시고 건강하신가요?

My mother is healthy, but father passed away.
어머니는 건강하신데 아버지는 돌아가셨습니다.

Do you have any brothers or sisters?
형제나 자매가 있나요?

I have two older brothers and one younger sister.
형 2명과 여동생 한 명이 있습니다.

I have a younger sister named -.
이름이 -인 여동생이 있습니다.

Is your sister married and has kids?
여동생은 결혼했고 애들도 있나요?

What do you do for a living?
What do you do?
What kind of job do you have?
What's your occupation?
What kind of work do you do?
직업이 무엇이죠?

I am running my own business.
개인 사업을 하고 있습니다.

I work for a company.
회사원입니다.

Which company do you work for?
어떤 회사를 다니시죠?

How many employees do you have in your company?
직장 인원이 얼마나 되나요?

How long have you been in your company (on your current job)?
지금 그 직장에(직업에) 어느 정도 있었나요?

I have been working in the company (at this job) for 7 years.
회사(이 직업)에서 일한지 7년 되었습니다.

What did you major in?
무엇을 전공하였나요?

I attended A University and majored in business administration.
A대학의 경영학을 전공했습니다.

228

(43) 날씨 (Weather)

What's the weather going to be like?
날씨가 어떨까요?

How is the weather going to be?
날씨가 어떨까요?

Did you hear the weather report?
일기예보를 들었나요?

What's the weather like today?
오늘 날씨는 어떤가요?

What's the weather like now?
지금 날씨는 어떤가요?

What's the weather supposed to be like evening?
오늘 저녁 날씨는 어떻다고 하던가요?

How will be the weather tomorrow?
내일 날씨는 어떤가요?

What is the weather report for tomorrow?
내일 일기예보가 어떻던가요?

What's the weather going to be like this weekend?
이번 주말 날씨가 어떨까요?

It's sunny and warm.
맑고 따뜻하군요.

The sky is clear.
하늘은 맑군요.

It's such a nice day.
날씨가 좋군요.

It's very hot outside.
밖이 매우 덥군요.

It's very hot and humid.
덥고 습기가 많네요.

It's very overcast.
매우 흐립니다.

The sky is getting overcast.
하늘이 점점 흐려지네요.

It's cloudy now. There is heavy gray cloud in the sky.
지금 흐린데 회색 구름이 잔뜩 있군요.

It's supposed to rain.
It's going to rain.
It's likely to rain.
It seems likely to rain.
비가 올 것 같군요.

It will probably rain.
Take an umbrella.
비가 올 것 같군요. 우산을 준비하세요.

It's raining.
비가 옵니다.

It's raining heavily outside.
밖에 비가 많이 옵니다.

Rain is coming down heavily out there(outside).
밖에 비가 많이 오는 군요.

It smells so fresh after raining.
비가 온 후 공기가 상쾌하군요.

It's very cold and windy outside.
춥고 바람이 많이 붑니다.

It's 7 degrees centigrade now.
지금 섭씨 7도입니다.

You should wear your jacket.
재킷을 입으세요.

It doesn't look very nice outside.
밖의 날씨가 별로 좋지 않네요.

It's kind of crazy weather outside.
밖의 날씨가 미친 것 같아요.

This weather will not be long.
이 날씨가 오래 가지는 않을 겁니다.

It looks like it may snow soon.
곧 눈이 올 것 같군요.

It's going to be warm.
따듯해 질 것입니다.

Rain is expected tonight.
오늘밤 비가 온다고 하더군요.

It's supposed to be colder tomorrow.
내일은 날씨가 더 추워진다고 하더군요.

The weather forecast said rain will continue for the next few days.
일기예보에서 비가 며칠 동안 계속된다고 하더군요.

It looks like a dry, sunny and warm.
맑고 따듯할 것 같아요.

It's going to be warm this weekend.
이번 주말엔 따뜻할 겁니다

Do you think it will rain tomorrow?
내일 비가 올까요?

I hope not.
그렇지 않길 바랍니다.

Do you think it will clear up tomorrow?
내일 날씨가 맑아질까요?

It's going to be clear and sunny.
It will be sunny tomorrow.
Tomorrow will be a fine day.
내일은 맑고 화창해질 것입니다.

When is it going to be cool?
언제 시원해질까요?

It's going to be hot for the time being.
당분간 더울 것입니다.

Weather is really unpredictable.
날씨는 예측을 못하겠어요.

Temperature are expected to cool off below zero.
기온이 영하까지 떨어진데요.

I hope it doesn't get cold.
I hope it isn't too cold.
I hope it doesn't cool off.
춥지 않으면 좋겠네요.

The weather report says a typhoon (hurricane) is coming.
일기예보에서 태풍이 온다고 합니다.

The typhoon is appraching.
태풍이 가까워졌습니다.

We have to brace for cyclone.
우리는 태풍에 대비해야 합니다.

Tornado watches are issued.
토네이도 주위보가 발령 되었습니다.

Thunderstorm watch is issued.
폭풍우 주위보가 발령 되었습니다.

Refrain from outdoor activities.
Don't go outside.
외출을 삼가해 주세요.

(44) 전화 (phone)

Hello. May I speak to Mr. James?
Hi. Is Mr. James there?
I'd like to speak with Mr. James.
I am calling for Mr. James.
Is Mr. James available?
제임스씨와 통화할 수 있을까요?

Who is calling please?
누구시죠?

This is Mr. Kim.
저는 미스터 김입니다.

Hold on please. (Hold the line.)
I'll transfer the line to him.
잠깐만 기다리세요.
그에게 전화를 연결해 드릴 게요.

He can't come to the phone.
He isn't available now.
전화를 받을 수 없습니다.

He is tied up in the meeting.
He is in a meeting now.
회의에 얽매여 있습니다.

He is not here right now.
그는 지금 여기에 없습니다.

When will he be available?
언제쯤 통화가 가능할까요?

Do you know when he'll be back?
Will he come back soon?
언제 그가 올까요? 곧 돌아오시나요?

He'll be here in this afternoon maybe about 2:00.
아마도 오후 2시경에는 있을 것 같습니다.

Probably he'll be gone for the rest of the day.
아마도 오늘은 퇴근하신 것 같은데요.

May I take a message?
Would you like to leave a message?
메시지를 전해드릴까요?

If you leave a message,
I'll pass it on to him.
메시지를 남기면 전해줄게요.

Could you tell him Mr. Kim called?
미스터 김이 전화했다고 전해주실래요?

I'll tell him that you called.
당신이 전화했다고 전해드릴게요.

Should I have him call you back?
Shall I tell him to call back later?
당신에게 전화를 드리라고 할까요?

Please tell him to call me back.
Could you tell him to give me a call?
전화를 주시라고 전해주세요.

I'll make sure he gets back to you.
당신에게 전화드리라고 꼭 말할게요.

I'll call back later.
나중에 전화 하겠습니다.

What is the best time to call?
어느 시간에 전화 하면 될까요?

Try to call again 30 minutes later.
30분 뒤에 다시 전화해 보세요.

Could I get his mobile number?
그의 휴대폰 번호를 알 수 있을까요?

I have trouble hearing you.
Connection isn't clear.
상태가 좋지 않아 잘 안들리네요.

Signal is bad.
연결상태가 좋지 않네요.

I'll call you this evening.
오늘 저녁에 전화 할게요.

Phone battery has run out.
The battery is dead.
폰 밧데리가 다 되었네요.

Can I use your phone for a minute?
당신의 전화를 잠깐 써도 되겠습니까?

Feel free.
부담 갖지 마세요.

Can I call you sometime?
언제 전화해도 되나요?

Feel free to call me any time.
언제든지 전화 하세요.

Where is the pay phone?
공중전화가 어디에 있죠?

Please get me the extension 77.
내선번호 77번 연결해 주세요.

If you leave a message,
I'll return your call.
메시지를 남기시면 곧 전화 드리겠습니다.

I am busy doing something. I'll get back to you after doing rush-job.
지금 무엇을 하느라 바쁩니다.
급한 일을 끝내고 전화를 드리겠습니다.

(45) 취미 (Hobby)

What do you like to do in your spare time?
What do you enjoy doing in your free time?
What do you like to do for fun?
What kinds of things do you like to do in your spare time?
What do you usually do in your free time?
여가 시간에 주로 무엇을 하세요?

Are there any hobbies you do?
What are your hobbies?
어떤 취미들이 있나요?

I just love taking pictures.
I enjoy taking pictures.
사진 찍기를 좋아합니다.

How many films do you see a month?
한 달에 몇 번 영화를 보죠?

I go to the movies a couple of times a month.
영화를 한 달에 2번 정도 봅니다.

How often do you travel abroad?
얼마나 자주 해외여행을 가나요?

I travel abroad with my family for every summer vacations.
매년 여름휴가 때 가족들이랑 해외여행을 갑니다.

Where did you travel(visit)?
어디를 여행하셨어요?

Have you ever been to Hawaii?
하와이에 가본 적이 있나요?

I've been there once before.
전에 그곳에 한번 가보았습니다.

I've never been there before.
그곳에 가본 적이 없습니다.

What kind of exercise do you usually do?
어떤 운동을 주로 하세요?

What kind of exercise do you like?
어떤 운동을 좋아하세요?

How often do you exercise?
얼마나 자주 운동을 하세요?

What sports do you like?
어떤 스포츠를 좋아하시죠?

Do you play any sports?
하시는 스포츠가 있으세요?

I like watching baseball.
저는 야구를 보는 것을 좋아합니다.

What is your favorite sports team?
가장 좋아하는 팀은 어디죠?

Which team do you root for?
어느 팀을 응원하시죠?

I root for Kia Tigers.
기아 타이거즈를 좋아합니다.

Who is your favorite athlete?
어느 선수를 가장 좋아하세요?

Have you ever been skiing?
스키를 타신 적이 있나요?

I go snowboarding several times every year.
매년 몇 번씩 스노보드를 타러 갑니다.

What do you do to stay healthy?
건강을 유지하기 위해 무엇을 하나요?

When I have time, I sometimes go climbing.
시간이 되면 등산을 갑니다.

Do you have any pets?
애완동물이 있으세요?

I have a puppy.
강아지를 기르고 있습니다.

What is your favorite kind of music?
What kind of music do you enjoy listening to?
What type of music do you like to listen to?
어떤 종류 음악을 들으세요?

I enjoy listening to quiet songs.
조용한 노래를 좋아합니다.

I like listening to KPOP.
KPOP 듣기를 좋아합니다.

Who is your favorite music artist?
좋아하는 가수가 누구죠?

Do you play any instruments?
연주하는 악기가 있나요?

Do you like to play computer game?
컴퓨터 게임을 좋아하나요?

(46) 렌트 하우스 찾기
(Finding Rental House)

I am looking for a room to rent.
(monthly low rent house)
월세방(저렴한 월세집)을 찾고 있습니다.

I'd like to rent a cheap and clean room close to A.
A와 가까운 싸고 깨끗한 방을 구합니다.

I want it, as little as 300 dollars and as much as 500 dollars.
최소 300달러에서 500달러로 원합니다.

How long will it take to find out one bedroom rent house?
원룸 렌트 하우스를 찾는데 얼마나 걸리죠?

I would prefer looking in the afternoon during the week.
이번 주 평일, 오후에 보고 싶습니다.

It is easier for me to take off work in the afternoon.
오후에 일을 쉬기 편합니다.

I have a good feeling about this rent house. But the price is high.
이 렌트 하우스가 맘에 드나 비싸군요.

Let's go look at another rent house.
다른 렌트 하우스를 보도록 하죠.

I want to take a look at that house.
저 집을 보고 싶군요.

How much is the rent?
How much is the monthly rental fee?
렌트료(한달 임대료)가 얼마죠?

That's way too much. It's expensive.
너무 많은데요. 비싸군요.

I was thinking $ -.
-정도로 생각했습니다.

How about $ -?
-가 어떤가요?

I can't pay much more than that.
그보다 많이 지불하지 못합니다.

Can I require the owner to fix the problems?
문제점을 고쳐주라고 집주인에게 요구할 수 있나요?

The problems need to be taken care of. Ask the owner to fix it.
문제점들을 주인에게 고쳐주라고 해주세요.

Hello. Can I speak with the rent house manager, please?
렌트 하우스 매니저와 통화할 수 있을까요?

I'm calling about the rent house on Apple Street.
애플거리에 있는 렌트 하우스 때문에 전화 했습니다.

I was wondering if the rent house is still available.
렌트 하우스가 아직 남아있나요?

I'd like to see it.
그곳을 보고 싶군요.

I am free today at around 3 P.M.
오후 3시경 한가합니다.

Can you make it?
그때 가능한가요?

I can be there at 3 P.M.
오후 3시에 뵙겠습니다.

Do I need to bring identification card or driver's license?
신분증이나 운전면허증이 필요하나요?

I need exact directions.
정확한 위치가 필요합니다.

Could you e-mail me?
이메일을 보내주실래요?

(47) 친구 사귀기 (Making Friends)

How are you feeling these days?
요즘 어떠세요?

I'm doing pretty good.
좋아요.

How about we grab a little lunch?
가볍게 점심 드실래요?

What's your plan for tonight?
오늘 저녁 무엇을 하세요?

I don't have any plans.
계획은 없습니다.

How about we have dinner?
저녁 드실래요?

Where shall we have dinner?
저녁을 어디에서 먹을까요?

What's your favorite food?
좋아하는 음식이 무엇이죠?

Would you like to come over to my house and have dinner with me?
집에 와서 저녁을 같이 드실래요?

How about we have a little get-together?
조촐한 모임이나 할까요?

Let's have a small dinner party at home.
집에서 조촐한 저녁 파티나 하시죠.

I'll bring the wine or beer to a party.
파티에 와인이나 맥주를 가져 갈게요.

Thank you for coming.
와 주셔서 감사합니다.

I am pleased that you have come.
와 주셔서 기쁩니다.

Thank you for inviting me to your dinner party.
저녁 파티에 초대를 해 주셔서 감사합니다.

Come on in. Just drop your coat here and make yourself at home.
들어오세요. 코트를 이곳에 두시고 편하게 지내세요.

Have a bite and see how it tastes.
(Here's a little something for you.)
이것 좀 드셔보세요. (별것 아닌데 드세요.)

I am pleased with this place.
이 장소가 마음에 드는군요.

Are you on vacation here?
이곳에서 휴가를 보내시나요?

Is this your first time here?
이곳이 처음인가요?

How are you enjoying your vacation?
휴가는 재미있게 보내고 계시나요?

I'm having a great time.
저는 즐겁게 보내고 있습니다.

Are you having a good time?
재미있게 보내시나요?

How long will you be staying?
How long are you going to stay?
How long are you going to be here?
얼마나 머무르실 겁니까?

I hope you will have a good time.
좋은 시간 가지세요.

I hope you had a good time.
좋은 시간 가지셨기를 바랍니다.

It's nice to make your acquaintance.
I'm happy to make your acquaintance.
I'm delighted to know you.
It's pleasure to make your acquaintance.
당신을 알게 되어 기쁩니다.

It's fun talking to you.
당신과의 대화가 즐겁군요.

I feel comfortable with you.
당신과 함께 있으면 마음이 편합니다.

I hope our acquaintance would develop further.
우리의 친분이 더 발전하기를 바랍니다.

Let's be friends.
서로 친구가 됩시다.

I hope you and I can be friends.
I hope we can stay friends.
당신과 내가 친구가 되길 바랍니다.

Having good friends is really important to my happiness.
좋은 친구를 가진다는 것은 저의 행복에 중요합니다.

How was today?
오늘 어떠했습니까?

How was your business?
일은 어떠했나요?

Things were going well.
좋았습니다.

So far so good.
지금까지는 좋습니다.

I've actually been busy lately.
최근 바빴습니다.

What a busy day. I'm tied up today.
정말 바쁜 날이네요. 오늘 꼼짝 못 하네요.

I've just been working really hard.
저도 정말 열심히 일했습니다.

I've also been busy.
저도 역시 바빴습니다.

Would you mind if I walk with you?
당신과 함께 걸으면 실례일까요?

No, I don't mind.
아뇨 괜찮습니다.

Yes, please don't.
네 그러지 마세요.

I will be working with you.
당신과 함께 일할 것입니다.

It was nice doing business with you.
It was a pleasure doing business with you.
같이 일을 하여 좋았습니다.

Do you live around here?
이 근처에 사시나요?

Do you live in this city?
이 도시에 사시나요?

What do you like to do to relax?
긴장을 풀기 위해 무엇을 하나요?

What is your favorite drink?
좋아하는 술은 무엇이죠?

How about we grab a beer?
맥주 한 잔 하실래요?

Let's go grab a drink.
Let's have some drinks.
Let's get a drink.
Let's go for a drink.
술 한 잔 하시죠.

Would you ever consider doing travel around the world?
세계여행을 생각해본 적 있으세요?

What are some of your goals?
당신의 목표는 무엇이죠?

What is your dream job?
당신이 꿈꾸는 직업은 무엇이죠?

Are you a saver or a spender?
저축하는 습관이나요? 소비하는 습관이나요?

Do you like to play video games or internet games?
비디오 게임이나 인터넷 게임을 즐기시나요?

Would you please tell me your cell phone number?
휴대폰 번호 좀 알려주실래요?

Let's keep in touch.
연락하고 지냅시다.

If you have any problems, feel free to give me a call.
무슨 문제가 있으면 언제든지 전화 하세요.

Drive safely(safe).
안전하게 운전하세요.

Drive home safely and have a good night.
집까지 안전하게 운전하시고 좋은 밤 보내세요.

Say hello to your family.
가족들에게 안부 전해 주세요.

(48) 약속과 만남
(Appointment & Meeting)

Can I have a few minutes of your time?
May I have a minute of your time?
Can I steal your time?
Can I have a second?
Got a minute?
Have you got some time?
Do you have a minute?
잠시 시간 좀 내 주실래요?

Could I make an appointment with you tomorrow?
내일 약속을 잡아도 될까요?

I wish I could, but I am not available on that day, I have something to do.
그러고 싶지만 할 일이 있어 안 될것 같아요.

When will you be available?
언제 시간이 되시나요?

Do you have any plans for this weekend?
이번 주 계획은 있으세요?

I am free this Saturday.
이번 주 토요일 시간이 됩니다.

Do you have a particular time in mind?
What time do you want to meet?
만나고 싶은 시간이 언제이죠?

What time shall we make it?
What time shall we meet?
When may I see you?
언제 만나는 것이 좋을까요?

Are you free at around 7 P.M?
저녁 7시경 한가하신가요?

Yes, I will be able to make it then.
네, 그때는 괜찮을 것 같습니다.

Where shall we meet?
Where would you like to meet?
어디서 만날까요?

Let's meet at 6 P.M. in front of the Severance mall.
세브란스 몰 앞에서 저녁 6시에 만나시죠.

Sure, I'll see you there then.
그럼 그때 그곳에서 보죠.

Do you know how to get there?
어떻게 가는지 아시죠?

I need directions.
약도가 필요하군요.

Can you send an email for directions?
길 안내를 위한 이메일을 보내 주실래요?

I'll see you later.
나중에 뵙겠습니다.

What time shall I pick you up?
언제 당신을 데리러 갈까요?

I'm sorry I'm a bit late.
I'm late. Sorry about that.
I'm sorry to have kept you waiting.
기다리게 해서 죄송합니다.

I was stuck in traffic.
교통 때문에 막혔습니다.

I got caught in rush-hour traffic.
교통정체가 있었습니다.

It's crowded on the road.
길이 붐비는군요.

It's terribly crowded during rush hours.
러시아워는 정말 붐빕니다.

Traffic is really backed up.
교통이 정말 밀립니다.

Downtown is frequently bumper to bumper.
시내는 길이 자주 막힙니다.

I haven't been waiting long.
얼마 기다리지 않았습니다.

It doesn't matter.
괜찮습니다.

Please, wait a minute.
조금만 기다려 주세요.

I am on my way.
지금 갈게요.

Is someone coming to get you?
누가 당신을 태우러 오나요?

Where would you like me to pick you up?
어디에서 픽업할까요?

I'll give you a ride.
제가 태워다 드리지요.

What time do you need to get there? By what time do you have to be there?
언제까지 그곳에 가야 되죠?

Would you like to meet at the hotel?
호텔에서 만날까요?

I will meet you at the hotel.
호텔에서 만나도록 하죠.

I'll drop you off wherever you need to go.
당신이 원하는 곳에 내려드리겠습니다.

What time do you arrive?
언제 도착하시죠?

I'll be able to pick you up.
당신을 픽업할 수 있을 것 같습니다.

I don't have a ride yet.
아직 탈 차가 없습니다.

May I trouble you for a ride?
Could you give me a lift?
Do you mind giving me a ride?
저를 좀 태워주실래요?

Would you be able to pick me up at hotel?
저를 호텔에서 픽업해 주실 수 있겠습니까?

If you could pick me up at hotel, that would be great.
호텔에서 저를 픽업해 주시면 정말 고맙겠습니다.

I was wondering if you could give me a ride to the airport.
공항까지 저를 태워다 줄 수 있겠습니까?

Can you come in early tomorrow morning?
내일 아침 일찍 오실 수 있으세요?

I have to go to the airport early.
일찍 공항에 가야 합니다.

I'd like you to come in at 7 A.M.
아침 7시까지 와주세요.

239

(49) 데이트 (Dating)

How was your day today?
오늘 어땠나요?

Did you do anything fun?
재미있는 일 있었어요?

Beautiful day today, isn't it?
오늘 날씨가 좋군요. 그렇죠?

Are you doing anything special tonight?
오늘 특별한 일이 있나요?

Do you have a minute?
Can you give me a few minutes?
Do you have some time now?
시간 좀 있으세요?

I'd like to start a conversation with the most beautiful girl in here.
이곳에서 가장 아름다운 여인과 대화를 시작하고 싶군요.

I was wondering if you have some time for me.
저에게 시간을 좀 내주실래요?

Would you like to hang(go) out with me?
저와 데이트를 하실래요?

Can we meet sometime today?
오늘 잠시 만나실 수 있나요?

I was just wondering if you'd like to hang(go) out today.
오늘 데이트 할 수 있을까요?

My friend is having a house party.
친구가 하우스 파티를 합니다.

Are you doing anything fun?
재미있는 일 있으세요?

If you're bored, let's plan on meeting up tonight.
지루하면 저녁에 만날까요?

If you don't have anything planned, I would like to take you to dinner.
계획이 없으시면 저녁이나 같이 할까요?

Could I make an appointment with you if you don't mind?
괜찮으시면 당신과 약속을 잡아도 될까요?

I was wondering you'd like to go out for lunch(dinner) with me.
저랑 같이 점심(저녁)을 드실래요?

I was thinking we could get a bite to eat somewhere nice.
괜찮은 곳에서 같이 간단한 식사나 할까요?

Would you like to go to(for) dinner or something with me?
저와 저녁이나 하실래요?

Are we going to the beach together?
함께 해변으로 갈까요?

Would that be all right with you?
그렇게 하는 게 괜찮겠어요?

I'd like to hang out with you and have a little drink.
당신과 같이 다니며 술 한 잔 하고 싶군요.

Can I buy you a drink?
술 한 잔 살까요?

I get nervous when I talk to girls.
여자들에게 이야기할 때는 긴장을 합니다.

I am looking forward to meeting with you.
당신을 만나길 고대할게요.

What kind of food would you like?
어떤 종류의 음식을 좋아하세요?

Where you would like to go for dinner?
어디서 저녁을 먹고 싶으세요?

Have you been to A restaurant?
A 식당을 가보셨나요?

Do you have any preference for dinner? You pick the place.
저녁식사 좋아하는 곳이 있나요? 정하세요.

How about going to a movie tonight?
오늘밤 영화 보러 가는 게 어떻습니까?

I hear Iron man is supposed to be good. It will be so much fun.
아이언 맨이 괜찮은 것 같다고 들었습니다. 아주 재미있을 것 같습니다.

Have you seen Iron man? I heard it was a good movie.
아이언 맨 봤나요? 그 영화 좋다고 하던데요.

Have you seen the latest Spielberg film? I heard it's fantastic.
스필버그 최신작 보셨나요? 환상적이라고 하던데요.

No, I haven't yet.
아뇨 아직 안 보았습니다.

It was released several days ago. Would you like to go see it with me?
며칠전 개봉했는데 저랑 같이 보러 가실래요?

Is there any fun movies that you might be interested in?
특별히 관심이 가는 재미있는 영화가 있나요?

Do you have a particular time in mind? What time shall we make it?
몇 시가 좋은가요?

Shall we make it at around 6 P.M?
저녁 6시 경으로 잡을까요?

I think it would be good time around 6 P.M. for dinner.
저녁을 위해 오후 6시경이 좋을 것 같습니다.

What's playing?
무엇을 상영하고 있죠?

Who is starring in the movie?
누가 주연이죠?

What's the show time in the evening?
저녁 상영시간이 언제죠?

When is the next show?
그 다음 시간은 언제죠?

I'll be buying tickets in advance.
미리 표를 살게요.

Where shall we meet?
어디에서 볼까요?

I'll see you then.
그때 뵐게요.

I'll be there on time.
제 시간에 그곳으로 가겠습니다.

I appreciate you asking me, but I'm afraid I'm doing something else.
그렇게 물어봐 주니 고맙지만 다른 무슨 일을 해야 할 것 같습니다.

I'm sorry, I already have plans.
죄송합니다. 이미 계획이 있습니다.

There are other things I need to take care of.
해야 할 일들이 있습니다.

I have personal matters(things) that I have to attend to.
처리해야 할 개인적인 일들이 있어요.

I have to get something done.
해야 할 일이 있습니다.

I am a little busy with work.
지금 일 때문에 약간 바빠요.

I'll be in touch, if need be.
필요하면 연락 드릴게요.

Are you working on me now?
저한테 작업거시는 건가요?

I just don't think of you in that way.
이런 방향으로는 생각해본 적이 없습니다.

You are just a business acquaintance.
당신은 그저 사업상 아는 사람입니다.

You are just a friend.
당신은 그저 친구일 뿐입니다.

Someday, you'll meet your soulmate.
언젠가는 마음이 맞는 이를 만날 것입니다.

I don't want to be more than just friends.
친구 이상으로는 원하지 않습니다.

Please stop bothering me.
Please stop pestering(bugging) me.
귀찮게 하지 마세요.

I am sorry to bother you.
I don't mean to be a pest.
귀찮게 해서 죄송합니다.

Let's start off being friends.
먼저 친구로 시작하도록 하죠.

Don't be that way.
Let's still be friends.
그러지 마세요. 친구로 계속 지내죠.

I am really not in the mood.
Can you give me more time?
그럴 기분 아니에요. 시간을 더 주실래요?

Are you seeing anybody right now?
지금 누구를 사귀는 중인가요?

I am seeing someone now.
지금 누구와 사귀는 중입니다.

I haven't met the right man yet.
아직 저에게 맞는 남자를 못 만났습니다.

I'll make sure you have a good time.
즐거운 시간이 된다고 약속할게요.

It will be fun.
재미있을 겁니다.

Sounds good.
It(That) sounds good.
좋습니다.

What's your favorite food?
좋아하는 음식이 무엇이죠?

I like Chinese food the most.
중국 음식을 가장 좋아합니다.

What time shall I pick you up?
What time would you like me to pick you up?
몇 시에 데리러 갈까요?

What time is the most convenient for you?
언제가 가장 편한 시간인가요?

Are you free at around 7 P.M.?
저녁 7시경 한가하신가요?

I've been on the go all day, so I am really tired. Rain check, please.
종일 바빠서 피곤한데 다음 기회로 할게요.

Have you ever been in love?
사랑에 빠진 적이 있었나요?

Do you believe in love at first sight?
첫눈에 반한다는 것을 믿으세요?

What's the first thing you notice about a guy (girl)?
남자(여자)를 볼 때 제일 먼저 어떤 것을 보게 되나요?

Tell me a little about yourself.
당신에 대해서 말해 주세요.

I feel like you seem to have good character.
당신의 성격이 좋은 것 같아요.

I am an introvert by nature.
저는 선천적으로 내성적입니다.

Do you prefer cats or dogs?
고양이나 개 중 어느 것을 좋아하세요?

What's your favorite season?
어느 계절을 좋아하죠?

Do you believe in luck?
I seem to be a lucky guy.
행운을 믿나요? 저는 행운아인 것 같아요.

What is the most valuable thing that you own?
당신이 가지고 있는 가장 소중한 것이 무엇이죠?

How did you enjoy it?
How was today?
오늘 어땠어요?

I hope you had fun.
즐거웠기를 바랍니다.

I am not much of a talker.
저는 말주변이 별로 없습니다.

I had a great time tonight.
I enjoyed spending time with you.
오늘 밤 즐거웠습니다.

It was so great talking to you.
당신과 대화를 나누어 즐거웠습니다.

Would it be possible to see you again?
당신과 다시 만날 수 있을까요?

Can I get your number?
전화번호 좀 주실래요?

Let me give you my number.
제 전화번호를 드릴게요.

Can I call you again?
다시 전화해도 될까요?

(50) 일과 (Daily Work)

What time is it now?
Do you know what time it is?
Have you got the time, please?
Do you have the time, please?
What time do you have?
지금 몇 시죠?

Take a break and have a cup of coffee with me.
잠시 쉬고 커피나 한 잔 하시죠.

That sounds great.
좋습니다.

Can I get you something to drink?
Would you care for something to −?
마실 것 (−) 좀 드릴까요?

No, thank you.
Please don't go to any trouble.
괜찮습니다. 저 때문에 신경 쓰지 마세요.

Would you like some coffee?
Care for some coffee?
커피 좀 드실래요?

I appreciate the offer, but I already ate a little while ago.
고맙습니다만 조금 전에 이미 먹었습니다.

We've been cooped up in here for too long. It's stuffy.
Shall I open the window?
너무 오랫동안 이곳에 갇혀있었네요.
답답하군요. 제가 창문을 좀 열까요?

Let's go to the staff lounge and get a drink or something.
직원 휴게실로 가서 뭐 좀 마십시다.

May I have a light, please?
May I trouble you for a light?
담뱃불 좀 빌려주실래요?

Do you smoke?
담배를 피우시나요?

I don't like smoking.
저는 담배를 싫어합니다.

I am a nonsmoker.
비흡연자입니다.

Smoking is bad for health.
흡연은 건강에 나쁩니다.

Let's go and get some fresh air.
I need to get some air.
신선한 바람 좀 쐽시다.

We've had enough rest.
충분히 쉬었네요.

Let's get started.
Let's be having you.
Let's get on with it.
자, 이제 시작하죠.

How about grabbing a bite?
Let's send out for a Pizza.
(Let's eat something.
 Let's order a Pizza.)
뭐 좀 먹을까요? 피자를 배달시키죠.

What's going on?
What's going on with you?
What's up?
What's up with you?
무슨 일이죠?

It's no matter.
It's nothing.
It's no big deal
별일 아닙니다.

Can you give me more details?
좀 더 자세히 말해주실래요?

Give me the rundown.
상세하게 보고하세요.

Give me a little more time.
It'll take time to go over documents.
시간을 좀 더 주세요.
서류를 검토하려면 시간이 걸립니다.

I need to think it over.
생각할 시간이 필요합니다.

I will tell you further details later.
나중에 더 자세히 말씀 드리겠습니다.

Let's go through the details.
자세하게 살펴봅시다.

I'll do my best until it's finished.
끝날 때까지 최선을 다하겠습니다.

I look forward to a favorable result.
양호한 결과를 기대하겠습니다.

We'll discuss further details later.
We'll talk in more detail later on.
다음에 더 자세하게 상의하도록 하죠.

Please fix this problem quickly.
Please expedite this problem as
soon as possible.
가능한 빨리 이 문제를 처리해 주세요.

Keep me informed of the progress.
일이 어떻게 되어 가는지 계속 알려주세요.

Please keep me posted.
Please keep me up to date.
계속 알려주세요.

You'll get a new assignment today.
당신이 할 새로운 일이 오늘 있습니다.

You won't be the only one under
pressure.
스트레스 받는 사람은 당신만이 아닙니다.

I want to hear your thoughts.
당신의 생각들을 듣고 싶습니다.

Speak your minds.
솔직히 말해보세요.

Do you get how to do this?
이것을 어떻게 하는지 아세요?

Can you help me get a handle on
this?
이것을 처리하는 데 도와주실래요?

Would you help me go through this
problem?
이 문제를 해결하도록 도와주실래요?

When you get a minute, could you
help me?
시간이 날 때 도와주실래요?

I have my hands full at the moment.
I am very busy now.
지금 너무 바쁩니다.

Is it almost finished?
거의 끝나가나요?

I am ahead of you.
제가 더 빠르군요.

It's actually a lot more complicated what it looks like.
보기보다 상당히 복잡하네요.

It'll probably be a little while longer.
시간이 더 걸릴 것 같습니다.

Let's go through this bit by bit.
이것을 조금씩 해결해보죠.

You performed very well in this business.
이번 일은 아주 잘했습니다.

Teamwork is the key to success.
팀웍이 성공의 열쇠입니다.

My favorite old saying is 'Nothing ventured, nothing gained'.
제가 좋아하는 격언은 '모험이 없으면 얻는 것이 없다'입니다.

My motto is 'No pains, no gains'.
제 모토는 '고생해야 얻는다' 입니다.

Thank you for your praise.
칭찬 감사합니다.

Let's call it a day.
Let's get off work.
Let's wrap it up.
It's quitting time.
그만 끝내죠.

Unless there is anything else, I am leaving for the day.
다른 일이 없으면 퇴근하겠습니다.

Can I ask about your private life?
What's your lifestyle?
사생활을 물어봐도 될까요?
생활습관이 어떻게 되죠?

I get up at around 6 in the morning and go to bed at midnight.
아침 6시경 일어나 밤 12시에 잠을 잡니다.

I am used to getting up early in the morning.
아침에 일찍 일어나는 습관이 있습니다.

I sometimes sleep late (oversleep) in the morning.
간혹 아침에 늦잠을 잡니다.

I oversleep until almost noon on Sunday.
일요일에는 거의 정오까지 늦잠을 잡니다.

I don't usually have breakfast.
아침은 잘 안 먹습니다.

I eat something light for breakfast.
아침은 간단한 것으로 먹습니다.

How was your weekend?
주말은 잘 보냈나요?

I spent the weekend doing nothing at home.
주말에 아무 것도 안하고 집에서 보냈습니다.

I am used to showering before bed.
자기 전에 샤워하는 습관이 있습니다.

I am busy taking care of my children every day.
매일 아이들을 돌보느라 바쁩니다.

I am used to living alone.
저는 혼자 사는데 익숙합니다.

How long does it take to get to your office?
사무실까지 가는데 얼마나 걸리죠?

How long is your commute?
통근 시간이 얼마나 걸리죠?

My commute time is about one hour.
통근 시간이 한 시간 정도 됩니다.

I go to work by subway.
지하철로 출근합니다.

What are your working hours?
근무시간이 어떻게 된가요?

I work 8 hours from 9 to 6, five-day workweek.
주 5일제, 9시부터 6시까지 8시간 일합니다.

We have one hour's lunch break.
점심시간은 한 시간입니다.

Let's do lunch sometime. My treat.
언제 점심이나 하죠. 제가 낼게요.

I have a few favorite restaurants near the company.
회사 근처에 자주 가는 식당들이 있습니다.

Let's hang out sometime.
언제 한 번 같이 놀죠.

Let's hang out soon.
조만간 한 번 보죠.

What are you going to do tonight?
오늘 밤 무엇을 하세요?

I plan on meeting friends.
친구들을 만나려고 합니다.

I am going to go to a night club.
나이트클럽에 가려고 합니다.

Do you have any plans for this weekend?
주말에 무슨 계획 있으세요?

I am going to meet some friends.
친구를 만나려고 합니다.

If you don't have anything special, how about meeting and hanging out?
특별한 일이 없으면 같이 만나서 놀까요?

Are you fond of drinking?
술 마시는 것을 좋아하나요?

I am a moderate drinker.
술을 적당히 마십니다.

How about a drink? Do you have a favorite hang out?
술 한 잔 어때요? 자주 가는 곳이 있나요?

Let's go grab a couple of beers.
맥주나 몇 잔 하시러 가죠.

Go first. I'll catch up with you soon.
먼저 가시면 곧 따라 갈게요.

Do you feel alone sometimes?
간혹 외로우세요?

If you look for the love, love actually is all around.
사랑을 원하면 사랑은 주변에 널려 있어요.

If you look for the love,
　　love actually is all around.

　　사랑을 원하면
　　　사랑은 주변에 널려 있어요.

APPENDIX 부록

Visiting Korea
한국 방문

Time really goes like the wind and clouds.
시간은 바람과 구름처럼 흐른다.
Months have passed and autumn, the fall of the leaf, is here.
달이 지나고 낙엽이 떨어지는 가을이 왔다.
Charlotte has come to Korea for vacation.
샬럿이 휴가차 한국에 왔다.

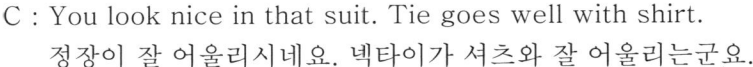

C : Hi. Is everything going OK with you?
　안녕하세요? 잘 지냈어요?

K : Things are great.
　좋습니다.

C : You look nice in that suit. Tie goes well with shirt.
　정장이 잘 어울리시네요. 넥타이가 셔츠와 잘 어울리는군요.

K : Thank you. That's a cute dress, blue really suits you.
　　How long will you stay in Korea?
　감사합니다. 옷이 멋있네요. 푸른색이 어울리는군요.
　한국에 얼마나 머물 예정이나요?

C : One week. What's the weather going to be like today?
　일주일요. 오늘 날씨는 어떤가요?

K : Weather forecast predicts sunshine.
　　What would you like to see in Korea?
　일기예보에서 화창하다고 하더군요.
　한국에서 어떤 것들을 보고 싶으세요?

C : Any place in Korea is fine.
　한국에 있는 어느 곳도 좋아요.

K : Where would you like to go in Seoul?
　　There are many attractions in Seoul.
　서울에서는 어디를 가고 싶으세요?
　서울에는 매력적인 곳이 많아요.

C : Anywhere. Is there a particular place?
　　어디든지 좋아요. 특별한 곳이 있나요?
K : I recommend you to go the National Museum of Korea and the traditional royal Gyeoungbok palace. These places are located nearby at your hotel.
　　국립박물관과 오래된 왕궁인 경복궁을 추천합니다.
　　이곳들은 당신이 머무르는 호텔 가까운 곳에 있습니다.
C : I'd like enjoy visiting museums.
　　박물관들을 가보고 싶네요.
K : The National Museum is the largest museum in Korea. You can feel the story of Korea's fascinating history, from ancient days to the modern era. Gyeongbok palace was the main seat of power for kings throughout 500 years. Gyeongbok means Shining Happiness or Great Good Fortune. The National Folk Museum sits in the northern section of the palace.
　　국립박물관은 한국에서 가장 큰 박물관입니다.
　　고대에서 현대까지의 매혹적인 한국의 역사를 느낄 수 있습니다.
　　경복궁은 500년 동안 왕들이 힘을 누렸던 곳입니다.
　　경복이란 큰 복 또는 큰 행운이란 뜻입니다.
　　국립 민속박물관은 경복궁 북쪽에 있습니다.

C : Where is the most famous shopping district in Seoul?
서울에서 쇼핑으로 가장 유명한 곳이 어디죠?
K : Myeongdong is the city's best known shopping destination for tourists. You can buy fascinating goods and hunt around for the latest trends. And shops along the street are worth browsing. Narrow alleyways lined with outdoor clothing stalls attract tourists. And there are also many new, creative items include shoes, hats, bags, vintage wears and accessories.
명동은 관광객들에게 쇼핑지로 알려진 곳입니다. 매혹적인 상품을 사거나 최신 유행을 구경할 수 있습니다. 그리고 거리를 따라 있는 가게들은 구경할 가치가 있습니다. 의류 가판대가 있는 좁은 골목들이 관광객들을 유혹하죠. 그리고 신발, 모자, 가방, 의류, 액세서리 등 많은 새로운 물건들도 있습니다.
C : I'm looking for a shop that sells inexpensive dresses. James told me that Dongdaemun market is good for a little shopping.
저렴한 옷들을 파는 가게를 찾고 있어요. 제임스가 동대문시장이 가볍게 쇼핑하기 좋다고 하더군요.

K : Dongdaemun is also one of the most famous shopping areas. Many fashion outlets attract nocturnal Korean and foreign shoppers due to low cost. Dongdaemun Market has more than 20 large shopping malls. A full range of fashion items that cover head to toe, are found in there at inexpensive and reasonable prices. Maybe it would be fun to go there.
동대문 역시 서울에서 가장 유명한 쇼핑 장소입니다. 많은 패션매장들이 낮은 가격으로 밤에 쇼핑하는 한국인과 외국인들을 유혹하죠. 동대문시장에는 20개가 넘는 큰 쇼핑몰들이 있습니다. 머리에서 발끝까지 모든 유행제품들을 싼 가격에 발견할 수 있습니다. 동대문 가게들은 가격이 상당히 싸고 합리적입니다. 아마도 그곳에 가면 재미있을 것입니다.

C : Thank you so much for all of the information.
여러 가지 정보 정말 감사해요.

K : You might be surprised how many shops they can fit in such a little space.
아마도 그 작은 공간에 얼마나 많은 가게들이 있는 지 놀랄 것입니다.

C : I am looking forward to it.
기대가 되는군요.

K : I'll show you around Insadong right now.
지금 인사동을 안내해 드릴게요.

C : Insadong? What is there to see?
인사동? 그곳에 볼 것이 있나요?

K : Insadong is a popular place where traditional Korean goods are on display. It's a good place to learn about Korean traditional culture. There are many galleries, traditional restaurants, craft shops and teahouses. Galleries have abundant traditional Korean paintings and sculptures.
인사동은 한국의 전통 상품들이 있는 유명한 곳으로 전통 문화에 대해 배우기 좋습니다. 많은 화랑들과 전통음식점, 기념품 가게, 찻집들이 있는데 화랑들에 한국전통의 그림들과 조각품들이 많습니다.

C : I love to go there.
그곳에 가고 싶군요.

K : You won't regret going to there. Let's take a taxi.
그곳에 간 것을 후회하지 않을 것입니다. 택시를 잡죠.

C : How far from here?
이곳에서 얼마나 멀죠?

K : Insadong is located in the middle of Seoul.
It will take 5 minutes if there are no traffic jams.
인사동은 서울 중심부에 있어요.
교통정체만 없다면 5분 정도 걸립니다.

C : It's not far from here.
이곳에서 멀지 않군요.

K : We are almost there. Let's get off. Look there.
 Insadong is a narrow corridor with antique shops,
 small galleries, craft shops and Korean restaurants.
 Let's look around briefly.
거의 다 왔습니다. 내리시죠. 저기를 보세요.
인사동은 골동품이나 화랑, 공예품 가게, 한국식당들이 있는 좁은 길입니다. 간단하게 둘러보죠.

C : Insadong is a really nice place. The old and the new coexist.
인사동은 정말 좋은 곳이군요. 전통과 현대가 공존하고 있군요.

K : This spiral-shaped mall of craft shops is Ssamzie-gil.
공예품 가게들이 나선형으로 있는 이곳이 쌈지길입니다.

C : Very impressive.
매우 인상적이군요.

K : There are many traditional handcrafts.
전통 공예품들이 많습니다.

C : These traditional masks are very unique and jewelry boxes are also very beautiful.
이 전통 탈들이 독특하고 보석함들도 매우 아름답군요.

K : Do you want to buy some souvenirs?
Teapots and cups are popular items for gifts.
기념품을 사고 싶으신가요?
찻주전자나 찻잔들이 선물로도 인기가 있습니다.

C : I have no idea what to buy for my niece.
조카에게 무엇을 사주어야 할 지 모르겠군요.

K : What kind of things does she like?
그녀가 어떤 것을 좋아할까요?

C : Well, she really likes pretty dolls.
예쁜 인형을 정말 좋아해요.

K : I am thinking that handmade Korean dolls dressed in native Korean clothes would be good.
한국 전통의상을 입은 인형이 좋을 거라 생각합니다.

C : Yes. But Korean personal ornaments are very impressive.
예. 하지만 한국의 장신구들이 인상적이군요.

K : I'm sure your niece will also love it.
조카 역시 그것도 좋아할 것입니다.

C : I'll take this traditional accessory.
이 전통 액세서리를 살게요.

K : It's good.
좋군요.

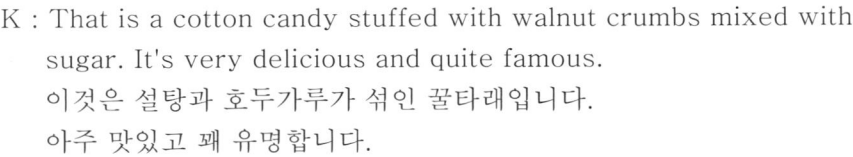

C : Look at that. What's that?
저기 좀 보세요. 저것은 무엇이죠?

K : That is a cotton candy stuffed with walnut crumbs mixed with sugar. It's very delicious and quite famous.
이것은 설탕과 호두가루가 섞인 꿀타래입니다.
아주 맛있고 꽤 유명합니다.

C : Hand skill is great.
손기술이 훌륭하군요.

K : Yes. Let's taste.
예. 맛을 보죠.

C : It's sweet and fantastic.
맛이 달콤하고 훌륭하군요.

K : How about having a cup of coffee and get some rest.
커피 한잔 하고 잠깐 쉬죠.

C : OK. I'm thirsty.
네. 목말라요.

K : Let's go there.
　　저곳으로 가죠.
C : Oh, that building is very oriental stylish.
　　아, 저 건물은 참 동양적이군요.
K : Yes. Let's go inside.
　　네. 안으로 들어가죠.
C : Well, Korean traditional cafe is really unique.
　　음, 한국 전통 찻집은 정말 독특하군요.
K : Korea has a tea based culture.
　　Now Coffee is gaining incredible popularity in Korea.
　　Coffee is actually part of Korean culture nowadays.
　　Most of the Koreans love coffee and you can find coffee
　　vending machines all over the street.
　　한국은 차 문화가 깊은 곳입니다.
　　지금은 커피가 한국에서 굉장한 인기를 끌고 있습니다.
　　커피는 사실 이제 한국문화의 하나입니다.
　　대부분의 사람들이 커피를 좋아하고 어느 거리에서든 커피자판기를
　　볼 수 있습니다.
C : There is no doubt that people all over the world love coffee.
　　세상 모든 사람들이 커피를 좋아하는 것은 틀림없어요.
K : The recent rise in the bean's popularity and growth of coffee
　　shop is due to young people. Starbucks is the most famous
　　and popular coffee shop in Korea. But Korea's fastest growing
　　coffee chain like Caffe Bene has gained a lot of popularity.
　　커피에 대한 최근의 유행과 커피숍들이 많은 이유는 젊은 사람들 때문
　　인데 스타벅스가 한국에서 가장 유명하고 인기가 많습니다. 하지만
　　빠르게 성장하고 있는 한국의 카페베네와 같은 커피 체인들이 인기를
　　얻고 있습니다.

C : There is hard competition among coffee chains in the US.
They are trying to deliver the best customer service.
미국의 커피 체인들 간에도 경쟁이 치열해요.
고객들에게 최상의 서비스를 제공하려고 노력하고 있죠.

K : By the way, do you want to get a city skyline view from the Seoul Tower?
그건 그렇고 서울 타워에서 시경을 구경하고 싶으세요?

C : Yes. I'd like to visit there.
네. 그곳을 보고 싶어요.

K : I'll show you. Seoul Tower is located in Namsan mountain.
But the car is not permitted to enter.
We have to use the cable car or ride a circulation bus.
Let's go there.
제가 보여 드리죠. 서울 타워는 남산에 있습니다.
하지만 차는 들어 갈 수 없습니다. 케이블카를 이용하거나
순환 버스를 타야 됩니다. 그곳으로 가시죠.

The weather is gorgeous
and the scenery is fantastic.
날씨도 좋고 경관도 훌륭했다.
She enjoys the view of the city
from Seoul Tower with a look of excitement.
그녀는 서울타워에서 도시 경관을
즐겁게 구경했다.

C : I love everything I am seeing here.
Sometimes I'd like not to go back to the real world.
여기서 지금 보는 것들이 다 사랑스럽네요.
때로는 현실세계로 돌아가고 싶지 않곤 해요.

Her blond hair is blowing in the wind, shining like sunlight.
그녀의 금발머리가 바람에 흔들리고 햇빛처럼 빛났다.
I am standing by her for a while in silence, lost in my own thoughts.
나는 잠시 생각을 잊고 조용히 그녀 곁에 서 있었다.

We have a dinner at a nearby Korean Restaurant.
우리는 근처 한국식당에서 저녁을 먹었다.

K : This is a good place for Korean food.
   It's not very big, but it's always busy.
   이곳이 한국음식이 좋은 곳입니다.
   크지는 않지만 항상 붐비는 곳입니다.
C : It's a nice place.
   좋은 곳이로군요.
K : Please, take off your shoes. Let me take your jacket.
   I'll hang it up.
   신발을 벗고 재킷을 주세요. 걸어 드릴게요.
C : Thank you.
   감사해요.
K : Please sit comfortably on a cushion with legs crossed.
   If you feel any discomfort, sit with both legs extended forward.
   다리를 구부려 방석에 편히 앉아요. 불편하시면 다리를 펴고 앉으세요.

C : OK.
　　알겠어요.
K : This restaurant has a variety good dishes and offers delicious foods.
　　이 음식점은 음식들이 다양하고 맛있습니다.
C : Atmosphere is really good.
　　분위기가 좋군요.

K : There are many side-dishes.
　　음식들이 많습니다.
C : Every dish is delicious.
　　음식들이 다 맛있네요.
K : Enjoy your meal and have as much as you want.
　　많이 드십시오.
C : Thank you.
　　고마워요.
K : How about Kimchi to go with your rice?
　　밥에 김치를 함께 먹는 게 어떻습니까?
C : Sure. But Kimchi is very spicy.
　　좋아요. 하지만 김치는 아주 매워요.
K : Yes, it is. But it will not spicy if you are eating with rice.
　　네 그렇습니다. 밥과 같이 먹으면 그렇게 맵지 않을 것입니다.
C : OK.
　　알았어요.
K : Koreans love it and eat it at every meal. Kimchi contains abundant vitamins, minerals, fibers and lactic acid bacteria. Therefore Kimchi promotes the functions of the digestive track.
　　한국인들은 이것을 좋아하고 매일 식사 때 먹습니다.
　　김치는 비타민과 무기질, 섬유질, 유산균들이 아주 풍부합니다.
　　그러므로 김치는 소화기능을 증진 시킵니다.

C : Are there many different recipes for Kimchi according to region?
지역에 따라 김치를 만드는 법이 다른가요?

K : Yes. You might taste various kinds of Kimchi in Korea.
네. 아마도 한국에서 다양한 김치를 맛보실 수 있을 것입니다.

C : I am not used to eat spicy food.
전 매운 음식을 먹는 것에 익숙하지 않아요.

K : Kimchi is unfamiliar at first, but if you have acquired taste, you will miss the flavor of Kimchi. It's like a good old Western cheese flavor. How do you like it?
김치는 처음에 이상하지만, 일단 맛을 알면 김치의 향이 그리워질 것입니다. 마치 오래된 좋은 서양의 치즈향기 같습니다. 어떠세요?

C : It's eatable.
먹을 만해요.

K : Why don't you try Bulgogi? Bulgogi is Korean beef barbecue. I am sure it will be delicious.
불고기를 먹어 보세요. 불고기는 한국식 소고기 바비큐입니다. 맛있을 것이라 장담합니다.

C : It's delicious.
맛있군요.

K : Try to make Ssam. Ssam means wrapped meat with leaf vegetables. Put some meat and soybean paste on the lettuce or leaf of sesame. Fold together and put it into your mouth. How does it taste?
쌈을 만들어 보세요. 쌈이란 야채로 고기를 싼다는 말입니다.
고기와 된장을 상추 또는 깻잎에 올리세요.
함께 접어서 입안에 넣으세요. 맛이 어떻습니까?

C : It tastes pretty good. Do you like to cook?
아주 맛이 좋아요. 요리하길 좋아하세요?

K : No I don't. I just can cook instant noodles.
   Are you good at cooking?
아닙니다. 라면만 할 줄 압니다. 요리를 잘하세요?

C : Yes, I love to cook.
네. 요리하길 좋아해요.

K : Can I offer you some Korean seasoned vegetables, Namul?
한국 양념채소인 나물을 좀 줄까요?

C : Yes. That looks yummy.
네. 맛있게 보이네요.

K : How about a drink?
These foods go well with Korean Vodka, Soju.
술을 한 잔 할래요? 이 음식들은 한국의 보드카인 소주가 제격이죠.

C : OK. James told me Korean national booze is Soju.
좋아요. 제임스가 한국의 국민 술은 소주라고 말하더군요.

K : Soju is one of the top beverages in Korea.
   How much do you usually drink?
소주는 한국에서 가장 잘 팔리는 술 가운데 하나입니다.
주량이 얼마나 되세요?

C : I enjoy drinking, but I am a slow drinker.
술은 좋아하지만 천천히 마시는 편이에요.

K : Me too. Koreans have a unique custom of sharing a glass when drinking. Never pour your own drink. After drinking up your glass, you pass it to me and fill it with the Soju. This is regarded as the symbol of friendship.
저도 그렇습니다. 한국인들은 술을 마실 때 나누는 습관이 있지요. 혼자 술을 스스로 따르지 마세요. 잔을 다 마신 후 저에게 잔을 건네고 소주를 채워 주세요. 이것은 우정의 표현이지요.

C : OK. It's unique drinking custom.
　　But why do you hold your glass with both hands?
　　알았어요. 독특한 음주문화이군요.
　　그런데 왜 잔을 두 손으로 잡아요?

K : It is a gesture of respect. When pouring for someone older than
　　you, put one hand to your pouring arm as a sign of respect.
　　When you offer a drink, give your glass with both hands.
　　존경의 표시입니다. 나이가 더 많은 분에게 잔을 따를 때도 존경의
　　표시로 한 손을 다른 손에 대고 따르세요. 잔을 권할 때는 두 손으로
　　잔을 잡고 주세요.

C : I understand. Koreans have polite drinking etiquette.
　　이해가 되네요. 한국인들은 예절 바른 음주 문화가 있군요.

K : Let's toast.
　　건배합시다.

C : Cheers!
　　건배!

K : Your glass is empty.
　　Would you like another drink?
　　잔이 비었군요. 한 잔 더 할래요?

C : Please, fill a glass halfway.
　　반만 채워 주세요.

K : Shall we order more food?
　　좀 더 음식을 주문할까요?

C : I've had plenty. Well, I think I am getting drunk.
　　많이 먹었어요. 음, 술이 좀 취하는군요.

K : I've had enough too. Did you enjoy Korean food?
　　저도 충분합니다. 한국 음식 괜찮았습니까?

C : Yes, I enjoyed it. The food was very wonderful.
　　I am really impressed with various foods.
　　네 좋았어요. 음식도 아주 훌륭했고 다양하여 정말 인상이 깊었어요.

K : I had a good day.
좋은 하루를 보낸 것 같네요.
C : It's been great talking with you.
대화가 즐거웠어요.
K : I really enjoyed talking to you.
당신과 이야기하는 게 좋았습니다.
C : Thank you for treating me to dinner.
저녁을 대접해 주셔서 감사해요.
K : It's my pleasure.
제가 좋아서 한일인데요.
C : I'll treat you next time.
다음에는 제가 대접을 할게요.
K : Try to enjoy yourself in Korea. I'll be tied up with my work
all day tomorrow, so let's meet the day after tomorrow.
This is Seoul tour and subway map. I put a mark on the map for
tourist attractions. I hope this will be of help to you.
I'll call you tomorrow night.
한국에서 재미있게 보내세요. 내일은 일 때문에 하루 종일 묶여 있어
모레 보도록 하죠. 이것은 서울 여행지도와 지하철 노선도입니다.
관광지를 지도에 표시해 놨어요. 이것이 당신에게 도움이 되길 바래요.
내일 밤에 전화할게요.

After returning home,
I take off my clothes, get into bed,
and lie there for a long time, staring at the ceiling,
thinking about her and the things we'd said to each other.
집으로 돌아온 후
옷을 벗고 침대에 오랫동안 누워
천장을 응시하며, 그녀와 함께했던 대화들을 생각했다.

Two days later, the sun comes up over the city,
I stand looking at various clouds
across the sky on my way to work.
이틀 후 태양이 도시 위로 떠올랐고
나는 출근하는 도중 잠깐 서서 잠시 하늘의 다양한 구름들을 보았다.

How long do I have to repeat the same things in this city?
이 도시에서 얼마나 계속 반복되는 일을 하여야 할까?
How can I cut the Mobius strip of my daily life
to change my future?
미래를 변화시키기 위해서
나는 어떻게 일상적인 삶의 뫼비우스 띠를 끊어야만 할까?
Maybe one day I'll want something different,
but not now.
아마도 언젠가는 다른 무언가를 원하겠지만
지금은 아닌 것 같다.

After finishing my half a day's work,
I meet Charlotte at 2 P.M. at COEX Mall.
오전 일과를 마친 후, 나는 오후 2시에 샬럿을 코엑스몰에서 만났다.

K : I'm sorry I'm a bit late.
   I took a bus, but I got caught in traffic jam.
   As you know, Seoul is terribly crowded.
   미안합니다. 조금 늦었습니다. 버스를 탔는데 교통정체가 있었습니다.
   당신도 알다시피 서울은 정말 붐빕니다.
C : Don't worry. I haven't been waiting long.
   Seoul seems to be frequently bumper to bumper.
   But public transport system in Seoul is very good.
   괜찮아요. 얼마 기다리지 않았어요. 서울은 길이 자주 막히는 것
   같아요. 하지만 서울의 대중교통은 아주 좋아요.
K : Did you easily find the way here?
   이곳을 쉽게 찾았나요?
C : Yes. Your directions were very clear. How was your day?
   당신이 알려준 길이 맞더군요. 오늘은 어땠어요?
K : Things were going well. What did you do in the morning?
   좋았습니다. 아침에는 무엇을 했습니까?
C : I had overslept until noon.
   정오까지 늦잠을 잤어요.
K : What did you eat for lunch?
   점심은 무엇을 먹었나요?
C : Toast and some orange juice.
   토스트와 오렌지 주스를 먹었어요.
K : What do you think of this city?
   이 도시가 어떻던가요?

C : It has many fine buildings. And the river that flows through the center of Seoul is very impressive and fascinating.
건물들이 멋진 것들이 많아요. 그리고 서울 중심을 지나는 강이 매우 인상적이고 매혹적이에요.

K : Yes. The scenery of Hangang(Han river) is very beautiful.
예. 한강의 경치는 매우 아름답습니다.
C : Seoul is active and dynamic city. I love atmosphere of this city.
서울은 활기차고 역동적인 도시더군요. 이 도시의 분위기가 좋아요.
K : I'm glad to hear that.
그 말을 들으니 기쁘군요.
C : I would like to take a look around more.
Are there any interesting places nearby?
더 둘러보고 싶어요. 근처에 볼 만한 곳이 있나요?
K : Did you look around Lotte department store & DDP yesterday?
어제 롯데 백화점과 동대문 디자인 플라자를 둘러봤나요?
C : Yes. Dongdaemun is really amazing. It's full of shops with so many things for sale.
네 동대문이 수많은 상품들을 파는 가게들로 가득 차서 정말 놀랐어요.

K : Did you have a good time in the department store?
  백화점에서는 재미있었나요?
C : Yes. I had fun at the store.
  It's one of the best place to kill time.
  Lotte company's 123-floors skyscraper is awesome.
  네. 즐거웠어요. 시간을 보내기에 아주 좋은 곳이더군요.
  롯데의 123층 고층빌딩은 굉장하더군요.

  By the way, I heard that most Korean temples are located at mountain valleys. Are there any temples in Seoul?
  그런데요 대부분의 한국의 절들은 산기슭에 있다고 들었는데, 서울에 혹시 절들이 있나요?
K : Of course. There are several famous temples in Seoul.
  물론이죠. 서울에는 여러 유명한 절들이 있습니다.
C : I can hardly wait to see it.
  지금 보고 싶군요.
K : Bongeunsa Temple is very close to here.
  It's right across the street.
  봉은사는 이곳 근처에 있습니다. 바로 길 건너편에 있어요.
C : Is it worth seeing?
  볼만하나요?

K : Yes. It's one of Seoul's largest and most impressive temples.
There is a 23m tall statue of Buddha.
네. 봉은사는 서울에서 크고 인상적인 절 중 하나입니다.
그곳에는 23m 부처상이 있지요.

C : I wonder what it looks like.
어떻게 생겼는 지 궁금해요.

K : Are you familiar with Buddhism?
불교에 대해 잘 아세요?

C : I know a little bit.
조금 알아요.

K : How did you get interested in Buddhism?
어떻게 불교에 대해 관심을 갖게 되셨죠?

C : Meditation is highly developed in Buddhism.
Sometimes, I try to meditate for my internal peace.
It purges away my complicated thoughts.
명상은 불교에서 아주 발달되었어요.
가끔 제 내부의 평화를 위해 명상을 하곤 해요.
복잡한 생각들을 정화시켜 주더군요.

K : Meditation is good for you. I also like it.
명상은 참 좋죠. 저 역시 명상을 좋아합니다.

After looking around COEX Mall,
we go to the Bongeunsa Temple.
코엑스몰을 둘러본 다음 봉은사로 갔다.

K : I was wondering if you'd like to taste some special Korean food.
조금 특별한 한국음식을 맛보시겠습니까?

C : I love most Asian food after meeting you.
당신을 만난 후로 대부분의 아시아 음식을 좋아해요.

K : OK. Let's start your culinary adventure in Korea.
　　알겠습니다. 한국에서의 음식 모험을 시작해보죠.

C : Sounds good to me.
　　좋아요.

K : Let's go to the nearby street food stall, Pojangmacha.
　　포장마차 가판 음식점으로 갑시다.

C : What's Pojangmacha?
　　포장마차가 무엇이죠?

K : It's the tent bar set up on the street.
　　We call it 'Pojangmacha', literally means 'covered wagon'.
　　One chef cooks and serves everything.
　　거리에 설치된 천막 음식점입니다. 우리는 포장마차란 뜻으로
　　그렇게 부르는데 한 명의 주방장이 모든 것을 요리하고 관리하죠.

C : Are there many places like that in Seoul?
　　서울에 그런 곳이 많나요?

K : At every street corner, there is someone selling something edible in Korea. Foreigners can taste various Korean foods in street food stalls.
　　한국에는 어느 길모퉁이에나 먹을 것을 파는 사람들이 있습니다.
　　외국인들은 음식 가판대에서 다양한 한국 음식들을 맛볼 수 있습니다.

C : I want to try all.
　　전부 먹어보고 싶군요.

K : Come with me.
　　저랑 같이 가시죠.

C : OK.
　　좋아요.

K : Look. Over there. Let's go in.
　　보세요. 저기입니다. 들어가시죠.

C : It's a cool place.
정말 좋은 곳이군요.

K : Where would you like to sit?
어디에 앉을까요?

C : Shall we sit in that corner?
저 구석에 앉을까요?

K : Yes, let's.
It seems to be quiet.
그러죠. 조용한 것 같군요.

C : This small tent bar has a really friendly atmosphere.
이 조그만 천막 음식점은 정말 분위기가 좋군요.

K : The food is pretty good.
음식이 꽤 맛있습니다.

C : It's a fantastic place to spend a night of eating and drinking. What are those?
먹고 마시며 밤을 보내기에 아주 좋은 곳이군요. 저것들은 무엇이죠?

K : Toppoki and Eomuk. The most favorite Korean street snacks. Toppoki is sliced rice cake smothered in red chili sauce.
떡볶이와 어묵으로 한국에서 가장 인기 있는 길거리 음식들입니다.
떡볶이는 고추장에 버무린 쌀로 만든 떡입니다.

C : Spicy food? OK. I can try again.
매운 음식이나요? 좋아요. 다시 도전해 보죠.

K : How brave! Eomuk is delicious. It's boiled fish cake.
용감하군요! 어묵은 맛있는데, 삶은 생선말이입니다.

C : It tastes good. What's this?
맛이 괜찮군요. 이것은 뭐죠?

K : This is a Soondae. It's a traditional Korean sausage made with pork blood and glass noodles. Let's taste popular Korean foods.
이것은 순대입니다. 이것은 돼지 피와 당면으로 만든 한국의 전통 소시지입니다. 한국의 대중 음식들을 맛보도록 하죠.

C : Sure.
좋아요.

K : Try all of these.
이것들을 다 먹어보세요.

C : I can eat anything.
무엇이든지 먹을 수 있어요.

K : You are brave enough to try all of these in one sitting.
한 좌석에서 이걸 다 맛볼 정도로 용감하시군요.

C : Soondae tastes weird, but not bad.
순대는 맛이 이상하지만 나쁘진 않군요.

K : This is my favorite Korean traditional pan cake, Pajeon.
그리고 이것은 제가 좋아하는 한국의 전통 피자인 파전입니다.

C : It's delicious. This is perfect for me.
맛있군요. 저에게 딱 맞네요.

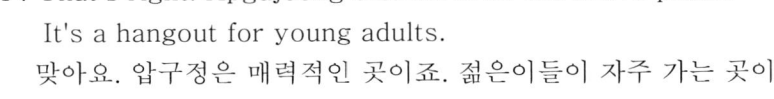

K : Help yourself.
많이 드세요.

C : Thank you.
감사해요.

K : How are we going to spend tonight?
What would you like to do?
오늘 밤 무엇을 하고 지낼까요? 무엇을 하고 싶으세요?

C : Actually, I'd like to go for a drink with you.
사실 저는 당신과 술을 마시고 싶어요.

K : OK. Is there somewhere you want to go?
좋아요. 어디 가보고 싶은 곳이 있으세요?

C : James told Apgujeong Rodeo Street is a favorite place in Seoul.
제임스가 압구정 로데오 거리가 서울에서 인기 있는 곳이라고 했어요.

K : That's right. Apgujeong district is an attractive place.
 It's a hangout for young adults.
맞아요. 압구정은 매력적인 곳이죠. 젊은이들이 자주 가는 곳이죠.

C : It has a good reputation.
그곳은 평이 좋더군요.
K : There are many boutiques, cafes, pubs, wine bars and restaurants.
그곳에는 많은 부티크 가게나 카페, 술집, 와인바, 식당들이 있습니다.
C : I hope that we can get some nice drinks at the fascinating pub.
멋진 호프집에서 술을 먹고 싶군요.
K : I'm sure we'll have a good time there.
그곳에서 좋은 시간을 보낼 수 있을 것입니다.
C : OK. Let's go there and have fun.
How can we get there?
좋아요 가서 즐겨요. 그런데 어떻게 가죠?
K : It's not far from here.
Let's take a taxi.
We will be there in several minutes.
이곳에서 가깝습니다.
택시를 타시죠. 몇 분이면 갈 것입니다.

We spend a pleasant evening.
우리는 즐거운 저녁시간을 보냈다.
We share a deep level of understanding about Korea and USA.
우리는 서로 한국과 미국에 대한 더 깊은 대화를 나누었다.
She asks me a lot of questions about Korean history.
그녀는 한국의 역사에 대해서 많은 것들을 물어보았다.

C : Can you tell me about the brief Korean history?
한국의 역사에 대해 간단하게 말해주실래요?

K : OK. Korea has 5000 years of history. History goes back to 2333 BC. According to the Korean creation myth, a prince and 3000 followers in heaven went down to the earth and settled on Korea. And the prince got married with a beautiful woman who was transformed from bear. Bear woman gave birth to a son, Dangun, the first king of Korea. He became the founding father of old Korea, Gochosun.

그러죠. 한국은 5000년 역사를 가지고 있는데, 기원전 2333년 전으로 거슬러 올라갑니다. 한국의 건국신화에 따르면, 하늘의 왕자와 3000명의 사람들이 지상에 내려와 한국에 정착했다고 합니다. 그리고 왕자는 곰이 변한 여인과 결혼하였다고 합니다. 웅녀는 한국의 첫 번째 왕, 단군을 낳았습니다. 그는 고대 한국인 고조선을 세우게 됩니다.

C : This story means the ancient shamanism of Korea.
한국의 고대 신앙을 의미하는가 보군요.

K : Yes. It reflects the totemism at the bronze age of Korea. Recorded history by the use of language extends as far back as 2100 years ago. Three kingdoms emerged in the 1st century BC in Korea. Goguryeo occupied the northern part, Silla dominated the southeast regions and Baekje dominated the southwest regions.

These 3 kingdoms actively engaged in China and Japan in order to promote the cultural exchanges and development.

네. 한국의 청동기 시대에 있었던 토테미즘을 나타내는 것입니다.
언어로 기록된 역사는 2100년 전으로 거슬러 올라갑니다.
기원전 1세기에 한국에 3 왕국이 생겨납니다.
고구려가 북쪽을 차지하고, 신라는 남동쪽, 백제는 남서쪽을 지배하게 됩니다. 세 왕국들은 문화 교류 증진과 발전을 위해 중국, 일본과 활발한 교류를 합니다.

C : Which country was stronger?
　　어느 나라가 강했죠?
K : Goguryeo was very strong at first and became a big kingdom expanding into Manchuria of the china. And Baekje played an important role in transmitting advanced cultures into ancient Japan, such as Chinese characters, building technology and Buddhism. Japanese imperial family has the royal blood of Baekje until now. Because princess of the Baekje and king of the Japan were married after Baekje helped him become the emperor. Therefore the current Japanese emperor is the direct descendant of Baekje kingdom.
　　고구려가 처음 아주 강했고 중국 만주까지 뻗어간 큰 왕국이었습니다. 그리고 백제는 고대 일본에 한자나 건축 기술, 불교를 전파하는데 중요한 역할을 합니다. 일본 황실은 지금까지 백제 왕실의 피를 이어 받고 있습니다. 왜냐하면 백제가 일본의 군주가 왕이 되는 것을 도운 후, 백제 공주와 일본 왕이 결혼을 했기 때문입니다.
　　그러므로 지금의 일본 황실은 백제의 자손입니다.
C : How long did that situation last for?
　　그런 상황이 얼마나 지속되었나요?
K : Allied with China, Silla conquered Goguryeo and Baekje, and unified the three kindoms in the 7th century. The Goguryeo people established the new kingdom called Balhae, and some of Baekje people immigrated into the Japan. The unified Silla kingdom experienced a golden age for about 300 years.
Its capital was Gyeungju which is known as the city of a thousand years.
　　중국과 동맹을 맺은 신라가 고구려와 백제를 정복하고 7세기경 삼국을 통일합니다. 고구려 민족은 발해라는 새로운 나라를 세우고, 일부 백제 사람들은 일본으로 이주하게 되지요. 통일신라는 약 300년간 황금의 시기를 맞습니다. 수도가 천 년의 도시로 알려진 경주입니다.

C : Why did Silla fall?
왜 신라가 망했죠?

K : Because Silla didn't integrate with conquered countries.
신라는 정복한 나라들과 융합하지 못했기 때문입니다.

C : And the next country was Goryeo? I remember that the English name of Korea was derived from Goryeo. Goryeo celadon have an international reputation because of its unique color and shape.
그 다음 나라가 고려인가요? 코리아란 이름이 고려에서 유래되었다는 말을 들은 것은 기억해요. 고려청자는 독특한 색깔과 모양으로 국제적으로 알려져 있더군요.

K : Yes. Besides, Goryeo published book by the using of metal type. It was the most oldest metal type printing in the world.
네. 게다가 고려는 금속활자를 이용하여 책을 발간하였습니다. 그것은 세계에서 가장 오래된 금속 활자입니다.

C : Oh. I don't know that.
아 그건 몰랐군요.

K : After the fall of Silla, Goryeo dynasty was established and continued 450 years. The last dynasty, Chosun was established about 500 years ago.
신라가 망한 후 고려왕조가 세워지고 450년간 지속됩니다. 마지막 왕조인 조선은 약 500년 전에 세워집니다.

C : What does Chosun mean?
조선이란 무슨 뜻이지요?

K : Chosun means the land of morning calm.
조선은 고요한 아침의 나라라는 뜻입니다.

C : Was Korean literature created at that era?
한글은 그 시대에 만들어졌나요?

K : Yes. Korean literature, Hangul was created in 15th century by King Sejong.
네. 한국의 문자인 한글은 15세기에 세종대왕에 의해 창조되었습니다.

C : How was Chosun?
조선은 어땠나요?

K : During this age, Confucianism's conservative ethics and values dominated Korea's social structure and attitudes. At the end of the 19th century, Korea had become a battleground for big countries because of its geographical location. Chosun dynasty came to an end when Japan invaded Korea in 1910. Eventually, Korea suffered from Japanese colonial rule.
이 시기는 유교의 보수적인 윤리와 가치관들이 한국의 사회구조와 틀을 지배하게 됩니다. 19세기 말부터 한국은 지리적 특성상 강대국의 전쟁터가 되고, 조선왕조는 1910년 일본이 한국을 침략하며 끝나게 됩니다. 결국 한국은 일본의 식민 지배를 받게 되었죠.

C : And at the end of World War II, Korea was freed from Japan. Right?
그리고 2차 세계대전이 끝날 때 한국은 일본으로부터 자유로워졌죠?

K : Yes. But the Cold War divided Korea.
하지만 냉전은 한국을 분단시켰습니다.

C : How many people are there in Korea?
한국 인구가 얼마나 되죠?

K : The population of the South Korea is 50 million and North Korea is 24 million. And there are about 6 or 7 million Koreans residing in oversea countries. Approximately 2 million Koreans reside in the United States, 2.5 million in China, 600,000 in Japan. And half a million Koreans live in Central Asia.
한국의 인구수는 5천만 명이고 북한은 2400만 명입니다. 대략 600만이나 700만 명의 한국인들이 해외 다른 나라에 살고 있습니다. 미국에는 2백만 명이 넘게 살고 있고, 중국에 250만 명, 일본에 60만 명, 그리고 중앙아시아에도 50만 명이 살고 있습니다.

C : Korean peninsula should be peacefully reunited in the near future.
한반도는 가까운 장래에 평화롭게 통일이 되어야 해요.

K : That is every Korean people's hope.
그것은 모든 한국인들의 바램입니다.

C : Could you explain about the Korean flag? I am supposed to contribute an article about the Korean culture to a magazine.
한국의 국기에 대해서 설명해 주실래요?
한국 문화에 관한 기사를 잡지에 기고하기로 되어있어요.

K : No problem. The Korean Flag is named Taegukki. It stands for perfect universal harmony and balance. The symbol in the center is derived from the traditional oriental philosophy. The red represents the plus energy of the nature, and the blue represents the minus energy of the nature. The red and blue are portrayed upside down to accommodate the harmony of natural power, and it means the power of creation. The white background is representative of the purity and peace-loving spirit. The four trigrams surrounding the circle mean combinations of the nature, such as heaven, earth, sun and fire, moon and water.
네 그러죠. 한국의 국기는 태극기라 부릅니다. 이것은 완벽한 우주의 조화와 균형을 의미합니다. 가운데 문양은 동양의 전통철학에서 나온 것입니다. 붉은색은 자연의 양의 힘을 뜻하고, 푸른색은 음의 힘을 뜻합니다. 위아래로 얽힌 붉은 색과 푸른색 문양은 자연의 힘의 조화를 묘사하고 있고, 이것은 창조의 힘을 뜻합니다. 하얀 바탕은 순수와 평화를 나타냅니다. 원 주위의 4개의 문양들은 자연의 조화인 하늘, 땅, 해와 불, 달과 물 들을 나타냅니다.

C : It has a deep meaning.
깊은 뜻이 있군요.

K : What are your thoughts on Asian culture?
아시아 문화에 대해서 어떻게 생각하세요?
C : Asia seems like to have something different ways of looking at things in comparison with West. Asian is more concerned with the high value of spirituality and morality.
아시아는 서양과 보는 관점들이 다른 것 같아요. 아시아 사람들은 정신적인 것과 도덕성을 더 중요시하는 것 같아요.
K : Asian culture has been influenced by Confucianism and Buddhism throughout its long history. Actually Confucianism has played an important role in making a Korean life style. Older people are still very much respected and all Korean people put a great value on one's dignity.
아시아의 문화는 오랜 역사 동안 유교와 불교에 영향을 받아왔습니다. 사실 유교가 한국의 생활 습관을 만드는데 중요한 역할을 했습니다. 고령자들은 아직도 매우 존경을 받고 있으며, 한국 사람들은 체면을 아주 중요하게 생각합니다.
C : Yes. Korean society looks like to be concerned with the traditional values and the ways of doing things.
네. 한국 사회는 전통적 가치와 일의 방법을 중요시 하는 것 같아요.
K : Korea is still one of the most Confucian nations in the world. Old custom like respecting the elderly people has been well maintained. For example, young people wait until the eldest person initiates activity, such as entering a room and eating.
한국은 아직도 유교가 성행하는 나라 중 하나입니다. 노인들을 공경하는 문화는 잘 유지되어 왔습니다. 예로써 나이가 가장 많은 분이 방에 먼저 들어가거나 식사를 시작하기 전까지는 젊은 사람들이 기다립니다.
C : That's a great custom.
좋은 풍습이군요.

K : Ancestor worship is also important in Korea.
　　Previous generations are remembered on Korean Thanks
　　Giving Day, Chuseok and Lunar New Year's Day.
　　Most of people visit relatives and graves of one's ancestors.
　　All families have gathered and prepared sacrificial foods to
　　perform the memorial rite. And deceased family is also
　　remembered and honored every year on the day of one's death
　　by the same method.
　　조상숭배 역시 한국에서는 중요합니다.
　　한국의 추수감사절인 추석이나 구정에는 조상들을 추모합니다.
　　대부분의 사람들이 친척을 방문하고 조상의 묘를 찾습니다.
　　모든 가족들이 모여 제사를 지내기 위해 음식을 준비합니다.
　　그리고 돌아가신 가족들 역시 제삿날 같은 방법으로 추모됩니다.
C : Many countries have similar customs.
　　많은 나라들이 비슷한 풍습을 가지고 있어요.
K : Americans have a great deal of optimism about the future.
　　미국인들은 미래에 대해 상당히 낙관적인 것 같아요.
C : Maybe every people wants to try to do so.
　　아마도 모든 사람들이 그렇게 하려고 노력하길 원하겠죠.

　　　　　　　　Time really flies like an arrow.
　　　　　　　　시간은 정말 화살처럼 빨리 간다.
　　　　　　　　One week goes by so quickly.
　　　　　　　　일주일이 정말 빨리 지나갔다.
　　　　Friendship sometimes makes an impact on
　　　　　　one's happiness and quality of life.
　　우정은 때로 누군가의 행복과 삶의 질에 영향을 미친다.
　　　　　　Charlotte seems to make me happy.
　　　　　　샬럿은 나를 행복하게 만드는 것 같다.

At the end of her one week trip to Korea,
I open my heart to her at the riverside of Hangang.
일주일 한국 여행의 마지막 날에 나는 한강변에서
그녀에게 마음을 내보였다.

K : I'd like to give you a ride to the airport.
What time do you need to get there?
공항까지 태워드릴게요. 언제까지 가야 되죠?

C : I am going to leave my hotel at 10:00 A.M.
아침 10시에 호텔에서 나가려고 해요.

K : What's your departure time?
떠나는 시간이 언제이죠?

C : My flight departs at 1:00 P.M.
So I have to get to the airport 2 hours before departure.
오후 1시 비행기인데, 출발 2시간 전에 도착해야 해요.

K : There will be a traffic jam. We'd better go early.
I'll pick you up at 9:00 A.M.
교통이 막힐 것입니다. 빨리 가는 것이 좋을 것 같습니다.
오전 9시에 데리러 갈게요.

C : OK.
알았어요.

K : Do you know where your terminal is?
터미널이 어디인지 아세요?

C : I am flying on American Air. Just drop me off at the curb.
아메리칸 항공으로 가는데 그냥 길가에만 내려주세요.

K : I'd like to spend the remaining time together before you leave.
당신이 떠나기 전까지 남은 시간 동안 같이 있고 싶군요.

C : Thank you. How sweet you are! This is a holiday I am going to remember for a long time.
고마워요. 정말 멋있네요! 이번 휴가는 오랫동안 기억될 것 같아요.

K : You're always welcome. See you tomorrow morning.
천만에요. 내일 아침에 뵐게요.

C : Thank you for your hospitality.
I will remember your kindness.
환대에 감사드려요. 당신의 친절을 꼭 기억할게요.

K : Your bright laugh gave me a lot of positive energy
and made me happy for the past few days.
당신의 밝은 웃음은 요 며칠간 저에게 좋은 에너지를 주고
행복하게 해주더군요.

C : The pleasure is mine.
오히려 제가 감사해요.

K : You are such a decent, honest person.
I like your openness.
I hope I can see you again.
당신은 품위 있고 정직하더군요.
당신의 개방성이 맘에 들어요.
다시 뵙기를 바랍니다.

    She gives me a bashful smile in silence for a moment.
       그녀는 잠시 동안 말없이 멋쩍게 웃었다.

C : Koreans live in a wonderful world that is full of peace and
beauty. A journey is best measured in friends who have met
rather than miles. Thank you.
I have seen more than I remember,
and remember more than I have seen.
You also have a great smile.
There is something infectious about it.

한국인들은 평화롭고 아름다운 세상에 살고 있네요.
여행이란 거리보다도 만난 친구들에 의해 평가되죠.
제가 기억하고 있는 것보다 더 많은 것을 보았고,
제가 본 이상으로 더 기억할게요.
당신의 웃는 모습 역시 아주 좋아서 끌어당기는 것이 있어요.

She smiles warmly at me after what she said.
그녀는 말을 한 후 따뜻한 미소를 나에게 보였다.

She stares deeply into my eyes
and gives me a kiss on the cheek.
그녀는 내 눈을 깊이 응시하더니
볼에 키스를 했다.

자신의 마음을
진취적이고 긍정적으로 바꾸어 주는 좋은 문구들

Think globally, act locally.
Manage yourself and time, and then lead others.
Be the self-motivated people and enjoy your work.
Try to keep good constitution.
Feel bio-energy and whole connected world.
Freedom has many different faces.
Enjoy commonality and ordinary life.
Try to fuse the technology and the liberal arts.
Love has unlimited ways.
Do your best and never give up.
Our thoughts become things.
Try to be more intelligent and brilliant.
Burst inspiration and inspire next.
Put focus on people relationship.
Proceed to next goal.
Keep smiling and keep yourself happy.
Keep emotionally healthy.
Insightful thinking and methodical approach.
Focus on what you are paying attention to.
Make no distinction and use positive terms.
Turn idea into reality.

Become intensely aware of what is happening in this moment.
　Respect privacy and individuality.
　　　　　　　　　　Patience is a virtue.
　　　　　　　　　　Be a warm hearted person.
　　　　　　　　Be diligent and live in the moment.
　　　　　　　　　Let it be and let it go.
　　　　　No waste time. Time is of the essence.
　　　　　　　Keep healthy and lively condition.
　　　　　　　　　　Simple is better.
　　　　　　　Enjoy working out and keep in shape.
　　　　　　　　　　No pain, no gain.
　　　　　　　　　　Love draws love.
　　　　　　　Rest in peace and act in passion.
　　　　　　　　　Free from any bias.
　　　　　　　　　　Just be yourself.
Be a citizen of the world.
　Don't attach to desire.

　　　Get organized to increase the power of creation.
　　　More understanding needed, not more persuasion.
　　　　Keep up to date with the latest thinking.
　　　　Feel the social change and use social stream.

Passion for knowledge and truth.
Gather information and become more adaptive.
Open your mind and level with others.
Don't wander off in the distractions of the past and future.
Building self confidence is the heart of self development.
There is nothing you can do to change a past moment.
Have a global mind.
Feel whole life energy and enjoy your life.
Follow your heart and humanity.
Getting ready is the secret of success.
Be in fashion and try to be confident.
Be one whom nobody can imitate.
Have a general idea of what is going on in the world.
Experience is the best teacher.
A sound mind in a sound body.
Focus on positive thoughts and forward thinking mind.
Step by step one goes very far.
Feel and understand the mainstream of society and modern life.
Creative thoughts and works impact the world.
Constancy of purpose achieves the impossible.
Power is in your thoughts.
Enjoy liberal mind.

Go confidently in the direction of your dreams.
Feeling happiness make you healthy.
Expectation is the powerful attractive force.
Your love attracts positive power.
Kindness is the golden chain.
Develop your general knowledge and ability to think.
Decide your fate for yourself.
Great capacity for patience and understanding.
Everything has the value, but not everyone sees it.
If you don't aim high, you will never hit high.
Great minds think alike.
Happiness is a perfume you cannot pour on others
without getting a few drops on yourself.
Spirituality is not about what you're doing,
it's about what you're being.
The more curious you are,
the more possibilities you will open throughout your lifetime.
It all depends on how we look at things,
and not how they are in themselves.
We were given two ears but only one mouth.
This is because God knows that
listening is twice as hard as talking.

한 권으로 끝내는 해외여행 영어회화

1판 1쇄 2015년 9월 1일
   4쇄 2022년 8월 1일

지은이 / 임창석
펴낸이 / 임준형
출판사 / 아시아 북스
등록 / 2015년 8월 5일 제 2015 - 000065 호
주소 / 서울시 송파구 문정동 법원로55 송파아이파크 오피스텔 C동 903호
전화 / 02-407-9091
팩스 / 02-407-9091
E-mail : Asiabooks@naver.com

저자와의 계약에 의해 아시아 북스 출판사에서 발행합니다.
본서의 내용 일부 혹은 전부를 무단으로 복제하는 것은 법으로 금지되어 있습니다.
파본은 교환하여 드립니다.
검인은 저자와의 합의 하에 생략합니다.

ISBN 979-11-955956-1-7 (13740)